THE TEXAS CONNECTION

A History of the Church Of God In Christ in Texas
Compiled by Pastor Kelvin W.C. Henry, Sr.

Volume I
COGIC HISTORY
TEXAS HISTORY
CHAPTER 1 & 2

QUADRENNIAL ISSUE
Election Edition

Choose Change Publishing
Spring, Texas 77379

email:Publisher@ChooseChange.pub
http://www.ChooseChange.pub

First edition, black and white. Also available in color.

ISBN-13: 978-1546410782
ISBN-10: 1546410783

© 1984, 2010, 2013, 2017, 2018 Pastor Kelvin W.C. Henry, Sr.

All rights reserved. No part of this publication may be reproduced, stored in a retrieval system, or transmitted, in any form or by any means, electronic, mechanical photocopying, recording, or otherwise, except for the inclusion of brief quotations in a review, without the prior permission in writing from copyright holder.

Copyright holder vigorously defends its copyright protection.

The Choose Change logo is a trademark of Choose Change Publishing. All other logos, pictures, trademarks and service marks shown in this book are the property of their respective owners.

Manufactured in the United States of America.

Cover design by Emerald Studio www.EmeraldStudioDesigns.com
Printed by CreateSpace, an Amazon company. Available from Amazon.com and other retail outlets.

ACADEMIC INSTITUTIONS, LIBRARIES, ORGANIZATIONS AND OTHER QUANTITY BUYERS: Discounts on this book are available for bulk purchases. Write or call for information on our discount programs.

This gathering together of these histories are only a small collection of excerpts from several accounts of these events, recorded facts, personalities and are not intended to be the whole record, nor is it recorded as original material or considered by the author/compiler as such, but simply as a simple limited record of these facts, persons, places and events.

Neither documentation nor footnotes to historical events or persons are provided in this simple chronological record of which would have been a cumbersome task, but the reader of this record will find shadows of these records as part of this history. The task to compile and record these histories, testimonies, historical events, places and people in one place is mine and mine alone. But as a Church Of God In Christ historian I am shaped by its total history, its people, its events and its record.

As a chronological scribe to these facts, persons, places and events, I cannot rightfully claim authorship to this history, only to its chronological interpretation and recording of the same.

Logos, pictures, trademarks and service marks are property of their respective owners and are only used for illustrative purpose only. We do not claim ownership to these.

If you have submissions please email: submissions@cogicstory.com
Visit us online at CogicStory.com
like us on Facebook @texasconnection

Important Note: *It is our goal to fully take the reader on a journey through this amazing and eye opening history. The reader will find that some of the individual histories, the history of the organization and its departments overlap and may repeat. This repeat or overlap in the record is due in part to the succession of leadership and to the chronological recording of this journey. This is hereby recognized and noted by the author/compiler.*

Table of Contents

Table of Contents.. i.

List of Illustrations and Pictures (*People, Places and Symbols*)...................v.

Acknowledgments...vii.

Introduction..ix.

Index Layouts..x.

Sample Entries..xi.

About the Author..xvii.

VOLUME I
Chapter 1   THE CHURCH OF GOD IN CHRIST, INC.................... 1
What Does That Mean..3
The Holiness/Sanctification Movement 5
Brief History of COGIC and Related Movements.............................5
The Holy Man of COGIC..5
Charles Harrison Mason 5
HIStory C. H. Mason 6
COGIC Holiness 14
Emergence of the Pentecostal COGIC 19
The Latter Day Quest 25
The Start of It 28
SENIOR AND PRESIDING BISHOPS' COGIC..........................39
Bishop C.H. Mason 43
Bishop O.T. Jones, Sr. 59
Bishop J.O. Patterson, Sr...63
Bishop L.H. Ford...69
Bishop C.D. Owens..71
Bishop G.E. Patterson 73
Bishop C.E. Blake, Sr...77
THE PRESIDIUM OF THE CHURCH OF GOD IN CHRIST 81
The Commission 83
The Executive Board...85
The Administrative Board..86
The General Board Notes...87
The General Board Yearbook..95

i.

GENERAL SUPERVISORS DEPARTMENT OF WOMEN 149
Mother Lizzie Woods Robinson 153
Mother Lillian Brooks Coffey 157
Mother Anne Bailey 159
Mother Mattie McGlothen 163
Mother Emma Crouch 165
Mother Willie Mae Rivers 167
Mother Barbara McCoo Lewis.. 171
PROFILES OF OTHER PIONEERING WOMEN 175
Elsie Washington Mason... 177
Neanza Zelma Jones 179
Deborah Indiana Mason Patterson 181
Margaret Ford 183
Shirley Owens 185
Louise D. Patterson 187
Mae L. Blake 189
THE OFFICE OF GENERAL SECRETARY. 191
GENERAL ASSEMBLY CHAIRMAN. 193
THE AUXILIARIES CONVENTIONS (AIM) 195
History UNAC and AIM... 197
History of the Sunday School Department 201
History of the Youth Department.. 203
History of the Department of Evangelism 207
History of the Department of Missions 211
History of the Music Department 217
Chapter 2   THE CHURCH OF GOD IN CHRIST IN TEXAS.......... 225
Charles Parham and William J. Seymour…………............................... 228
The Anointed Handmaid... 229
The Mother group of COGIC Saints 229
Elder D.J. Young…………………………………………....................230
Bishop E.M. Page.. 232
Mother Molly Page 233
The Bible Training School.. 233
The Page Normal School.. 235
Bishop J.H. Galloway... 238
Mother Hannan Chandler 241
Texas is Divided…………………………………………….................. 242
The New Bishops of Texas 243
The New Supervisors of Texas 243
The Galloway Home….. 246
Other notable Women from Texas... 253
1st and 2nd Bishop of Texas.. 253
First Church / Greater First Church…... 254
Report of Bishop Page 1926 COGIC Burial Association........................ 255

The following sections cover the various jurisdictions of Texas, fellowships of Texas, COGIC events and other related events in Texas.

VOLUME II

Chapter 3	TEXAS CENTRAL METROPOLITAN JURISDICTION............	
Chapter 4	TEXAS EASTERN JURISDICTION.................................	
Chapter 5	TEXAS EAST CENTRAL JURISDICTION........................	
Chapter 6	TEXAS GREATER SOUTHEAST 1ST JURISDICTION..............	
Chapter 7	TEXAS GULF COAST JURISDICTION............................	
Chapter 8	TEXAS LONE STAR JURISDICTION..............................	

VOLUME III

Chapter 9	TEXAS NORTH CENTRAL JURISDICTION................................	
Chapter 10	TEXAS NORTHEAST 1ST JURISDICTION.................................	
Chapter 11	TEXAS NORTHEAST 2ND JURISDICTION................................	
Chapter 12	TEXAS NORTHEAST 3RD JURISDICTION................................	
Chapter 13	TEXAS NORTHEAST 4TH JURISDICTION................................	
Chapter 14	TEXAS METROPOLITAN JURISDICTION..........................	

VOLUME IV

Chapter 15	TEXAS NORTHWEST JURISDICTION...	
Chapter 16	TEXAS SOUTH CENTRAL JURISDICTION................................	
Chapter 17	TEXAS SOUTHEAST 1ST JURISDICTION.................................	
Chapter 18	TEXAS SOUTHEAST 2ND JURISDICTION................................	
Chapter 19	TEXAS SOUTHEAST 3RD JURISDICTION................................	

VOLUME V
Chapter 20 TEXAS SOUTHWEST JURISDICTION..............................

Chapter 21 TEXAS WESTERN JURISDICTION.................................

Chapter 22 TEXAS INTER JURISDICTION......................................

Chapter 23 Fellowships and others..

Chapter 24 COGIC and other Events in Texas.................…...............

Appendix A...

Appendix B...

Appendix C...

Notes...

Indexes..

Definitions..

Lists of Illustrations and Pictures
-People-

Bishop C. H. Mason	Bishop J. Neaul Haynes	Bishop R.E. Woodard, I
Bishop C. P. Jones	Bishop S.L. Green, Jr.	Bishop R.E. Woodard, II
Charles Fox Parham	Bishop G.D. McKinney	Bishop R. Kyles, Jr.
Bishop W. J. Seymour	Bishop N.W. Wells	Bishop R.E. Ranger
Bishop O.T. Jones, Sr.	Bishop E.J. Wright, Sr.	Bishop C.L. Bryant
Bishop O.T. Jones, Jr.	Bishop L.E. Willis, Sr.	Bishop C.H. Nelson
Bishop J.O. Patterson, Sr.	Bishop F. O. White	Bishop NH Henderson, Sr.
Bishop J.O. Patterson, Jr.	Bishop S. Daniels	Bishop P.E.W. Bryant, Sr.
Bishop L.H. Ford	Bishop J.A. Blake, Sr.	Bishop T.D. Iglehart
Bishop C.D. Owens	Bishop E.R. Driver	Bishop S.E. Iglehart
Bishop G.E. Patterson	Bishop D.J. Young	Bishop W.B. Houston
Bishop W.A. Patterson. Sr.	Bishop E.M. Page	Bishop D.R. Houston
Bishop C.E. Blake, I	Bishop J.H. Galloway	Bishop F.L. Haynes
Bishop P.A. Brooks, II	Bishop M.G. Grady	Bishop D.S. Smith
Bishop J.W. Macklin	Bishop A. L. Thomas	Bishop C.F. Porter
Bishop W.W. Hamilton	Bishop J.E. Alexander	Bishop J.E. Lee
Bishop R.L. H. Winbush	Bishop W. H. Watson, II	Bishop Juan Lawson
Bishop W. H. Watson, III	Bishop L. M. Wooten, Sr.	Bishop A. L. Thomas, Jr.
Bishop Frank Fanniel, Sr.	Bishop N. J. Gatlin	Bishop James Hornsby
Bishop Venson Nobles, Sr.	Bishop R.L. Williams	Bishop R. L. Sample
Bishop Nathiel Wells	Bishop Darrell Hines	Bishop Matthew Williams
Bishop J. Tates	Bishop D. Bell, Sr.	Bishop T.T. Terry
Bishop R.L. Nichols, Sr.	Bishop T.D. Williams	Bishop K. Thompson

-Places-

Mason Temple
Azusa Street Mission
Bethel Bible School
1. Evangelist Temple COGIC (TSE 1st)
2. Compton Temple (TSC)
3. Saintsville COGIC (TN1st)
4. Holy Light COGIC (TW)
5. Smith Temple COGIC (TN2nd)
6. Porter Temple COGIC (TL)
7. Hunter's Memorial COGIC (TSE 3rd)
8. Christian Tabernacle COGIC (TE)
9. Lilly of The Valley COGIC (TM)
10. Agape Temple COGIC (TNW)
11. Pentecostal of Faith COGIC (TSE2nd)
12. Holy Temple COGIC
13. (TNE3rd)
14. (TNC)
15. (TNEM)
16. (TNE4th)
17. Christ Temple of Deliverance (TGC)
18. (TEC)
19. Powerhouse COGIC (GTSE 1st)

Note: Numbered places are the Jurisdictional headquarters or the Bishop's church of each of the 19 jurisdictions of the Church Of God In Christ in Texas.

-Symbols-

COGIC Seal	Seal of the Bishop	Evangelism
Presiding Bishop's	AIM	Music
Youth Department	Sunday School	General Assembly
The Women's Department	Missions	General Secretary

Acknowledgments

Firstly, I thank God for such a great and awesome task; that he has laid at my charge. It is my hope and prayer that this is what he wants. Secondly, I thank God for the memory of my family line that runs so deep in this, the Grand Ole Church Of God In Christ.

Especially the memory of my grandparents the late Pastor Elder Odis Terry (*OT*) Taylor (*Unc*) and Licensed Evangelist District Missionary Viola C. Taylor (*Mame*), who's rearing afforded me the memories and living history, which I cherish still to this day.

This rearing is due in large part to my mother's wisdom and understanding in allowing the request of my upbringing to be in the hands of my grandparents. So I thank also my late mother for not being selfish and affording me this experience.

To the memory of my great-grandparents Pastor Archie Taylor (*Grandpa*) and Mrs. Ida (*Mother Ida*) Taylor. Mr. John B Childs, Sr. (*Big Daddy*) and Mrs. Annie Mae Childs (*Medea*) who allowed my sister (*Patricia*) and myself to share in these families summer vacations both in Chatham, Louisiana (*Taylor*) and Bryan, Texas (*Childs*). My great-great-grandmother an ex-slave who started my family's history in the Church of God in Christ (*seven generations so far*). In the person of Sister Sara Taylor-Peoples. She was my great grandfather's mother a mighty praying woman. She would raise my grandfather (*OT*) and one of his sisters (*Rose Ann*). I remember my grandfather telling me of how she would pray for OT and all those that would follow OT. So she prayed for me and the generations after me as well. It not only includes me but also my wife, my son and all those that follow Him. Thanks great-great grandma Sara.

To my father's side of the family the Butlers – The memory of my father the late Bro. Jimmie Lee Butler, Sr., and Mama Nellie, *(who were members of the Christ Way COGIC Supt. Eddie Dillon, Founding Pastor)*. Aunt Frankey (*my father's baby sister*), my late Aunt Mandy, my late Aunt Rabbit (*Eunce*), Uncle Tom (*Tommy*), my late Uncle Pee-Wee (*Earnest*) my late Uncle Bo-Pete (*Alex*) and every cousin aunt and uncle I didn't mention.

To my siblings- My one and only brother Duna (*Jimmie Lee Butler, Jr.*), all my sisters Antis, Lori Ann, Trenis, Sonja (*my twin*), Angela, Patricia, Dana (*in order of age not linage*)

To my long awaited son Kelvin W. C. Henry, Jr. It is my prayer that when the time is right that you will pick up where I leave off of this great work.

To all the saints that grew me up in this way called holiness and made such valuable contributions to my walk with Christ, whose names are too numerous to name. THANK YOU.

The late Supt. Luther Swindell, Sr., and the Norton Temple Family. Special thanks to the Mother Clarice Burks and the late Mother Ruth Dove for your material contributions, without which this great work would be greatly lacking.

To Dr. Merdice Brown and the Salt Mine Family. Thank you for your love, support and encouragement through the years. The Salt Mine Church. My place of refuge.

And the last is really the first. To my partner in ministry and in life; the one I confide in, my bride, my best friend, my confidant and my most ardent supporter; the mother of our one and only son. This is being completed because of your inspiration. The one and only Missionary Maveya J. Henry, my wife Thank you dear for all of your support. I love you.

My Family Heritage in the Church Of God In Christ
Seven Generations so far

My family's legacy in the Church Of God In Christ starts with my great-great grandmother Sister Sara Taylor-Peoples, who was an ex-slave and was married to Bob Peoples. Bob Peoples was not saved but, he was known for his good aim with a shot gun. He was said to be so good that at night he could shoot a coyote between the legs of a cow (*which was attacking his livestock*). He would kill the coyote and not hit the cow (*although he would be inebriated at the time*).

Before her marriage to Bob she was married to Lemuel Taylor who was saved and in the church and from that union one child was born. My great grandfather Archie Taylor (*aka A.R.*). Sara Taylor was known as a mighty praying woman. My grandfather would tell me stories of how she was always praying. While she was doing her house work, she was praying. While she was cooking, she was praying. While she was washing, she was praying. She was always praying.

Because my great grandfather had so many children and his wife, their mother (*Mattie Lee Ziegler Taylor*) had passed away shortly after child birth. To help him, great-great grandma Sara would raise my grandfather OT and one of his sister's Rose Ann. Great-great grandma Sara during that time would be found praying for her child and all his children. She would be the ***first generation*** of my family in the church in the state of Louisiana.

Her son Archie Taylor was the ***second generation*** of my family in the Church Of God In Christ in Louisiana. He was known as Pastor A. R. Taylor and he pastored seven churches in the state of Louisiana. We called him "*grandpa*." When we would visit, he would take me with him to cut yards there in Chatham, Louisiana and surrounding areas. At that time they called me Wayne (*my second middle name*). I loved going with him to cut yards and I loved hearing all the stories he would tell me. I enjoyed him introducing me to those in the community. I remember him saying this is "*OT's grandson, Wayne*". He was so proud of Wayne and I was so happy to be his great grandson. These memories I still cherish to this day.

Grandpa's 8 children one of which was Pastor O.T. Taylor (my grandfather and his wife my Grandmother) District Missionary Viola Taylor which represents the ***third generation*** of my family in the Church Of God In Christ. My grandfather pastored five churches in Texas and my grandmother was the district missionary of 2 districts. The Fairbanks Mission District-TSC, Bishop C.H. Nelson and the Holy Light District-TSE 1st, Bishop R.E. Woodard, Sr. Three of the churches were in different jurisdictions (*TSE1st, TSC and TSE 2nd*). At the request of my grandmother my mother allowed her parents to raise one of my sisters (*Patricia*) and me. A decision that was hard for my mother and one I didn't understand at the time, but one I thank God for today.

My Mother Lois Marie who was a great soloist and was known for singing "*Walk with me Lord*". In my eyes she was the greatest mother ever, always providing for me and my sisters (*Patricia and Dana*). She was a hard working beautician and a hard worker in the church. My mother and my aunts uncles and cousins represents the ***fourth generation*** of my family in the Church Of God In Christ. I Pastor Kelvin W.C. Henry, Sr., along with my siblings and my cousins, we represents the ***fifth generation*** of my family in the Church Of God In Christ. My nephew Minister Kenneth R. Childs and my son Kelvin W.C. Henry, Jr., represents the ***sixth generation*** of my family in the Church Of God In Christ.

My nephew Minister Kenneth R. Childs' daughter Kennedi Childs represents the ***seventh generation*** of my family in the Church Of God In Christ. To God be the glory.

Introduction

PURPOSE OF THIS RECORD

We believe that these volumes are a must have for every member of the Church Of God In Christ, in Texas. The Texas Connection will be prepared quadrennial as part of what we hope will become a state by state, or country by country volume set. Currently in the state of Texas there are 19 jurisdictions. These jurisdictions represent hundreds of districts and thousands of local congregations, which represents hundreds of thousands, if not millions of individual members.

The bringing together of all these histories under one title in and of itself is a historical marker of the growth and strength of the Church Of God In Christ, in Texas. No where else is there a greater coverage of these jurisdictional, district, and local churches histories as well as the National History of our church.

UPDATING THE RECORD

The record of each jurisdiction, district, and local history as well as our National history will be extensively updated, revised and recorded. To be sure that all histories recorded are accurate, reliable and current we will: (1) contact reliable sources of this information. (2) collect new information on all local, district and jurisdictional histories, as well as our National history that are in the last volume. (3) search extensively for any histories that may have not been included in the past volume. *(Unfortunately, despite our best efforts, some histories may not be covered; this may be caused by a failure of some to respond to our request. Consequently these histories are not included.)*

The next edition of the Texas Connection completely revises and updates the previous edition. Any sources of local, district or jurisdictional or national histories are welcomed and many of these we understand are actual testimonies of actual events and or personalities.

ARRANGEMENT OF THIS RECORD

The Texas Connection is divided into Chapters: Chapter 1's focus is on a limited record of the Church Of God In Christ's History and Leadership. This includes the limited history of the Senior and Presiding Bishops, the General Supervisors and other notable Women, the five major auxiliaries, the office of General Secretary and Chairman of the Assembly.

Chapter 2 covers the beginning history of the Church Of God In Christ in Texas.

Chapter 3 thru 22 covers the 19 jurisdictions of the Church Of God In Christ in Texas, which includes the district of each jurisdiction and the local churches of each district.

Chapter 23 focuses on conventions/fellowships which can and have become a jurisdiction on the approval of the Presiding Bishop, the General Board and General Assembly of the Church Of God In Christ. This Chapter also covers other fellowships and churches with similar doctrines of the Church Of God In Christ. Some of these churches may have at one time been a part of the Church Of God In Christ and any past jurisdictions that are no longer operating.

Chapter 23 focuses on various Church Of God In Christ News worthy events of the church in Texas.

Indexes   The six indexes included in the Texas Connection will help you locate histories of the Church Of God In Christ, in Texas and our national history. These are the histories of local churches, districts, jurisdictional histories in Texas and a limited International Church of God In Christ history.

>**International Officers**   This index list the two Senior Bishops of the Church Of God In Christ and the five Presiding Bishops. It list the seven General Supervisors of Women and other national officers both past and present.
>
>**Jurisdictional Officers**   This index lists the past and present Jurisdictional Prelate of each of the Jurisdictions in the great State of Texas. It lists the past and present State Supervisors of the Women's Department for each of the Jurisdictions in Texas. It may also list other jurisdictional officers past and present.
>
>**District Officers**   This index lists the past and present District Superintendents and District Missionaries in the 19 Jurisdictions of Texas. It also lists other district officers of each district.
>
>**District's**   This Index lists the Districts of each Jurisdiction.
>
>**Local Churches**   This Index lists the local Churches of each Jurisdiction.
>
>**Others**   This Index lists Fellowships and other Churches that may have once been a part of the Church of God in Christ or that shares similar doctrines.

WHAT MAKES THIS RECORD UNIQUE?

For the first time in the history of the Church of God In Christ, in Texas the histories of all the Jurisdictions, the District and local Churches are compiled in one volume set. A history that officially was started here in 1914 (*although the Church Of God In Christ was already operating in Texas*) with the appointment of Bishop Emmitt Moore Page as the overseer of Diocese No. 1, which included Texas, Oklahoma, Kansas, Western Missouri, Eastern Illinois and Iowa. TC will bring this history to life in one place.

We have set out to record every local congregation's history as well as the Districts history and Jurisdictions history. This is an awesome task to say the least and not every ones history will be fully covered in every volume. But we hope to update this volume every 4 years (quadrennial) with new and or updated histories as needed.

SAMPLE ENTRIES
(The next page is an actual sample of the Jurisdictional Entry)

Jurisdictional Entry

(1) Texas Greater Southeast First Jurisdiction
(2) Church Of God In Christ

(3) Bishop Johnny Tates	(5) Mother Lena I. McClain
(4) Jurisdictional Prelate	(6) Jurisdictional Supervisor

(7) **Districts**

(8) Beaumont	(9) Supt. Gary L. Cantue	(10) Msny. Ellaner Cook

DEFINITIONS
(1) The name of the Jurisdiction
(2) Identifies the International Church body
(3) Identifies the Jurisdictional Prelate (Bishop)
(4) Identifies the title of the Jurisdictional Prelate
(5) Identifies the Jurisdictional Supervisor (Mother)
(6) Identifies the title of the Jurisdictional Supervisor
(7) Heading for the Jurisdiction's Districts
(8) Name of the Districts
(9) Identifies the District Superintendent
(10) Identifies the District Missionary

Note: *The jurisdiction also known as the state is the direct arm of the COGIC to the International church. It is on the 6th level (a1) in the ecclesiastical structure of the Church Of God In Christ. Each jurisdiction is headed by a Jurisdictional Prelate also known as the State Bishop. Each jurisdiction also has a Women's Department which is headed by the Supervisor of Women or also known as the State Mother. The State or Jurisdiction mimics the International Church, but its functional structure and administration is left to the discretion of the Jurisdictional Prelate.*

Texas Greater Southeast First Ecclesiastical Jurisdiction

Church Of God In Christ, Inc.

Bishop Johnny Tates
Jurisdictional Prelate

Mother Lena I. McClain
Jurisdictional Supervisor

Districts of Texas Greater Southeast First

District Name	District Superintendent	District Missionary
1.) Baytown	Supt. John L. Bank	Msny Mae Scott
2.) Beaumont	Supt. Dr.	Msny Ellaner Cook
3.) Galveston	Supt. arry	Msny Ida Ward
4.) Greater Kountze	Supt. oe Chatha	Msny Beulah Jones
5.) Greater Northside	Supt. Cedric	Msny Mattie Jones
6.) Higher	upt. hae	Msny E. A. Collins
7.) Houston	Supt. Ha ilton	Msny L. Johnson
8.) East Te	Supt. rry Co er	Msny B. Henderson
9.) Jasper	Supt. Je Dav	Msny Joyce Tyler
10.) New Dim	Sup Elm	Dr. Lena McClain
11.) North Ho st	Sup astle	Msny Y. Singleton
12.) Northeast	Supt. Aaron L. Houston, I	Msny C. Tompkins
13.) Saints Prog E angelistic	Supt. Connie Cooper	Msny Y. Randle
14.) South Houston	Supt. Johnny Rhodes	Msny Gloria Fuller

SAMPLE ENTRIES
(The next page is an actual sample District Entry)

District Entry

(1) Higher Dimensions

(2) District Superintendent (4) District Missionary
(3) Supt. Michael R. Jordan (5) Msny. Elizabeth Collins

(6) **District Churches**
(7) Palm Lane COGIC
(8) Elder Clarence Collins, Pastor

DEFINITIONS
(1) Identifies the name of the District
(2) Heading for District Superintendent
(3) Identifies the District Superintendent
(4) Heading for District Missionary
(5) Identifies the District Missionary
(6) Heading for the District Churches
(7) Identifies the Local Church in the District
(8) Identifies the Pastor of the local Church and his Title

Note: *The district is the direct arm of the COGIC to the jurisdiction also known as the state. It is on the 6th level (a2) in the ecclesiastical structure of the Church Of God In Christ. Each district is headed by a District Superintendent. Each district is made up of local churches. Each district also has a Women's Department which is headed by the District Missionary of Women. The district mimic the State (Jurisdiction), but its functional structure and administration is left to the discretion of the District Superintendent.*

Higher Dimensions District
Texas Greater Southeast First Ecclesiastical Jurisdiction
Church Of God In Christ, Inc.

Supt. Michael R. Jordan, Sr.
District Superintendent

Missionary Elizabeth A. Collin
District Missionary

Churches of the Higher Dimensions District

Church Name	Pastor's Name
1. Greater Crosby Temple COGIC	Elder Ralph Wells, Sr.
2. Holy Light Temple COGIC	Elder Kelvin W.C Henry, Sr.
3. Holy Temple COGIC	**Supt. Michael R. Jordan, Sr.**
4. Moreh COGIC	Elder Raymond Hunt, Sr.
5. Palm Lane COGIC	Elder Clarence E. Collins

*Church Name and Pastors name in bold is the District Superintendent and the church he pastor's

SAMPLE ENTRIES
(The next page is an actual sample Local Church Entry)

LOCAL CHURCH ENTRY

(1) **Norton Memorial Temple COGIC**
(2) Supt. Luther Swindell, Sr., Pastor

(3) Church Address
(4) 5008 Lucille Street
(5) Houston, Texas 77026
(6) Phone (713) 675-2356
(7) Fax: (713) 675-2356
(8) Email:
(9) Website:www.nortontemple.org

(10) Mailing Address
(11) Same

(12) Church History
(13) In the year of 1946, Norton Temple had its

DEFINITIONS
(1) Identifies the Name of the listed Church
(2) Identifies the Pastor of the listed Church
(3) Heading for the listed Church's Address
(4) Identifies the Address for the listed Church
(5) Identifies the City, State, and the Zip Code of the listed Church
(6) Identifies the Phone number for listed Church
(7) Identifies the Fax number for the listed Church
(8) Identifies the Email address for the listed Church or Pastor
(9) Identifies the Web address for the listed Church
(10) The Heading for the listed Church's Mailing Address
(11) Identifies the listed Church's Mailing Address
(12) Heading for the listed Church's History
(13) Identifies the listed Church's History

Note: *The local church is the direct arm of the COGIC to the district. It is on the 6th level (b) in the ecclesiastical structure of the Church Of God In Christ. Each local church is headed by a Pastor who is an Ordained Elder. Each local church is made up of local members that have confessed their faith in Jesus Christ as Lord and Saviour and their belief in and acceptance of the doctrines of the Church Of God In Christ. Each local church also has a Women's Department. The local church's functional structure and administration is left to the discretion of the local pastor.*

Norton Memorial Temple COGIC

Supt. Luther L. Swindell, Sr.

Norton Memorial Temple Church of God in Christ
Supt Luther Swindell, Sr., Pastor

Church Address
5008 Lucille Street
Houston, Texas 77026
Phone (713) 674-8254
Fax: (713) 674-8254
Email:
Website: www.nortontemple.com

Mailing Address
Same

Church History
In the year of 1946, Norton Temple had its beginning with Elder R.L. Norton as founder, and purchasing of the property at 5008 Lucille Street, Houston, Texas 77026. His first attempt was to build an arbor which was torn down at the request of his Pastor, Elder David Anderson, who said, "It is not time yet…" with only his wife and children as his first members Elder Norton continued to have faith that God was no shorter than His promise and would soon come to his rescue.

In 1947, plans were made and the first building was erected. With constant prayer and zeal to do a great work for God, many souls were added to the church and it became necessary to rebuild in order to accommodate the growing congregation. The second building was completed; however, this did not satisfy Elder Norton's desire to do a greater work for the Lord. On February 8, 1973, God called Elder Norton from his untiring, unselfish, and devoted services to his deserving reward. Immediately following the demise of Elder Norton, Elder W.C Harris served as pastor of Norton Temple for a very brief period of time.

In July, 1973, Elder J.B. Allen was appointed pastoral minister of Norton Temple Church. During his administration he was successful in building Our present beautiful edifice which stands at 5008 Lucille Street today as Norton Memorial Temple. This is the last work that he did for God in his declining years. Elder Allen went home to be with the Lord, July 5, 1981.

In November, 1981, Elder Luther Swindell, Sr., of Hitchcock, Texas was appointed shepherd over the flock of God at Norton Memorial Temple. Under his leadership various accomplishments have been made. His contributions include the enlargement of the church cafeteria, addition of a finance room, concreting the church park lot, purchase of a church van, renovating the church cafeteria, implementing the Irene Swindell & Dr. Barbara Jones Scholarship fund – which was founded by the late Dr. Barbara Jones in recognition of Mother Irene Swindell, the acquisition of additional surrounding properties, and the winning of many souls for Christ.

Pastor Swindell is to be highly commended for his excellent leadership and availability as he continues to work for the glory and honor of God.

ABOUT THE AUTHOR

Kelvin W.C. Henry, Sr. is a fifth generation Church Of God In Christ member, Servant/Leader. His family is as of this publication seven generations strong in the Grand Ole Church Of God In Christ. He is the pastor of the Holy Light Temple Church Of God In Christ, Inc., located in Houston, Texas. He has served in the local, district, state and the national level.

He has served in the local church before his pastorate as the local Sunday School Superintendent, the Chairman of the Board of Trustees of Holy Light Temple COGIC, and as Co-Pastor of Holy Light Temple, just to name a few.

He served in districts as a youth in the 1970's and a teen in the 1980's under **Supt. L.H. Marine** Fair Banks Mission District-TSC Bishop C.H. Nelson, **Supt. W.L. Jordan, Sr.**, South Houston District and Mid-Way District-TSE 1st, Bishop R.E. Woodard, Sr., **Supt. Clayton**-North Houston District-TSE 1st Bishop R.E. Woodard, Sr., **Supt. Prince Spurlock**-TSE 3rd Bishop R.E. Ranger, **Supt. Sherman Gee**-TSE 3rd Bishop R.E. Ranger, **Supt E.L. Glenn**-TSE 3rd Bishop R.E. Ranger. **Bishop Teagues**-TSE 2nd-Bishop M.G. Grady.

He has served on the District level as the District Sunday School Superintendent in the Holy Light District under District Superintendent Leroy Herbert, Sr., in the Texas Southeast First Jurisdiction, Bishop R.E. Woodard, Sr., Jurisdictional Prelate.

He has served as the expeditor in the Northern District under Superintendent W. L. Bowie, Sr., in the Texas Southcentral Jurisdiction, Bishop N.H. Henderson, Sr., Jurisdictional Prelate.

He has served in the Houston Central District as the Director of Education under Superintendent Luther L. Swindell, Sr., Texas Southeast First Jurisdiction, Bishop Rufus Kyles, Jr., Jurisdictional Prelate.

He's served as the District Sunday School Superintendent under Superintendent Luther L. Swindell, Sr., Texas Southeast First Jurisdiction, Bishop Rufus Kyles, Jr., Jurisdictional Prelate.

He is now serving in the Higher Dimensions District as the District Y.P.W.W. President under Superintendent Michael R. Jordan, Sr., Texas Greater Southeast First Jurisdiction, Bishop Johnny Tates, Jurisdictional Prelate.

He has also served on the Jurisdictional level as one of the regional Sunday School President's under the leadership of Jurisdictional Sunday School Superintendent Wesley Virgin, Texas Southeast First Jurisdiction, Bishop Rufus Kyles, Jr., Jurisdictional Prelate.

He has also served on the Jurisdictional level as the Jurisdictional Sunday School Administrator under the leadership of Jurisdictional Sunday School Superintendent Terence K. Kirk, Texas Southeast First Jurisdiction, Bishop Rufus Kyles, Jr., Jurisdictional Prelate.

He has also served on the Jurisdictional Sunday School Department as one of the regional Sunday School President's under the leadership of Jurisdictional Sunday Superintendent Terence K. Kirk, Texas Southeast First Jurisdiction, Bishop Rufus Kyles, Jr., Jurisdictional Prelate / Bishop Brandon B. Porter Interim Jurisdictional Prelate.

He is married to the love of his life, the beautiful Missionary Maveya J. Henry and they share one handsome son Kelvin W.C. Henry, Jr.

Chapter 1

The Church Of God In Christ, Inc.

organized 1907

Contents of this Chapter
"What does that mean?"
Brief History of COGIC and related Movements
Senior and Presiding Bishops' of COGIC
The Presidium of COGIC
The Women's Department of COGIC
AIM History (also UNAC)
Sunday School, **M**ission and **E**vangelism **(ME)**,
Music and **Y**outh **(MY)**

"What does that mean?"

The seal I remember from my childhood Created in 1973

The seal adopted in the April session by the General Assembly in 1981

How it was explained to me

As a child growing up in the Church Of God In Christ, in the seventies. I remember always associating our church with our seal or some may say our logo.

I would often describe our seal as *"a tree or bush in the middle"*, *"with lines around the outside of the tree or bush"*, *"inside a circle"* with the words *"The seal of the Church Of God In Christ, Inc.,"* and *"Established 1907"*. As an inquisitive child, (*and as I do as an adult, even today*), I asked: *"What does that mean?"* My very patient and loving grandfather *Pastor O.T. Taylor* (and others) helped me to understand the seal that represents our church. In those days we were taught to say the whole name, the Church Of God In Christ even when it is listed as C.O.G.I.C.

It was explained to me that there are a total of **5 parts** that make up the seal of the Grand Ole Church Of God In Christ. **(1)** The first part of the seal that was brought to my attention was the thing in the middle that I described as a tree or a bush (*see the seal above"The seal I remember from my childhood"*) is actually **Garnered Wheat** which is symbolic of all the members that make up the Church Of God In Christ.

(2) The second part of the seal, that was brought to my attention (*and by the way I didn't notice it, as a child*) was there is something that looks like a belt, holding the wheat together. It was explained to me that the belt was actually a **Rope of Wheat**; which represents our founder; Bishop C.H. Mason, that banned our churches together back in 1907, as a holiness/sanctified/Pentecostal body.

(3) The Third part that was brought to my attention was the year **1907**. It was in this year that Bishop Mason was filled with the Holy Ghost (in *March of 1907, at the Azusa Street Revivals*) and after his return with others from the Azusa

Revival; with his testimony of his personal experience of this great outpouring, he and those that accepted this great outpouring of the Holy Ghost and the doctrine thereof, were dis-fellowshipped from the (*Holiness*) Church Of God In Christ (1896). Upon them being expelled, Bishop Mason called those that believed together, that agreed with this new doctrine, and organized the (*Pentecostal*) Church Of God In Christ (in *1907*).

(4) The Fourth part that I described as the lines outside of the tree or bush, actually represents for the saints, the **Latter Day Rain**, the awaited Revivals of the End-Time. These revivals such as the Azusa Revival, which caused our church and many other like-minded Holiness, sanctified and Pentecostal churches to come into existence. I later learned that the rain also reminds us that, Christ is our center and as our center, he should be the focus of our worship and the example of our service.

(5) The Fifth and final part of **The Seal of the Church Of God In Christ** represents the name God gave to our founder Bishop C.H. Mason, while he was walking down a street in little Rock, to distinguish our church from others of like named groups at the time. This name was given with a promise by God that if you (*at the time Overseer Mason, Overseer Jones and the Church of God members*) would take the name (**Church Of God In Christ**); that *"there would not be a building larger enough, to hold all those that would come"*. As we see today a promise that was well met. To date there has been a total of three seals the corporate seal, the one I remember as a child created in 1973 and the current version that was adopted by the general assembly in April 1981.

The Corporate Seal

The one I remember as a child Created in 1973

The current Seal adopted in April 1981 at the Spring Call Meeting

Chapter 1
THE CHURCH OF GOD IN CHRIST

How did the Church Of God In Christ get its start in Texas? To answer this question we must go where the Church Of God In Christ finds its roots. It starts with sweeping movements that were found in the late 1800's; sweeping their way across the south.

There was a call for a different religious experience; this call for a different service and worship experience was an initial call for that of *"True Holiness"*. This longing for such an experience evolved into the *Holiness/Sanctification movement* of which the participants believed that the born in sin man could be cleansed by faith in Jesus Christ and experience sanctification through the word of God.

These doctrines teaches among other things that one has the ability to live a holy and separated life in this present world. This movement later evolved into the combined *Holiness/Sanctification/Pentecostal* movement.

Many of the early believers were often referred to as *"holy rollers"*. This was due in part to when the believer would experience being filled with the Holy Ghost; they would experience what is called Glossolalia. *Glossolalia* or being filled is the experience in which the believer would speak in tongues and would often shout and/or roll uncontrollably.

Of these groups the *Church Of God In Christ* can find some of its earliest roots, but the story of the church finds the infancy of its history like others of God's people in the personal story of its *"HOLY MAN."*

The Holy Man of COGIC
Charles Harrison Mason

Bishop C.H. Mason

Like Moses was to the children of Israel looking for the Promised Land, so the Church Of God In Christ finds that its story is tied to the history of Bishop Charles Harrison Mason. His story starts on a certain day in September of 1866, on a farm near Bartlett, Tennessee. The Mason family was a resident of Prior Lee's farm, this type of farm was also called a sharecropping farm.

America in 1866, shortly after the American Civil War; was a dark period in America's history. During this time the south was still feeling the after effects of slavery and its effects on the local landscape and a blot on America as a whole. This blot was being slowly righted, by the then 16th President of these United States of America, Abraham Lincoln.

President Lincoln led his beloved country through its greatest internal crisis by ending slavery while having the awesome task of preserving the Union of the Northern and Southern States.

This righting of the half a century's long injustice treatment of the America Negro was started down a long road of change with the signing and issuing of the Emancipation Proclamation in 1863 and the passage of the Thirteenth Amendment to the Constitution of the United States. This was a new time and different experience in the history of the newly freed American Negro.

HIStory C. H. Mason

For the first time in the history of the America negro, he as a people were free, and as newly freed slaves Jerry and Eliza Mason were excited to welcome into this world, on this wintry Sabbath day of September 8, 1866, their new addition to their young family.

These new parents of a child, whose life would change the religious and social landscape of this country and of the world, were strong Baptist Christians. Their conversion happened during those dark days of slavery on Prior Lee's Farm. This new male child of the Mason family was given the name of Charles Harrison Mason.

Eliza Mason was a fervent prayer warrior. She was a devoted prayer partner of her close friend and co-resident of the farm Ms. Saxton. These two women were known by those on the farm to be women of great prayer and faith. These were two mothers of young children. Eliza was the mother of Charles and Ms. Saxton the mother of Alice.

"Charlie" as Eliza would call him prayed that God would save him at an early age. The example of Eliza's fervent prayer life would follow Charles for the rest of his life. As a young child Charles prayed for the kind of religion and relationship with God that he witnessed of his parents.

During this time in young Charles' life, Jerry Mason would leave his family and join the Union army, which was shortly after the Civil War. But he wasn't gone for long, for he did return, and in 1878, Jerry Mason, moved Eliza and the 12 year old Charles, 12 miles north from Prior Lees' Farm to the swamp-like plantation of John Watson located in Plumersville, Arkansas. This move was thought to be in response to a local epidemic of yellow fever. This same epidemic in a short time after the move, would end the live of Jerry.

Young Charles was described as *"an industrious helper"*, whom Jerry felt that he *"could not coral long enough to educate."*

It was apparent by what would next happen to Charles at this age that the prayers of *"Charlie"* and his mother would be answered early in his life. Charles would later testify that at this tender age he would have magnificent visions of heaven and horrific like nightmares of hell.

These very vivid dreams and visions of heaven and hell would cause the young boy to lay on his bed and think on these visions many days. These visions is what Charles would testify to as his seeing the need to be saved and accept Christ as his Savior.

In November of 1878, at the tender age of 12 years old, Charles was saved. He was then baptized in the same month by his brother the Rev. I.S. Nelson, the pastor of Mt. Olive Missionary Baptist Church, near their new home in Plumersville. After his conversion, Charles became even more dissatisfied with the lifestyles of those his fellow residents of the plantation. Because of the ungodly lifestyles of the people,

Charles had a longing and a desire to move back to his birth home on Prior Lee's Farm. Charles was a very religious child that had the respect of those on the plantation.

He had a belief system that he stuck to even though the temptation to be like those around him was great. It was noted by those that knew him at this time that: *"He, was so different from those other bad boys around about."*

These were indeed conditions that Charles didn't like both naturally and spiritually. To say the least, they were deplorable conditions. And near the end of the summer of 1880, the 13-year-old Charles became very sick.

This sickness included among other things a severe spell of fever and chills. Charles was so sick that some thought that this was a sickness that he would not recover from.

This kind of sickness usually resulted in death. So many thought that the bed that Charles was now laying in was his death bed. It was the thought of many on the plantation that his young life would come to a quick end by the latter part of August.

But God would use this sickness as a start of the signs that his hands were on the life and destiny of this, his servant. This approval of God on the life of young Charles would be seen, when, what some though was a quick end, would be turned around to a quick recovery.

It is now three days from *"Charlie's"* 14th birthday and a miraculous change in his condition came. The day was the first Sunday in September 1880. This first Sunday of September the 5th, day of 1880, young Charles would experience the healing virtue of his God. On what was considered to be His deathbed would become the place where God would reveal his glory. The still weak Charles arises only with the strength of God, with no human help from this, his bed of affliction and this act of faith alone would be the medium by which God would show his healing hand.

This miraculous healing presence of God caused Charles to seek to praise him early in the morning, to testify of his goodness and renew his covenant with Christ.

This renewal caused him to feel the heavy burden of the deplorable state of his living conditions to be lifted. The surroundings of ungodliness, made the already swampy atmosphere even the more so depressing. This was his re-commitment to Christ: *"Lord I, have done all that I can do."*

Our story now picks up some 11 years later in 1891 and Charles is now 25-years-old and ready to start the process to achieve three of his set major life goals.

This list of major life goals were: (1) to receive a college education (2) buy a home and (3) as the scripture reads: find *"a good thing"*, a wife that would be a life long companion.

During this time in his life he would spend a lot of time testifying to anyone who would listen, to the goodness of God and the entire wonderful thing God had done in his life.

Charles knew that his life was destined to be a life of service to God and his people, but Charles wanted to accomplish his set major life goals before, as he puts it, *"my life may be completely turned over to the ministry."*

So with this frame of mind Charles sets out to complete his list of goals and puts on hold God's perfect will for his life. At this time Charles was during what is called lay preaching, which is a little more than testifying. He has decided to ask the Mother of Alice Saxton for her hand in marriage.

This choice of a life partner met with the approval of both the Saxton family and the Mason family. The Saxton family was fond of Charles. This choice to follow what he wanted instead of the perfect will of God for his life, would soon lead to turmoil.

Charles and Alice were married in 1891, and Charles felt that he was well on his way to accomplishing his personal ambitions, his set of major goals for his life. Even though Charles was happy with his choice of life mate, the happiness would be interrupted by his need to travel and preach the word of God.

Some two years into their marriage in 1893, Mason would accept his Minister's license from the Mt. Gale Missionary Baptist Church, which was located in Preston, Arkansas.

Accepting his license is what Charles felt as a fulfilling of his promise to God; *"that if God would allow Charles to marry Alice then Charles will preach his word."* This new call on Mason's life would cause him to have to travel and preach the word of God. Mason had a passion for church work and the work of the church. He would labor over souls night and day that were seeking the Lord.

The new Mrs. Alice (Saxton) Mason expressed the fact that she did not want to be married to a preacher. And this now once happy couple has now become two people with different ambitions for their lives.
Finally after only two years of being married, Alice decided that she could no longer be the wife of a preacher, which had to spread God's Word. So Alice leaves Mason and due to her leaving, he would experience a deep level of depression, which would cause him to be so troubled that he thought about ending it all.

Mason began to see that his life was not on track with the perfect will and the work of God concerning his life. This depression caused him to seek help from the leaders of his local church.

These leaders were the Rev. E.C. Morris (*the president of the Arkansas Baptist State Convention in 1891; he also cofounded the Arkansas Baptist College in 1884*).

Rev. C.L. Fisher was the Academic Dean of the Arkansas Baptist College and one of the leaders in the Arkansas Baptist Convention. Rev. A.M. Booker was the President of the Arkansas Baptist College.

These men would take Mason under their caring wings, encourage him and inspire him to overcome the trouble that he was now experiencing in his life. At this point in his life God allowed a book that many were reading across the south to fall into his hands, which would change his life.

The book that would change Mason's Life

An Autobiography
The Story of the Lord's dealings with Mrs. Amanda Smith
The Colored Evangelist

It was the autobiography of Amanda Smith who was called the *"Colored Evangelist."*

THE TEXAS CONNECTION
The Church Of God In Christ *(Holiness)*

Amanda was born in 1837 and was a member of the African Methodist Episcopal Church. She was a traveling evangelist that had a holiness experience. The testimony of Smith was published in 1893, and this book made such an impact on Mason that it would cause him to see his life like looking in a mirror. This revelation of where his life stood was an eye opener.

Mason soon began to see that he needed to experience the Holiness that he had been reading about for himself. And so Mason would be converted into Holiness this same year (1893) and after being sanctified through the Word of God, he would preach his first sermon in Holiness. His message text would be taken from II Timothy 2:1-3 *"Thou therefore endure hardness as a good soldier of Jesus Christ."* This *"the first message of Mason in holiness"* would describe the walk and life of Mason from that moment on. It was indeed significant of the calling and battles he would have on his life and ministry from that moment until his transition from this world.

Two weeks after preaching his first sermon in Holiness, the after effects of this sermon would cause a revival to breakout. This was the first of many revivals that the message of holiness, that Mason would preach, would cause.

A mother figure to Mason, who was the wife of A.M. Booker and who served as the secretary of the Arkansas Baptist College, convinced Mason to enroll in the College, and by November 1, 1893 Mason was enrolled in the Arkansas Baptist College.

Mason was soon dissatisfied with the methods of teaching and presentation of the Bible, and after only three months, he withdrew from school and returned to every open pulpit declaring Christ by Word, example and precept.

(There was a meeting that would forever change Mason's life. This was the meeting of a soon to be close ministerial companion. This, the meeting of Mason and Jones. But before we get to this historic meeting we must go back a few years to catch Jones' life story up to Mason's story.)

Jones' Story

Overseer Charles Price Jones

The story of Charles Price Jones starts in 1865, in the state of the Georgia peach. Charles Jones was born to a newly freed slave on December 9, 1865, near Rome, Georgia. Jones' mother was a slave during the American era of slavery, but God had his birth to come only a few years after this dark time in our history.

It was common for most slaves, to be as Jones' mother was, very religious, and believed greatly in the power of God and in living and leading a God-fearing life.

The young Jones was an industrious child that had a good work ethic. This desire to work and find a better way caused Jones to search for work outside of his birth state. This search took him to Arkansas. He would settle in Crittenden County Arkansas.

At this time during Jones early life, he would have an experience just shortly after December of 1884. A call for a deeper experience and knowledge of God led him to join the Locust Grove Baptist Church.

At this tender age of 19 years old, Jones was baptized in the Mississippi River on Cat Island in Arkansas. This was the start of Jones quest to get to know what this new convergence to Christianity really meant. In the following year (that of 1885) Jones would announce his call to the ministry. He was then licensed to preach the gospel later in the year of 1887.

Some four years after Jones was saved, and one year after receiving his license to preach in January of 1888, he registered for his religious education.

This great start for Jones was the connection that cause him to gain the respect of many there at the College and those associated with the school. This in turn caused him to be pushed up the hierarchy of the Arkansas Baptist Convention.

By July of 1888, Jones would accept his first Pastoral assignment and pastor the Pope Creek Baptist Church. Jones was ordained October of 1888, by the dean of the Arkansas Baptist College (*C.L. Fisher*).

In November of 1888, one month after his ordination, Jones would be chosen to pastor his second, church the St. Paul Baptist Church in Little Rock, Arkansas.

By 1891, Jones would pastor three churches. The last of these churches was the Bethlehem Baptist Church in Searcy, Arkansas. This was a common practice in those days with rural (*country*) churches.

Most rural congregations would have services on 1st and 3rd Sundays or on 2nd and 4th Sundays.

This was usually due to economics and a shortage of ministers, because of such it was a common practice for most ministers of these churches to either pastor more than one church and/or also have an outside job, (*as many ministers do today.*)

In 1891, the 26 year old would experience a great year. This would be the year that would greet major changes that would lead to some great leadership roles in his life.

First, he would graduate from the Arkansas Baptist College; second he would be elected the corresponding secretary of the Arkansas Baptist Convention and third he was the editor of the Baptist Vanguard which was Arkansas Baptist Convention's faith-based newspaper.

Fourth and lastly, he was a trustee of the Arkansas Baptist College all this again while pastoring three churches. He would also marry the woman he loved *Miss. Fannie Brown.*

Another life changing year would be 1893. This year Jones would leave all his work in Arkansas to accept a call to pastor the Tabernacle Baptist Church in Selma, Alabama.

This change and move was not just a whimsical happing, but rather it was a God arranged opportunity of two God ordained paths to meet. It was in 1893, that Charles Price Jones would meet Charles Harrison Mason.

The 28 year old Jones would meet the 27 year old Mason. These two young preachers shared much in common. They both attended the Arkansas Baptist College (*Jones graduated, but Mason withdrew after only 3 months.*) They also shared in the wise counsel of E.C. Morris the cofounder of the College.

Even though the two shared different views of the promotion methods of the message of Christ, they both shared a common thought of dissatisfaction and the shared view of a new doctrine, that of holiness which gave new life to the old Baptist way.

Mason preferred that *"old time religion"* that he experienced as a boy, that old slave type of spirituality. Jones preferred to use those ideas and equipment that he received through his education at the Arkansas Baptist College.

In 1895, Jones would leave his pastorate of the Tabernacle Baptist Church in Selma, Alabama to accept a call to pastor the Mt. Helm Baptist Church in Jackson, Mississippi. At this same time Mason had relocated to Mississippi somewhere around the Lexington area.

This was no chance move for Jones, but a God arranged move.

For it is now that Mason *"is now in God's will"* for his life and on tract for the work of God. Mason's teaching is now seeing the effects of God's plan for a new Church. A holiness church slowly is unfolding. The time and place is now set for Mason and Jones to meet.

The members of the Mt. Helm Baptist Church was at first happy with their new pastor. He was one that could really speak and sing. He was also a learned man. The only immediate problems as they saw it, was his teachings of a new doctrine called Holiness.

This move to Jackson Mississippi was also a timely move for Jones in another way. Little did Jones know that a new Baptist Convention was being formed, for which he was in time to be a forming delegate. The name chosen for the new convention was the National Baptist Convention.

During the first convention of the National Baptist Convention, Jones became dissatisfied with the convention's complete resolution to cause a change on racism in America.

This position of the National Baptist Convention focused on two main areas to cause improvements for blacks in America.

The two main areas of concentrations of this position were to address: (1) the political disfranchisement of blacks and (2) the dehumanization of blacks.

These were indeed great concerns that needed to be addressed, but the groups' focus was not on a spiritual solution, but rather on the worldly secular nature of these areas of needed improvements. Their solutions addressing these important issues was stated in their resolution.

The main resolve was addressing these solutions in the area of education, social and political change for the black man. This, as Jones saw it, had little or rather no focus on a spiritual solution.

These views by the Convention caused Jones to be disenfranchised with the National Baptist Convention. The newfound doctrine and teaching of holiness by Jones and Mason was also causing a small but noticeable change in the mindset of some of the National Baptist Convention delegates.

Jones and Mason were not the only ones disenfranchised by what they witnessed. The cause of this disfranchisement could be called a more secular view of a problem that should be solved with a more spiritual slanted solution, as they viewed it.

The following were the group of men looking for a more excellent way: W.S. Pleasant of Hazelhurst, Mississippi; C.P.

THE TEXAS CONNECTION   The Church Of God In Christ *(Holiness)*

Jones of Jackson, Mississippi and C.H. Mason of Lexington, Mississippi. These men would soon be described as *"Militant Gospel Holiness Preachers."*

It is now 1896 C.P. Jones and C.H. Mason made a call to all those that were disenfranchised to hold the first holiness convention and revival in the city of Jackson, Mississippi. This meeting was said to have had such an impact on the city, (*due in most part to the holiness/sanctification preaching of Jones and Mason*); that many of the once open church doors to Jones and Mason had now become closed.

During this time a request was made for C.P. Jones to come and preach in Natchez, Mississippi at the Asia Baptist Church that was pastored by J.L. Young. Jones took with him on this trip his new found teaching and revelations on sanctification and holiness.

Jones with power and effectiveness preached these doctrines and the lasting effect was a great stir in the church that caused a split between those that had accepted these new teachings and those that didn't.

This split caused Pastor Young to make another call to Jones to return and amend the doctrines he taught. This request was made due to the fact that most religious leaders at the time were not subscribing to these doctrines.

Most believed that it was impossible to live a life that was free from sin and its control.

This was a request that Jones could not fulfill, due to a conflict of scheduling. He was already committed to fulfill a prior scheduled engagement. His friend C.H. Mason agreed to go and run a revival meeting to address these issues. This was the solution to the request made by Pastor Young.

The revival would lasts one week. During this time of Mason's sanctification and holiness preaching, there was only one person that would come and receive the message to the point of conversion. This one new convert was Charles Pleas and he received sanctification by the word in 1896. Pleas would follow Mason until his transition. (*Elder Pleas was the Bishop of Kansas for 55 years, he was appointed by Bishop Mason.*)

Two great things would happen for Jones in 1896, he had two great publishings. The Holiness magazine called the *"Truth"* and a pamphlet called *"The Work of the Holy Spirit in the Churches"*.

One year later in 1897, would become a year known for the *"burning of black churches"* in the south. This occurrence would cause those that suffered these great losses to have to worship under brush abhors. When this persistent pioneering preacher (*Mason*) returned to Jackson, Mississippi, his first message back in the city was delivered from the south entrance of the courthouse, a location that he was force to accept due to these acts of terror.

At this time of such hardship, it was a common occurrence for these faithful worshippers that accepted this new doctrine to become deprived from their families, home and churches.

This disenfranchisement caused many to wonder what could be done, because thousands throughout the south were being given the cold shoulder for their beliefs in these new doctrines. This treatment was not just limited to individuals, but also to groups.

It was reported that in Mississippi, the State Convention, dis-fellowshipped a complete Baptist Association from the convention because of their acceptance of these doctrines.

This attempt at assimilation was not limited to those without the circle. Some that witnessed these events first hand even tried to convert Mt. Helm into a holiness church, but their attempt was rebuffed.

By June of 1897 Jones would call others that were in the Baptist Church, but were shifting toward Holiness to a conference. Jones was active in the holiness movement but was still an active member of the Jackson Missionary Baptist Association *(his membership in the Association would continue until 1900.)*

These hardships were stumbling blocks for the new movement, but not a cause to stop the new fledging group. A Mr. John Lee was so touched by the ministry of Mason that he allowed him to use his living room to become the meeting place for this new group of believers.

This was a suitable location for only a short period of time. This new teaching was in great demand and drew a large crowd, so much and so until Mr. Lee's living room could not contain those in attendance.

This new problem of outgrowth was soon solved by an owner of a cotton gin house no longer in use in Lexington, Mississippi.

This gin house set just off the bank of a little creek. With the consent of its owner, this site would become the new meeting place of these seekers and worshippers.

This great outpour of these new teachings in Holiness/Sanctification would of course cause the Devil to rear his ugly head. He did so in such a manner that we would in today's terms, would be called a drive by shooting.

Someone filled with great indignation for the success of these meetings shot into this group a pistol five times and two shots from a double barrel shotgun. God's hand was at work during this condemnable act. While the saints shouted a prayed some were injured by this act, but no one was killed.

The old Cotton Gin house

This meeting was so successful that organizing the people into a recognized religious organization, a church that would cause those that believed to become a part of, was necessary.

This new religious organization would teach the doctrine of entire sanctification and a life style of true Holiness. There was a need to call those that believed together to form this new religious organization. Elder Jones, Elder Mason and Elder Pleasant made this formulation call jointly.

This call yielded a total of sixty charter members in response. This new holiness body was known as the *"Church of God."*

The next thing to be done was to purchase a piece of land that the new organization could call their own.

THE TEXAS CONNECTION — The Church Of God In Christ *(Holiness)*

This new need was met a short time later with the purchase of a parcel of land on Gazoo Street, which was located just beyond the corporate line.

The land was purchased from Mr. John Ashcraft. With the purchase of this land, the next need was a facility where the people could worship. This task was accomplished with the building of a small but permanent building, which the size was 60 x 40. The next major task before the group was that they needed a new name.

In 1897, there were many organizations using the name the *"Church of God"* and so the leaders began to seek God for a name that would mark them different from those of like name.

God answered the urgent task through its cofounder C.H. Mason. While he was walking down a certain street in Little Rock Arkansas. God revealed a name to him that would forever set this group apart from those of similar name.

The name that God revealed to Mason had a promise attached to it. The promise was simple, *"If you take this name there will not be a building built large enough to hold those that would follow."* This name is the *"CHURCH OF GOD IN CHRIST."*

This revelatory name was supported by I Thessalonians 2:14. When Mason presented this name to the brethren it was agreed upon by all. Once the brethren agreed to change the name, Mason made it legal by incorporating it in Memphis, Tennessee.

The next phase of change to the church was reorganization. The brethren agreed upon a new structure and Elder C.P. Jones was chose as the General Overseer. Elder Mason was then chosen as the Overseer of Tennessee and Elder J.A. Jeter was chosen as the Overseer of Arkansas.

This original call of the 1896 group of men to hold the first holiness convention and revival in the city of Jackson, Mississippi was by 1898, an annual holiness convention of the Church Of God In Christ (Holiness). C.P. Jones the General Overseer was now hosting at the Mt. Helms Baptist Church, even though a larger number of Mt. Helm members found these new doctrine unsettling.

To add logs to the fire, Jones, along with a few members, proposed something that caused a lawsuit to be pursued by members of the Mt. Helm Baptist Church.

This proposal was that the name of the Church be changed to Church of Christ, Holiness. This proposal would cause the church to split into two separate congregations.

A lawsuit was filed against Jones and those that wanted to change the name of the church.

The court issued an order that would rule against Jones and those that agreed with him. The ruling noted that: *"the land that the church was built on was donated for the express purpose of establishing a Baptist Church and neither Jones nor anyone else had the power to neither change its original purpose, nor its name, nor change its original doctrinal teachings or beliefs."*

There was a prevailing view between Baptist of the day that this new doctrine of holiness could not find a sound place in scripture. It was further believed that it would change what it meant to be a Baptist, if this new teaching was left unchallenged.

THE TEXAS CONNECTION — The Church Of God In Christ *(Holiness)*

By 1899, E.C. Morris, the president of the Arkansas Baptist College, used his annual address to stop what he saw as an erosion of the Baptist belief, by these new outside doctrines (*Morris was a mentor of both Jones and Mason*).

The following was Morris' address, which proclaims his official view as a Baptist on the subject of perfection and he stated: "*That there is such a doctrine as sanctification taught in the Scriptures must be admitted. And that this doctrine has been wantonly perverted and misunderstood must also be admitted. But I am Charitable enough to say that many who have misunderstood and misinterpreted this doctrine have done so from honest convictions which had formed in their hearts on account of incompetent teachers.*"

Morris taught and believed that the only time one would become holy would be upon one's death.

This teaching is evident by the following excerpt from the same address: "Having received the sanctifying influence of the Holy Spirit on our hearts, we set about a cultivation of it with an anxious desire that we may become more like Christ each day. The deformity which sin has brought on us will only be lost in the regeneration of the world."

To hear ones mentor descent your view or beliefs would cause some to be disheartened, that it would cause some to have a crisis of faith. This was not the attitude of Jones and Mason, but rather they both felt that their one time trusted wise counselor was just misinformed and just not clearly understanding the true holiness/sanctification message.

Later on, Jones put on record addressing his mentor and others that questioned his belief in these doctrines with the following statement: "*Having reached my decision to follow my convictions and my Lord, I was looked upon as a fanatic by some, by others as of weak brain; by yet others as a sharper trying to distinguish myself by being different, by nearly all as a heretic.*"

Dissenting and critical views of these two persistent pioneering preachers did not stop their believing nor living these doctrines.

These militant preachers continued to preach these new doctrines as the organization that they cofounded began to grow and take hold on the Baptist and other religious communities. Jones and Mason would find themselves dis-fellowshipped from both the State and the National Baptist Conventions. This explosion and effect thereof was not just on a State and National level but also on a local level. Jones would soon find himself removed as Pastor of Mt. Helm (*this action was a forced action by the Jackson Baptist Association.*)

After his forced outing from Mt. Helm Baptist Church C.P. Jones founded Christ Temple Church, which was a full participating church, now joined into the Church of God in Christ (Holiness). The founding of the Church Of God In Christ (Holiness) gave those then African American Holiness Baptist, Methodist and all people a new organization from which to base their strength as a religious group.

Bishop Mason married his second wife Sister Lelia Mason sometime in 1905, after the death of his first wife Alice Saxton, who divorced him. CP Jones was the minister that married Charles and Lelia. They would enjoy 31 years of marriage until her transition in 1936. Lelia Washington Mason would be the bearer of the eight Mason children. *(Bishop Mason would marry for the last time to Miss Elise Washington in 1943 and this union would remain until his transition in 1961.)*

The year is now 1906, and the revival that was sweeping through the west coast had reached the earshot of Mason and Jones. This revival would be a turning point in the life of Mason. On the other hand upon getting the news of the revival and its happenings, Jones was almost against it from his first hearing of it.

Jones did not believe that receiving the Holy Ghost required the evidence of speaking in tongues.

He would write the following concerning receiving the Holy Ghost: *"Now Christ and the Holy Spirit are one; and the Holy Ghost is the Spirit of Christ, and when one who has asked and received the Holy Ghost lets some sort of Spirit cause him to deny the witness of the Spirit that he has received in order to get that other spirit, I ask you what has he done.*

Seymour, the conductor of this revival in Los Angeles, was no stranger to either Mason or Jones.

For they were familiar with him due to the revivals he conducted in Mississippi.

This revival being ran by Pastor Seymour had peaked the attention of Mason and by March of 1907, caused him to want to go and see for himself its happenings.

Mason asked Jones to accompany him to Los Angeles to visit the Azusa Street Revival, but this request fell on deaf ears. Mason would make this journey to California to attend this great Pentecostal revival with two of his other closest companions; that of Elder D.J. Young and Elder J.A. Jeter.

Apostolic Faith Mission

Mason, Young and Jeter would enjoy the fellowship of the saints while there in Los Angeles for this Revival. Upon arriving there they heard the message of Elder William Joseph Seymour taken from Luke 24:49, *"And behold I send the promise of my father upon you; but tarry ye in the city of Jerusalem until ye be endued with power from on high."* This Pentecostal message would convince Mason of his need to experience this great outpouring.

D.J. Young
One of the two that traveled with Mason to California

J.A. Jeter
One of the two that traveled with Mason to California

The following is some of the testimony of his experience of this great outpouring:
"The first day in the meeting I sat to myself, away from those that went with me. I began to thank God in my heart for all things, for when I heard some speak in tongues, I knew it was right though I did not understand it. Nevertheless, it was sweet to me. I also thanked God for Elder Seymour who came and preached a wonderful sermon. His words were sweet and powerful and it seems that I hear them now while writing. When he closed his sermon he said, "All of those that want to be sanctified or baptized with the Holy Ghost, go to the upper room; and all those that what to be justified, come

to the alter." I said that is the place for me, for it may be that I am not converted and if not, God knows it and can convert me." "Glory!" The second night of prayer I saw a vision. I saw myself standing alone and had a dry roll of paper in my mouth trying to swallow it. Looking up towards the heavens, there appeared a man at my side. I turned my eyes at once, then I awoke and the interpretation came. God and Him only, he would baptize me. I said yes to Him, and at once in the morning when I arose, I could hear a voice in me saying. "I see..." I got a place at the alter and began to thank God. After that, I said Lord if I could only baptize myself, I would do so; for I wanted the baptism so bad that I did not know what to do. I said, Lord, you will have to do the work for me; so I turned it over into His hands..." "Then, I began to seek for the baptism of the Holy Ghost according to Acts 2:41 which readeth thus: "Then they that gladly received His word were baptized, "Then I saw I had a right to be glad and not sad." The enemy said to me, there may be something wrong with you. Then a voice spoke to me saying, if there is anything wrong with you, Christ will find it and take it away and will marry you... Some said, let us sing. "I arose and the first song that came to me was "He brought me out of the Miry Clay." The Spirit came upon the saints and upon me ... Then I gave up for the Lord to have His way within me. So there came a wave of Glory into me and all of my being was filled with the Glory of the Lord. So when He had gotten me straight on my feet, there came a light which enveloped my entire being above the brightness of the sun. When I opened my mouth to say Glory a flame touched my tongue which ran down to me. My language changed and no word could I speak in my own tongue. Oh! I was filled with the Glory of the Lord My soul was then satisfied.

This Baptism of the Holy Ghost was the power of God in a great outpouring. Two of these three would take back with them to their Holiness/Sanctification brothers a new experience, that of Pentecostalism.

This new Pentecostal experience which Elder Mason found for himself, he began to proclaim to others upon his return home to Memphis, Tennessee as a New Testament doctrine.

This new Pentecostal experience was not widely accepted among those that Elder Mason was in fellowship with.

The then General Overseer of the Church of God in Christ (Holiness), Elder C.P. Jones didn't agree to the idea of incorporating this new doctrine in with the Holiness doctrine.

This division between Mason and Jones was not the only division that would arise as of a result of this new Pentecostal experience.

This division was also felt between Young and Jeter those that traveled with Mason to California.

Even though Jeter witnessed for himself the outpouring at the Azusa Revival, he and others sided with Overseer Jones to disregard this new outpouring as an addition to the Holiness message.

This difference in the teaching of this new addition to the Holiness message went on from May of 1907 to August of 1907.

By August of 1907, there was a call for the General Assemble to meet for a doctrine discussing convention of the Church of God in Christ (Holiness) in Jackson, Mississippi.

This convention was called to discuss and present a resolution of the Church of God in Christ's (Holiness) official position on this new doctrine of Pentecostalism.

THE TEXAS CONNECTION   The Church Of God In Christ *(Holiness)*

At this meeting of the General Assembly of the Church of God in Christ (Holiness); Jones, Jeter and others brought the matter before the general assembly.

Jones and his group held the view that this new Holy Ghost experience of speaking in tongues was simply a delusion and believed that this new doctrine and/or experience of Pentecostalism should not be added as a official part of the already hard fought and Semi-established Holiness doctrine.

Much like Holiness was to the Baptist way, so was Pentecostalism to the Holiness way. After a vote on the matter, the general assembly decided to terminate Mason's membership and all those that believed as he did.

This was done by the general assembly with the simple act of withdrawing *"the right hand of fellowship"* from Mason and those that held this belief on Pentecostalism.

Official of the Church Of God In Christ

Poster of Bishop C.H. Mason
Showing some miracles of nature

General Overseer C.H. Mason
Founder of the COGIC

Some Early Leaders of the Church Of God In Christ
Bishop E.R. Driver, Bishop E.M. Wilson, Bishop S.M. Crouch
Bishop C.H. Mason and others.

The emergence of the Pentecostal COGIC

This decision by the general assembly caused C.H. Mason to leave and take with him some of the congregations of the Church Of God In Christ (*Holiness*). C.H. Mason called a special meeting in Memphis, Tennessee. The brothers that attended this meeting were E.R. Driver, J. Bowe, R.R. Booker, R.E. Hart, W. Welsh, A.A. Blackwell, E.M. Page, R.H.I. Clark, D.J. Young, James Brewer, Daniel Spearman and J.H. Boone.

E.R. Driver
the first State Bishop of California

This group of godly men made-up and organized the first Pentecostal General Assembly of the Church Of God In Christ. This new group of the Church Of God In Christ decided to keep the name. This new assembly of the *(Pentecostal)* Church Of God In Christ chose as their new leader Elder C. H. Mason.

E.M. Page
the first State Bishop of Texas

Mason now bore the title of General Overseer and Chief Apostle of the Church Of God In Christ. This decision of the assembly in keeping the name the Church Of God In Christ was a decision that would again cause some contention between Jones and Mason.

Jones felt that he and his group should be able to keep the name of the organization that he served as the original General Overseer. As Mason and his group believed that they had the right to use the name because God had given the name to Mason and also made the promise to him.

This disagreement between the two groups caused this case to ultimately be decided by a Tennessee Court in which the court decided that the name would be exclusively used by Mason and his group.

Jones would reorganize those that stayed with his group into a new non-Pentecostal, but still a Holiness denomination called the Church of Christ (Holiness) USA. Jones would remain the leader of this group until his transition on January 19, 1949.

Jones was met with a great emotional loss in 1916, at the transition of Fannie his first wife. He would later marry Pearl E. Reed 2 years later in 1918. At the start of his new denomination Jones was elected the president; this title was changed to the office of Senior Bishop by 1927.

Bishop Jones was known for his song writing ability and he composed over a thousand songs. These songs were later immortalized with their inclusion in the Church of Christ (Holiness) Official Hymnal titled: Jesus Only, Songs and Hymnal." The Church that Jones would pastor from 1917, until his transition in 1949 would be the Christ Temple Church in which he founded in Los Angeles, California.

Bishop Mason as the Chief Apostle of the *(Pentecostal)* Church Of God In Christ was give the authority by the general assembly to organize auxiliaries for the church, completely establish doctrine for the church and to appoint Overseers (*Bishops*).

The first appointments he made to the office of State Overseer (*Bishop*) were as follows: Dr. Hart for Tennessee; Elder J. Bowe for Arkansas and sometime later he appointed another, the Elder J.A. Lewis for the state of Mississippi.

After more growth came to the church and leadership was needed in other regions. Bishop Mason made other appointments and they were as follows: Elder E.M. Page as Overseer for Texas; the Elder R.R. Booker as Overseer of Missouri; Elder E.R. Driver as Overseer of California and as the National Field Secretary Elder W.B. Holt, who was a white minister in the Church Of God In Christ.

Bishop C.H. Mason as the Chief Apostle made an immediate decision about the time of year for the National Meeting of the Church which would be called the "*Holy Convocation.*" This name was chosen for the meeting based on scriptures such as Lev. 23:1&2.

The timing of the meeting each year would be crucial to the success of the meeting. The time of the year that Bishop Mason chose and dedicated was twenty days, and these dates were from November 25th through December 14th.

This time of the year was chosen so that the saints could fellowship and conduct all the business of the Church. This time of the year was ease for the saints who were mostly farmers, and by this time of the year they would have gathered in their crops, which would allow them to support the meetings in two ways; with their time and have resources that would allow them to financially support the Convocation.

The site of the first of these "*Holy Convocations*" was at 392 South Wellington Street Memphis, Tennessee. The success of these first meetings led to the Church Of God In building its first National Temple on 958 South Fifth Street, in Memphis, Tennessee. This first Tabernacles was completed in 1925.

The Church Of God In Christ during this time proved to be an important organization to the then newly developing Pentecostal movement to both Black and White preachers. Although many were members of the Church Of God In Christ, many others were not. These where given ministerial credentials or were ordained by Bishop Mason between the time of 1907 to 1919.

During this time the Church Of God In Christ was one of the few, if not the only, Pentecostal denomination in the United States that was incorporated and charted as a religious organization with this status.

This legal designation of the Church Of God In Christ allowed those issued credentials though the church, though they were independent ministers, to legally operate as Pastors.

It was also customary for ordained and licensed ministers to receive certain benefits such as half priced train ticket. These credential were also used when these ministers came before the draft board during World War II.

Many of these independent ministers, both Black and White, were not a part of a recognized Pentecostal religious body with the power to give them bonafide credentials, which would allow them to perform recognized ministerial functions such as marriages, burials and etc.... Bishop Mason and the Church Of God In Christ would ordain these ministers.

White members of the COGIC

To address segregationist laws of the time for those ministers that were white, there was an agreement between Bishop Mason and these ministers called a *"Gentlemen's Agreement."*

This agreement allowed the white ministers with credentials from the Church Of God In Christ the ability to issue to those ministers that would come in under their ministries to be also issued credentials from this legally recognized Pentecostal organization.

It is noteworthy to recognize that the first National Field Secretary Elder W.B. Holt of the Church Of God In Christ was a white pastor of a *"white"* Church Of God In Christ that was organized in Memphis, Tennessee at 930 Louisiana Street. Elder Holt was later appointed as Superintendent in California.

By 1913, the line that had been washed away at the American Jerusalem was starting to reappear because of the Southern Segregation laws and practices. A call was made to *"all Pentecostal Saints and Church Of God In Christ followers"* to meet in Hot Springs, Arkansas in April of 1914. This invitational call was made on December 20, 1913 by Elder E.N. Bell and Elder H.A. Goss. This call to convene a General Council was advertised in the Word and Witness. Its subscribers were mostly Caucasian saints.

The organizing General Council

Founders of the Assemblies of God and the article that called the white COGIC ministers, published in word and witness 12/20/1914

In 1914, an organizing convention was being held in Hot Springs, Arkansas. This organizing convention was organized by White Pentecostal ministers, many of which were licensed and ordained by Bishop Mason and held credentials of the Church Of God In Christ.

These men established and organized the General Council of the Assemblies of God. The council established doctrines that didn't put emphasis on Sanctification and Holiness as requirements to receive the baptism of the Holy Ghost.

This was not a complete break from the Church Of God In Christ; the fellowship was still there.

The Assemblies of God council invited Bishop Mason to preach at the organizing convention in which he would address 400 white Pentecostal Ministers, many of which held credentials with his name on them.

THE TEXAS CONNECTION — The Church Of God In Christ (Pentecostal)

This is a cordial relationship that exists between the two denominations even today.

At this time most blacks that had a religious experience under the banner of Christianity had this experience by the way of the Methodist or Baptist Church. The Holiness and Pentecostal movements of which the Church Of God In Christ would lead the charge would change this religious landscape.

Bishop Mason would plant the seeds of Pentecostalism on the east coast and in the north that would grow when blacks would migrate to these regions.

These seeds were watered when the Evangelists of the Church Of God In Christ would travel to these locations preaching this new and powerful Holiness/Pentecostal message.

The growth of the Church Of God In Christ was evident in the North by 1917, with churches in Philly, Brooklyn and Pittsburgh.

Mason Temple
*The International Headquarters
of the Church Of God In Christ
located in Memphis, Tennessee, USA*

The site of the first "*Holy Convocation*" of the Church Of God In Christ was held at 392 South Wellington Street, Memphis, Tennessee. The success of these first meetings led to the Church Of God In Christ building its first National Temple on 958 South Fifth Street, in Memphis, Tennessee this first Tabernacle was completed in 1925.

This remained the National meeting place from 1925 until 1936. In 1936, the National Organization was visited by a tragic fire that left the Church Of God In Christ without a National Temple. Bishop Mason the General Overseer and Chief Apostle of the church provided the local church that he pastored as the temporary site for the National meeting place which was located at 672 South Lauderdale. This site was used from 1936 to 1945.

By 1945, Bishop Mason and the Church Of God In Christ was able to see a dream and project that seemed impossible at the time come to full fruition. The same year of 1945, saw the completion and dedication of what was then the largest black owned religious facility of its day that of Mason Temple Church Of God In Christ.

Mason Temple was built during World War II. This is amazing because it was wartime and a national steel ration was in place. But in spite of this rationing God saw Bishop Mason and the Church through this time with no problem in acquiring enough steel to complete this larger facility, which was built for less than $400,000.00.

Mason Temple upon its completion became the largest church or hall that was black owned and operated facility in the country. Mason Temple has three levels which is estimated to seat a total of 9,000.

This seating capacity is as following: 5,000 main seating 2,000 balcony and a 2,000 capacity in the assembly room.

When Mason Temple was opened it was a one stop shop state of the art facility for its day. It had located between its walls a state of the art sound system for sound both inside and outside, a complete air condition and heating system, a post office, a nursery, both male and female showers and bath, restrooms, a beauty salon and a barber shop, shoe shine parlor, baggage-check and registration room, first aid and an emergency ward, picture booth, 2 professional kitchens, 2 cafeterias and concessions and in the business area 36 administration offices.

Mason Temple over the years has seen many historical and cultural events unfold between its walls. It is not widely known but Dr. King actually spoke twice at Mason Temple. His first speech at Mason Temple was a "get out the vote" rally held on July 31, 1959.

The last public speech of Dr. King (*I've Been to the Mountain Top*") which was in support of sanitation workers what were striking for a living wage, was given on April 3, 1968.

Many gospel stars have performed at Mason Temple such as Mahalia Jackson, Richard White, The Clark Sisters and many others.

Because of the grace of God the (*Pentecostal*) Church Of God In Christ grew from a few congregations in 1907 to the largest Pentecostal Organization in America, which was due in large part to the obedience of one of his servants, that of Bishop Mason.

Bishop Charles Harrison Mason's leadership and direction was both spiritual and apostolic.

After the transition of Sister Leila (*Washington*) Mason, Bishop Mason's second wife, the mother of his eight children. Bishop then married Sister Elsie Washington Mason in 1944 (*no children were born of this union*).

The Masons

Bishop C H. Mason & Mrs. E.W. Mason

From 1951 until his transition in 1961 Bishop Mason knew that his health was declining and knew that he alone would not be able to adequately see to the ecclesiastical and secular matters of the Church. After much prayer he appointed a special seven man commission to assist him with these and other national matters. The official name later chosen for this commission was the Executive Commission. This Commission was given complete authority to conduct and execute apostolic business formerly performed by Bishop Mason.

These activities of the commission included, but were not limited to making all appointments. The following were the initial appointments to this Commission by Bishop Mason: On June 5, 1951 three men were appointment and they were Bishops A.B. McEwen, J.S. Bailey and O.M. Kelley. On May 19, 1952 one man was appointed to the commission in the person of Bishop J.O. Patterson, Sr., and on October 12, 1955, three m were added Bishops U.E. Miller, S.M. Crouch and O.T. Jones, Sr., (*six were later added and its name changed.*)

At the God blessed age of 95 in Detroit, Michigan, Bishop Charles Harrison Mason closed his eyes for the last time on November 17, 1961, at the Harper's Hospital.

At Bishop Mason's funeral there was an estimated 10,000 people in attendance at Mason Temple. Bishop Mason's resting place is a tomb located on the second level of the headquarters of the Church Of God In Christ in Memphis, Tennessee at Mason Temple.

The estimated members of the Church Of God In Christ is currently six million six hundred thousand (6,600,000).

There are currently estimated a total of Fifteen thousand five hundred (15,500) churches under the parent body of the Church Of God In Christ headquartered in Memphis, Tennessee.

These churches can be found in the United States, in 52 countries, and on the islands in the seas.

Plaque registering Mason Temple as a National Historic Place by the
United States Department of Interior

Below are a few of the many historic photos inside of Mason Temple from the civil rights movement to a visit from a sitting United States President.

Dr. Martin Luther King, Jr. and his aide Jessie Jackson just before he delivered the *"Mountain Top"* Speech

Dr. Martin Luther King, Jr. at Mason Temple delivering his last speech *"Mountain Top"* on a stormy Thursday night on April 3, 1968 before more than 2,000 people

President Clinton greeting Presiding Bishop L.H. Ford before addressing the Church Of God In Christ in Mason Temple at the National Holy Convocation on November 13, 1993.

Inside Mason Temple Church of God In Christ which was built during World War II during a time of a steel rationing because of World War II. The approximately seating is a total 9,000.

The Azusa Street Revival

Apostolic Faith Mission site of The Azusa Street Revival

W.J. Seymour

Standing Left to Right (*possibly Sister Prince*), G.W. Evans, Jeannie M. Seymour, Glen Cook, Florence Crawford, unidentified man, Lucy Farrow. **Seated:** Mary Evans, Hiram W. Smith, unidentified child, William Joseph Seymour and Clara Lum.

The revival that would launch Pentecostalism finds its origins in a watch meeting revival on December 31, 1900, in Topeka, Kansas. It would move to Houston, Texas, pick up Pastor Seymour and then head to Los Angeles, California in April 1906 and would last until sometime in 1909.

*Historical Marker of Bishop Mason and the Church of God in Christ in Mississippi
Recognized by the Mississippi Department of Archives and History, 2014*

Bishop C.H. Mason
*founder of
The Church of God in Christ*

Overseer Charles Pleas
Bishop Mason's first convert
into holiness in 1896

*A postcard of **Holmes County Court House**
Lexington, Mississippi (see reference above)*

The old cotton Gin House
(see reference above)

*Mother Elsie W. Mason (wife) and Bishop C.H. Mason
at the Annual Holy Convocation of the Church of God
in Christ in Memphis, TN*

The Latter Day Quest
"The American Jerusalem"

The phenomenon of speaking in tongues for the Church Of God In Christ, had its spark and its inception when the paths of two men given credit for being used by God to further the Holiness/Pentecostal movements crossed. These men were Charles Fox Parham and William Joseph Seymour. The following is that story:

William J. Seymour
"The Leader of the Azusa Street Revival"

Sometime after September 22, 1862, Simon Seymour joined the union Army and served as a member of the United States Colored Troops. As a foot solider he would march across the southern states. During this march through what was swamp land, Simon contracted a disease that he would never fully recover. Some have speculated that it was most likely a bout of malaria.

It was on May 2, 1870, that former slaves Simon and Phyllis Seymour (*Phyllis Salabar*) welcomed one of their many children into this world on the Sugar Plantation owned by Asiland Carlin in Centerville, St Mary's Parish, Louisiana. This was the same place where the Seymour's were married and was the site of Phyllis's slave residence.

Like many during this time the Seymour's didn't have much and to say that they were poor is a under statement. By 1896, the only things the family had as earthly possessions were described as *"one old bedstead, one old chair and one old mattress."* At the stated worth of a whole fifty-five cent.

The Seymour family were various religious participants. This can be what contributed to William's open religious insight and his acceptance of divers' views of religion.

These diverse experiences include the following: *Simon and Phyllis were married by a Methodist minister; The five month old baby William was baptized on September 4, 1870, at the Catholic Church in Franklin, Louisiana; and at the end of their days both Simon and Phyllis found their final resting place in a cemetery that was a part of a Baptist Church.*

Young William would receive his initial education from the Freedman's School in Centerville, Louisiana where he learned to read and write. After becoming an adult William was ready to see and experience more that life had to offer outside of the poverty that was a way of life for him and others in South Louisiana.

While traveling and working he came in contact with the Holiness movement in Cincinnati, Ohio that was led by Wells Knapp (1853-1901). This group was called *"God's Revivalist."*

Seymour's travels which were a search for his family and for a better way of life took him to places like Indiana, where he worked as a waiter. While there working as a waiter in an upscale hotel restaurant, he was saved at a Methodist Church.

After hearing and accepting the teaching on entire sanctification, Seymour joined the *"Evening Light Saints"* which later became the *"Church of God Reformation"* which was headquartered in Anderson, Indiana. The teaching that they were known for was that there would be a great outpouring of the Holy Ghost before the rapture of the Church.

During this time Seymour would experience sanctification and accept his call to preach. In 1895, Minister Seymour would fall victim to a common illness of the time. He contracted smallpox. This illness caused two changes in the life of this young minister. First his contracting smallpox left him blind in one eye and scars of the disease would cause him to wear a beard the rest of his life to cover the scars on his face.

The loss of the vision in his one eye caused Seymour to pray to God that He would restore his vision. God answered his prayers, but not as he would suppose. Even though his natural vision was never restored in his eye, he gained great spiritual vision.

The start of it.

There was another event about to happen that would also have a life long effect on Seymour, the Holiness/Sanctification movements and the world.

Charles Fox Parham
"The Leader of the Bethel Bible School"

There was a question raised during a revival held in December 1900. The question that caused this event was *"is speaking in tongues evidence of the undisputable sign of the baptism of the Holy Ghost?"* This is an observable occurrence that is also called Glossolalia. Glossolalia was in some circles a common place occurrence and even though it was common, it was discussed and misunderstood by many in these inside and outside of these circles.

A former Methodist pastor in Kansas who was now operating the Bethel Bible School in Topeka, Kansas asked his students to do a home work assignment. This assignment

Bethel Bible School
"in Topeka Kansas 1900"

was to study a phenomenon that happened in the book of Acts. This phenomenon was the falling of the Holy Ghost on the day of Pentecost and being filled. The aforementioned question was studied by the class to substantiate the undisputable sign of this filling.

This was a discussion that Parham wanted his students to interact with because of his acceptance of the teachings of the group the *"Fire-Baptized Holiness Church"*. The main teaching of the FBHC was that receiving of the Holy Ghost was the *"third work"*.

As all Christians believe the *"first work"* is that of salvation. The *"second work"* as many of the Holiness churches taught was that of sanctification which is recognized as the work of grace. And finally as Pentecostals believe and teach the *"third work"* is that of the baptism of the Holy Ghost or Holy Spirit.

This doctrine of the *"third work"* was a doctrine that was accepted and taught by Parham. The only thing about this doctrine that he disagreed with was what he classified as: *"the extreme emotionalism"* that was characteristic of those of FBHC when this filling would take place.

In 1895, there were many leaving the Methodist Church among whom Parham was one. In this exiting from the Methodist Church there was a common doctrine being taught and accepted by those that left. There was a well known school of thought among those of this exodus concerning speaking in tongues as the generally accepted sign of the baptism and the filling of the Holy Ghost.

Parham taught this doctrine, but with the exception that this baptism in the Holy Ghost came not as part of an extreme display of emotionalism, but rather due to and as a part of a common worship.

Also as part of his version of this teaching, Parham taught that the *"second work"*, sanctification was the process where the believer was cleansed and made Holy.

This doctrine taught that the *"third work"* happened when the believer was filled, the believer was then empowered by the Holy Ghost and was then ready for the work of God by receiving his spirit by the evidence of speaking in tongues.

This homework assignment culminated into a prayer vigil which was a New Year's Eve vigil on December 31, 1900 at the Bethel Bible School.

This was the site of the initial recorded event that would later kick start the Azusa Street Revivals. It was the request of one of the students that had completed the homework assignment and wanted to experience the events she read about in the book of Acts. She made a simple request that Parham would lay his hands on her and pray that she would experience the baptism of the Holy Ghost with the evidence of speaking in tongues.

Agnes Ozman
"The first of Parham's group to receive the baptism of the Holy Ghost with the evidence of speaking in tongues"

The student making this request was Agnes Ozman. It was now January 1, 1901 and Ozman's prayer request was answered and she was baptized with the Holy Ghost with the evidence of speaking in tongues.

Some two years and a little over 700 miles away. William J. Seymour arrives in Houston, Texas sometime in 1903.

This move is believed to be among other things a search for his family. This was a search for siblings of his parents that were sold during the time of slavery. This was a common search for newly freed slaves.

What Seymour thought was a search for a connection to his family was actually a divine connection to his future.

True to his religious upbringing Seymour would look for a house of worship for which he could worship God as he believed.

He found such a place in Houston, Texas in the form of a little Holiness Church. This little holiness church was pastored by Lucy Farrow.

Pastor Farrow was a black woman, who was the niece of Frederick Douglass *(Frederick Douglass was one of this nations first great internationally known black speakers and Pre-Civil War activist who was also a leading abolitionist.)*

A change in the spiritual life of Seymour would occur in 1905, some two years after his arrival in Houston. Charles Fox Parham asked Pastor Farrow to come to Topeka, Kansas and be the Governess in his home.

This was a position that Farrow felt honored to be offered. The only problem was that by accepting this position it would leave the little Holiness Church she pastored without spiritual leadership.

This problem was solved by a faithful member of the church. Farrow asked Seymour if he would pastor the small holiness church in her absence so she could accept the position as governess in the home of Parham.

Seymour accepted the work and thus began his pastoral service in ministry. This first pastoral assignment would prove to be the training ground for the awesome ministry that lay ahead for this soon to be leader in the *Holiness/Pentecostal movement.*

Pastor Seymour would pastor the small church for a space of time before Farrow would return from Kansas. When Farrow returned to Houston, Texas she was speaking in tongues.

During this same frame in time Parham would come to Orchard, Texas on an invite from Walter Oyler and his wife. He later made a visit to Houston at the request of Mrs. John C. Calhoun. This visit would be the first time that Pastor Seymour would hear the Pentecostal message. At the request of those same friends, Parham decided to move his Bible School to Houston, Texas to train workers in the ministry.

The Bible Training School
"Formerly was Bethel Bible School moved from Topeka

On July 13, 1905, Parham and the Bible school moved to Houston, Texas and it was renamed "The Bible Training School". A year and a month after this move the Houston Chronicle would run an article entitled *"Houstonians Witness The Performance Of Miracles"* being held at Bryan Hall in Downtown Houston, Texas. As so read the article that ran in the August 13, 1905 edition of the Houston Chronicle.

Houston Chronicle Article
August 13, 1905 edition

Parham is given credit as the founder of the Apostolic Faith Movement and the modern Pentecostal/Charismatic revival. Parham taught the initial evidence of the baptism in the Holy Ghost was speaking in tongues.

In Texas where Parham and Seymour would have their Godly appointed meeting there was a separation law that was practiced by many in the state.

At the onset this law would seem to be the one thing that would curtail this great appointed happening. Texas at the time had set segregation laws that were not just laws on the books, but rather strongly upheld laws of separating the races in both the religious and secular circles.

To someone other than the young Pastor Seymour these laws would seem to be the straw that would break the camel's back. But his strong desire to receive this new teaching on the Pentecostal awakening of our age was strong enough to overcome these seemingly insurmountable odds. This strong desire of Pastor Seymour would lead him to matriculate into *"The Bible Training School"* in October of 1905.

This enrollment of Pastor Seymour presented a problem for Parham, because of the laws of Texas he could not allow Pastor Seymour to sit in the same class with the other white students. So Parham came up with an inventive way for Pastor Seymour to still get the benefit of his class room teachings on the experience of Pentecost. The solution was simple, when the class was conducted, Parham would simply leave the door open and Pastor Seymour would sit on the floor outside the classroom to hear the teaching.

It is recognized that Pastor Seymour was a quick study. After hearing and receiving this new doctrine for only a few weeks on the baptism of the Holy Ghost with the initial evidence of speaking in tongues he began to teach this new doctrine on his own, even though at that time he was not a recipient of this experience.

The segregation laws of Texas again proved to be a problem which caused Seymour's teaching of this new doctrine to be limited to only blacks, but again this would be solved by the joint meetings of Parham and Seymour. In these meetings Parham would address the white audience and Seymour would address the black audience.

This arrangement would seemly work to Parham's advantage, because Parham saw this as an opportunity to reach the African America community in Texas through Seymour. Which would help to spread the Apostolic Faith message among them. Seymour would carry this message through revivals in Texas, Mississippi and other states.

Little did Parham know that God would use Pastor Seymour to spread more than just the Apostolic Faith message, but God would carry Seymour from Houston to California and this move came about because of a faithful visit of Sister Neely Terry a resident of Los Angeles and a member of the Second Baptist Church in Los Angeles, California.

Sister Terry made a visit to Houston to visit relatives and while there she visited the little Holiness Church pastored by Seymour. Terry had no idea that this visit was not a chance meeting, but rather an arranged visit by God for his future time and purpose.

In February 1906, in Los Angles a new doctrine was being taught at the Second Baptist Church by a Sister Julia Hutchins. This new doctrine was the teaching of Holiness and Sanctification as a separate work of grace, after and in addition to being born again. This separate work as Hutchins taught was that the believer could live holy in this present world.

This doctrine was taught in such a convincible manner that it caused eight families along with Sister Hutchins to be expelled from the Second Baptist Church.

When this group of eight families was expelled from the church, they were not stopped, but rather they started a mission on 9th and Santa Fe Street in Los Angeles. One of these families expelled was Brother Richard Asbury and his wife Sister Ruth Asbury.

A short time after this group started the mission *(which possibly took the name Nazarene Mission)*. Sister Julia Hutchins was impressed upon by the Lord that this assembly needed a male pastor. Sister Hutchins came before the members of the mission and made this known to them and asked for any suggestions.

Sister Neely Terry who was the cousin of Sister Ruth Asbury and a member of the Second Baptist Church had returned from Houston where she found that her family and friends were dis-fellowshipped from the Second Baptist Church.

Terry upon rejoining her family and friends at the newly formed mission made the suggestion of a Minister that she had just met while visiting in Houston that was a great teacher on Holiness.

This suggestion was taken under advisement and a call was made for Pastor Seymour to come to California.

Pastor Seymour accepted this call and he started his travel to the mission with only a ticket that was paid for by Parham and others.

On his way after leaving Houston with no money or possessions he stopped by and stayed in the headquarters of the *"Pillar of Fire" in Denver, Colorado*, lead by Sister Alma White. This was a small Holiness group that also taught the sanctification message and furthermore taught and believed that the Holy dance was part of this work.

As history tells us this was not a warm reception. For Seymour was a preacher that did not fit everyone's mold of what they thought a man of God should be *(this was the case on this occasion of Sister White meeting him)*.

Upon arrival at the Pillar of Fire, Seymour would simply inform Sister White that he was a man of God and needed a place to stay and food. By so many imposters preceding him and by what some accounts would later report, White described Seymour's appearance as "*one of untidiness*" and would cause her reception of him to be not so welcoming.

Finally Pastor Seymour made his arrival in Los Angeles to the mission on Santa Fe; he came preaching Acts 2:4 this message simply proclaimed the teaching that the Baptism of the Holy Ghost with the evidence of speaking in tongues was necessary to experience Pentecost.

This was not the message that Hutchinson was expecting out of what she thought was a holiness preacher. The message was not in the context of the holiness teaching or doctrine as she believed it.

This message so dismayed her that she called upon the president of the Southern California Holiness Association (SCHA) of which the mission was a member with her concerns.

Her actions after disagreeing with the message that the new minister of the mission was preaching, caused Azusa Street to forever be known as the place of the American Revival of the Century, *"The Pentecostal Awakening of America."*

At the advice of President J.M. Roberts of the SCHA, Hutchins padlocked the doors to the mission on Santa Fe to keep out what she perceived as a new and unsettling doctrine.

What Hutchins didn't realize was that this new doctrine had already taken root in the heart of some of the members and thus those in reception of such had already received and agreed with this revelation.

With the actions of Hutchins, Pastor Seymour who had arrived in Los Angeles with nothing, but a prayer was now in the city with no house of worship, no money for lodging thusly in need of places of spiritual and natural refuge.

Pastor Seymour's residential needs are met by Mr. Edward Lee, one who heard this new doctrine and took it to heart. Mr. Lee didn't have much as a janitor of one of the local banks, but what he did have he offered to the man of God as a place of natural refuge.

The second need which was the primary need, a place for worship was provided for when two of those that were locked out by Hutchins actions as well stepped up. These two locked out members of the mission on Santa Fe provided their home as a place for the newly locked out group to meet, thusly providing the spiritual refuge.

This new group would soon begin to have regular prayer meetings in the welcoming home of Richard and Ruth Asbury at 214 North Bonnie Brae in a small but comfortable home. Mr. Asbury was employed as a janitor.

The Asbury House
214 North Bonnie Brae

This new prayer group's meeting was mostly made up of those that were locked out of the mission on Santa Fe, which was for the most part attended by African Americans. Every now and then there would be white attendees. They would seek God for the outpouring that they heard Seymour preaching.

The first to receive an answer to the request of this outpouring was on April 9, 1906, only after about five weeks removed from the mission on Santa Fe Street, the provider of Seymour's place of residence began to speak in tongues.

This was testified to by Seymour at the next meeting which witnessed others upon the hearing the news following suit. Much like wild fire, the news of this outpouring caused great attendance and one of the Asbury's neighbors began to do something that she had never done.

The neighbor was Jennie Evans Moore (*Seymour's future wife*) who began to sing in an unknown tongue and play the piano. It was believed by those present that the language that Moore was singing in was Hebrew. This outpouring caused many to be curious and attend the meetings that soon moved to the porch of the Asbury home. But the day that would be significant for this young 36 year old Holiness/Pentecostal preacher would be April 12, 1906, this would be the day that the Lord would allow him to experience what he had preached for six months.

When Pastor Seymour and others received just what they had been praying for and began to speak in tongues. It was such an outpouring until it was reported that the daughter of the Asbury's was so amazed at what she was witnessing that the sight of such caused her to fall through the kitchen door.

This was the start of the Pentecostal Revival of the west cost that would change the world. It is said that the events of the outpouring was truly hard to describe. One description simply says *"People fell to the floor as if unconscious, others shouted and ran"*.

Hundreds began to gather, this crowd included blacks and whites who freely mingled. The streets were filled as Seymour preached from the Asbury's porch. This meeting outgrew the Asbury's home and a search was made for a new meeting place.

Apostolic Faith Mission
William J. Seymour pictured at AFM around 1910

This new now expanded group found their building at 312 Azusa Street and held its first meeting there on April 14, 1906. This site was located in a black low economic neighborhood where the rent was only $8.00 a month. A local article called the new location of this group a *"tumble down shack"*.

This description was due in part to the fire that caused the once church, to no longer look like a church. The once pitched roof was now gone and the once grand church now looked like a storage building.

Those in charge of the reconstruction found it to be more cost effective to change it to a flat roof.

This new home for this outgrown prayer group didn't resemble a church although it was built as such.

The only thing left that resemble a house of worship in this now 60 x 40 square building was the gothic style window that was featured on the front of the structure on the second level.

The first floor of this used to be AME church was now being used as storage and as horse stables. The second level of the structure had been reconstructed into living quarters that were rented out as apartments.

This was not a cathedral grand, but it was just what was needed. This simple and humble new home was the perfect place for the outpouring that was to come. There needed to be a place where both the elite of society could come and those that were not influential could feel comfortable.

As one article in the Apostolic Faith noted *"It is noticeable how free all nations feel...No instrument that God can use is rejected on account of color or dress or lack of education. This is why God has so built up the work."*

This new home needed a name and the name chosen was the Apostolic Faith Mission. The simplistic and humble home of the mission was not furnished with matching pulpit furniture that matched the pews, communion and offering tables.

But it was with wooden boards (*or as some reports have named them old planks*) laid across empty nail barrels as pews and odd chairs as seating.

The consecrated desk or pulpit as it is named was made up of old milk crates simply stacked on top of each other and covered with spare pieces of cloth.

It has been recorded that Pastor Seymour would oft times been seen with his head in one of the crates receiving a message for the people from God.

It was in this simple place with its simple people in these simple surrounds that the message filled with the fire of Pentecostalism would draw those seeking from all over the world.

They came from far and near. They were of all races. They were the young, the middle age and the old. They were rich and they were poor. They were sick and they were well. No matter what they were or who they were it really didn't matter. They were there to experience this great Pentecostal Revival.

The news of this great revival reached and had the attention of those in the news media. The leading newspaper of the day *"The Los Angeles Daily Times"* published an article on the Happenings of Azusa Street that ran in the Wednesday Morning Edition on April 18, 1906.

Los Angeles Daily Times Articles
Wednesday April 18, 1906 edition

The writer of this article had no way of knowing that on the morning of the publishing of this article at exactly 5:12 a.m. that the great Earthquake of San Francisco 1906, would hit. This article was less than appealing, but rather it was highly critical of the revival and its evangelist.

The headline read *"WEIRD BABEL OF TONGUES"* this article called Pastor Seymour *"AN OLD COLORED EXHORTER"* it would also call the testimony of Sister Moore as *"Gurgles of WORDLESS TALK"* and describe the meeting as a *"New Sect of Fanatics Is Breaking Lose."*

This Latter Day outpouring was described as a *"frenzy of religious zeal."* A prophecy of one of the ministers in attendance was also noted in this same article. It simply read: *"awful destruction to this city unless its citizens are brought to a belief in the tenets of new faith."*

Certainly this divine revelation that foretold of God's awesome power truly had an Azusa Connection. This awesome display of God and the pre-doomsday prophesy caused Southern Californians to be in search of answers.

The earthquake of San Francisco 1906
7.8 magnitude earthquake

One of the lay ministers who attended the Azusa Street Meetings produced a track that kept those interested informed of these end time evens. The Minister, a Brother Frank Bartleman, would put out thousands of these tracks, about the earthquake of April 18, 1906 and the events of the Azusa Street Revival.

Frank Bartleman
A participant at Azusa Street

This along with other faith-based articles that carried the word of these events and the revival caused those in search of answers to attend the Azusa Street Revival in droves by the hundreds. These droves filled the dirt floor of this humble building and filled the streets.

One of these faith based papers that covered these events was produced by Seymour and the Mission called *"The Apostolic Faith"*. This paper reached many with the printed sermons of Seymour. It also covered the going-on of this great revival that lasted for 3 years.

It is noted that the circulation for the Apostolic Faith numbered passed that of 50,000. Before the days of the television ministry, these papers literally spread the Pentecostal message across the globe.

It was noted that the Azusa Street revival was not an organized meeting. It was a free flowing meeting that allowed the pure unadulterated move of God. There was no big I's or little u's, there was truly neither male nor female, neither black, nor white or respect of person. In the words of Frank Bartleman, "the blood of Jesus washed the color line away", *at what he later described as the American Jerusalem."*

The Apostolic Faith Paper
Newspaper published by Seymour

Many would seek the Lord on the first floor and there was also on the second level what was called the upper room. This also doubled as the living quarters for Seymour and some of the other members of the mission. This was said to be the place where you seeked for the Pentecostal outpouring.

As soon as it was going good and the people were being blessed the *"Devil"* in his usual fashion stuck his head up. The revival would face those that didn't want for one reason or another, see it succeed. This was not always by those that were outsiders, but rather by some that were close.

There were three main events that caused the success of this great outpouring to be overshadowed with a crippling cause and effect set of happenings. The first of these came from the mentor of Seymour, in the person of that of Charles Fox Parham. When Parham received news of the Revival he made a visit, to see for himself what the talk was all about.

In this visit by Parham, he was disturbed by two factors that he noted was not right.

Firstly by Parham the *"meeting of all the races in one place was insulting"*. Secondly, by Parham as noted previously *"the emotionalism of the meeting was too much"* and by his view *"not necessary"*. This published view brought about the first major split of the mission.

The Second major split came when what was a very happy day for Seymour, was not a happy day for all. On May 13, 1908, Seymour married the jewel that would be his soul mate. This marriage between William Seymour and the neighbor of the Asbury's Miss. Jeanne Evans Moore caused another group to leave the mission.

The Seymour's
Bishop W.J. and Jeanne Seymour

The last of the three major crippling blows came when two of Seymour's trusted workers in an act of discord left the mission and took with them the main mailing lists of the *"The Apostolic Faith"* newspaper. *(These are viewed as the three major crippling blows to the Mission, but many more would follow)*

The end of the initial revival that began in April of 1906, came to an end sometime in 1909. Many of the Holiness Churches and others of the time would harshly rebuke the events at Azusa Street. Some would describe the events of Azusa Street as *"strange spells and jibberish"* in their open public rebuke.

Only a few years after the start of this great outpouring, there was a great falling away. The charge of keeping the *"fire burning"* fell to the original prayer group that met at the Asbury's home. *(It is said that Lucy Farrow traveled to California to assist Pastor Seymour)*

Bishop Seymour was faithful to the call of pastoring the church until the Lord called him from Labor to reward. Pastoring was not his only given task. He also had a true apostolic call of establishing churches around the world. This call even led to him writing the church manual *"The Doctrines and Discipline of the Apostolic Faith Mission"* the book served as the doctrine book to the churches that were under his authority.

The legacy and leadership of Bishop W.J. Seymour, the leader of Azusa, was ended when on September 28, 1922, Bishop Seymour experienced chest pains and shortness of breath. Even though medical attention was given, he was called on this day from labor to reward.

On his headstone in the Evergreen Cemetery in Los Angeles it simply denotes *"Our Pastor"* and a memorial plaque denotes his contribution as the founder of the Azusa Street Mission, the Apostolic Faith Church of God and The Azusa Street Mission Churches.

It was reported that his last words were *"I love my Jesus so."* The call of leadership of the mission fell on Jeanne Seymour, Bishop Seymour's widow and she pastored the mission until her transition on July 2, 1936.

THE TEXAS CONNECTION
The Latter Day Quest

It is a true saying: *"what happened at Azusa Street shall never be forgotten."*

Even though some generations after the original Azusa Street revival and even after the property was lost *"due to the nonpayment of taxes"* and the building was torn down *"due to neglect"* this testament of what happened there shall never be forgotten and lives on in the history of all those that the revival and the churches effected.

These histories include all those that find their history in the various holiness churches, the various Pentecostal churches, the various Sanctified churches and all those churches that identify with the fall of the "Latter Day Rain."

> The Headstone and Memorial plaque honoring Rev. William J. Seymour leader of the Azusa Street Revival and his contribution as the founder of the *"Azusa Street Mission"*, the *"Apostolic Faith Church of God"* and *"The Azusa Street Mission Churches"*.

The resting place of Rev. William J. Seymour in the Evergreen Cemetery in Los Angeles, California

The headstone and memorial plaque

The headstone of Rev. William J. Seymour
May 2, 1870 to Sept. 28, 1922

JENNIE M. Seymour
March 10, 1874 to July 2, 1936

Memorial plaque honoring W.J. Seymour

The Senior and Presiding Bishop

Office of Senior Bishop
established 1907

established 1968

established 1968

The Church Of God In Christ has had as International Leaders two Senior Bishops and to-date five elected Presiding Bishop's, which is a total of seven Chief Apostles. The original office of Leadership was initially called General Overseer and was later changed to Senior Bishop and Chief Apostle. The office of the Senior Bishop was abolished and replaced by the Office **of the Presiding Bishop and Chief Apostle** (*by the 1968 Constitutional Convention and its adaptations of the historic amendments to the church's constitution and its bylaws*).

Important Note: It is our goal to fully take the reader on a journey through this amazing and eye opening history. The reader will find that some of the individual histories, the history of the organization and its departments will overlap and may repeat. This repeat or overlap in the record is due in part to the succession of leadership and to the chronological recording of this history. This is noted and recognized by the compiler.

Important Note: As noted above this repeat or overlap in the following personal history of Bishop C.H. Mason, Bishop O.T. Jones, Sr. and Bishop J.O. Patterson, Sr., is due in part to the succession of leadership and to the chronological recording of this history. This is also noted and recognized by the compiler.

Senior Bishops and Presiding Bishops of the Church of God in Christ, Inc.

* Tenure as leader of the Church

Bishop Charles Harrison Mason
Founder & 1st Senior Bishop
*1907-1961

Bishop Ozro Thurston Jones, Sr.
2nd Senior Bishop
*1961-1968

Bishop James Oglethorpe Patterson, Sr.
1st Presiding Prelate
*1968-1989

Bishop Louis Henry Ford
2nd Presiding Prelate
*1989-1995

Bishop Chandler David Owens, Sr.
3rd Presiding Prelate
*1995-2000

Bishop Gilbert Earl Patterson
4th Presiding Prelate
*2000-2007

Bishop Charles Edward Blake, Sr.
5th Presiding Prelate
*2007-Present

Bishop C.H. Mason

Bishop Charles Harrison Mason
Founder and First Senior Bishop 1907-1961
First Chief Apostle

For the first time in the history of the America Negro, he as a people were free. As newly freed slaves Jerry and Eliza Mason were excited to welcome into this world on this wintry Sabbath day of September 8, 1866, their new addition to their young family in Bartlett, Tennessee.

These new parents of a child, whose life would change the religious, social landscape of this country and of the world; were strong Baptist Christians. Their conversion happened during those dark days of slavery on Prior Lee's Farm. This new male child of the Mason family was given the name of Charles Harrison Mason.

Eliza Mason was a fervent prayer warrior. She was a devoted prayer partner of her close friend and co-resident of the farm, Ms. Saxton. These two women were known by those on the farm to be women of great prayer and faith. These were two mothers of young children Eliza, the mother of Charles, and Ms. Saxton the mother of Alice.

"Charlie" as Eliza would call him prayed that God would save him at an early age. The example of Eliza's fervent prayer life would follow Charles for the rest of his life. As a young child Charles prayed for the kind of religion and relationship with God he witnessed of his parents

During this time in young Charles's life Jerry Mason would leave his family and join the union army, which was shortly after the Civil War.

But he wouldn't be gone for long, for he did return, and in 1878 Jerry Mason moved Eliza and the now 12-year-old Charles twelve miles north from Prior Lee's farm to the swamp like plantation of John Watson located in Plumersville, Arkansas.

This move was thought to be in response to a local outbreak of yellow fever. The same epidemic that would shortly claim the life of Jerry Mason.

Young Charles was described as *"an industrious helper"*, whom Jerry felt that he *"could not coral long enough to educate."*

It was apparent by what would next happen to Charles at this age that the prayers of "Charlie" and his mother would be answered early in his life.

Charles would later testify that at this tender age he would have magnificent visions of heaven and horrific like nightmares of hell. These very vivid dreams and visions of heaven and hell would cause the young boy to lay on his bed and think on these visions many days.

These visions is what Charles would testify as his seeing the need to be saved and accept Christ as his Lord and Savior.

And so in November of 1878, at the tender age of 12-years-old Charles was saved. He was then baptized in the same month by his brother the Rev. I.S. Nelson the pastor of the Mt. Olive Missionary Baptist Church near their new home of Plumersville. After his conversion Charles became even more dissatisfied with the environment of those of his fellow residents of the plantation. Because of the ungodliness of the people, Charles had a longing and a desire to move back to his birth home on Prior Lee's Farm.

Charles was a very religious child that had the respect of those on the plantation. He had a belief system that he stuck to even though the temptation to be like those around him was great. It was noted by those that knew him at that time: *"He, was so different from those other bad boys around about."*

These were indeed conditions that Charles didn't like both naturally and spiritually. To say the least they were deplorable conditions. Near the end of the summer of 1880 the 13 year old Charles became very sick. This sickness included among other things a severe spell of fever and chills.

Charles was so sick that some thought that this was a sickness that he would not recover from. This kind of sickness usually resulted in death. So many thought that the bed that Charles was now laying in was his death bed. It was the thought of many on the plantation that his young life would come to a quick end by the latter part of August.

But God, would use this sickness as a start of the signs that his hands were on the life and destiny of this, his servant. This approval of God on the life of young Charles would be seen when, what some thought was a quick end, would be turned around to a quick recovery.

It is now one day from *"Charlie's"* 14th birthday and a miraculous change in his condition came. The day was the first Sunday in September 1880. This first day of September the 5th, day of 1880, young Charles would experience the healing virtue of his God. On what was considered to be his deathbed, had become the place where God would reveal his glory. The still weak Charles arises only with the strength of God! With no human help from this, his bed of affliction and this act of faith alone would be the medium by which God would show his healing.

This miraculous healing presence of God caused Charles to seek to praise him early in the morning, to testify of his goodness and renew his covenant with Christ.

This renewal caused him to feel the heavy burden of the deplorable state of his living conditions to be lifted. The surroundings of ungodliness, made the already swampy atmosphere even the more so depressing.

This was his recommitment to Christ: *"Lord I, have done all that I can do."*

Our story now picks up some 11 years later in 1891, and Charles is now 25-years-old and ready to start the process to achieve three of his set major life goals.

This list of major life goals were: (1) to receive a college education (2) buy a home and (3) as the scripture reads: find *"a good thing"*, a wife that would be a lifelong companion.

During this time in his life he would spend a lot of time testifying to anyone who would listen, to the goodness of God and the entire wonderful thing God had done in his life.

Charles knew that his life was destined to be a life of service to God and his people, but Charles wanted to accomplish his set major goals before, as he puts it, *"my life may be completely turned over to the ministry."*

So with this frame of mind Charles sets out to complete his list of goals and puts on hold God's will for his life. At this time Charles was during what is called *"lay preaching"*.

(*Which is considered to be, a little more than testifying*), he has decided to ask the Mother of Alice Saxton for her hand in marriage. This choice of a life partner met with the approval of both the Saxton family and the Mason family.

The Saxton family was fond of Charles, but this choice to follow what he wanted instead of the perfect will of God for his life, would soon lead to turmoil.

Charles and Alice were married in 1891, and Charles felt that he was well on his way to accomplishing his personal ambitions, his set of major goals for his life. Even though Charles was happy with his choice of life mate the happiness would be interrupted by his need to travel and preach the word of God.

Some two years into their marriage in 1893, Mason would accept his Ministers license from the Mt. Gale Missionary Baptist Church, which was located in Preston, Arkansas.

Accepting his license is what Charles felt as a fulfilling of his promise to God; that if God would allow Charles to marry Alice then Charles will preach his word. This new call on Mason's life would cause him to have to travel and preach the word of God. Mason had a passion for church work and the work of the church. He would labor over souls night and day that were seeking the Lord.

The new Mrs. Alice Mason expressed the fact that she did not want to be married to a preacher. And this now once happy couple has now become two people with different ambitions for their lives.

Finally, after only two years of being married, Alice decided that she could no longer be the wife of a preacher, which had to spread the word. So Alice leaves Mason. Due to her leaving he would experience a deep level of depression. Which would cause him to be so troubled that he thought about ending it all.

Mason began to see that his life was not on track with the perfect will and the work of God concerning his life. This depression caused him to seek help from the leaders of his local church.

These leaders were the Rev. E.C. Morris *(the president of the Arkansas Baptist State Convention in 1891; he also cofounded the Arkansas Baptist College in 1884)* Rev. C.L. Fisher *(the Academic Dean of the Arkansas Baptist College and one of the leaders in the Arkansas Baptist Convention)* and Rev. A.M. Booker *(the President of the Arkansas Baptist College).*

These men would take Mason under their caring wings, encourage him and inspire him to overcome the trouble that he was now experiencing in his life. At this point in his life God allowed a book that many were reading across the south to fall into his hands, which would change his life.

It was the autobiography of Amanda Smith who was called the *"Colored Evangelist"*. Amanda was born in 1837, and was a member of the African Methodist Episcopal

Church. She was a traveling evangelist that had a holiness experience; the testimony of Smith was published in 1893. This book made such an impact on Mason that it would cause him to see his life like looking in a mirror. This revelation of where his life stood was an eye opener.

Mason began soon to see that he needed to experience the Holiness that he had been reading about for himself. And so Mason would be converted unto Holiness this same year (*1893*) and after being sanctified through the word of God; would preach his first sermon in Holiness. His message text would be taken from II Timothy 2:1-3 *"Thou therefore endure hardness as a good soldier of Jesus Christ."*

This *"the first message of Mason in holiness"* would describe the walk of Mason from that minute on. It was indeed the signification of the fight that he would have on his hands from that moment until he closed his eyes.

Two weeks after his preaching of his first sermon in Holiness, the after effects of this sermon would cause a revival to breakout. This was the first of many revivals that the message, of Holiness that Mason would preach would cause.

A mother figure to Mason was the wife of A.M. Booker, she served as the secretary of the Arkansas Baptist College. By November 1, 1893, Mason was enrolled in the Arkansas Baptist College due in a large part to Mrs. Bookers urging.

After only three months enrolled in the College, Mason was so dissatisfied with the methods of teaching and presentation of the Bible that he soon withdrew from school and returned to every open pulpit declaring Christ by the word, example and precept.

There was a meeting that would forever change Mason's life. This was the meeting of a soon to be close ministerial companion. This, the meeting of Mason and Jones.

This change and move was not just a whimsical happing, but rather it was a God arranged opportunity of two God ordained paths to meet. It was in 1893, that Charles Price Jones would meet Charles Harrison Mason. The 28-year-old Jones would meet the 27-year-old Mason. These two young preachers shared much in common, they both attended the Arkansas Baptist College (*Jones graduated, but Mason withdrew after only 3 months*) they also shared in the wise counsel of E.C. Morris the cofounder of the College.

Even though the two shared different views of the promotion methods of the message of Christ, they both shared a common thought of dissatisfaction and the shared view of a new doctrine, (*that of Holiness*) which gave new life to the old Baptist way.

Mason preferred that old time religion that he experienced as a boy, that old slave type of spirituality. Jones preferred to use those ideas and equipment that he received through his education at the Arkansas Baptist College.

In 1895, Jones would leave his pastorate of the Tabernacle Baptist Church in Selma, Alabama to accept a call to pastor the Mt. Helm Baptist Church in Jackson, Mississippi. At this same time Mason had relocated to Mississippi somewhere around the Lexington area.

This was no chance move for Jones, but a God arranged move. For it is now that Mason *"is now in God's will"* for his life and on tract for the work of God. Mason's teaching is now seeing the effects of God's plan for a new Church, a holiness church slowly is unfolding. The time and place is now set for Mason and Jones.

The members of the Mt. Helm Baptist Church was at first happy with their new pastor. For he was one that could really speak and sing. He was also a learned man. The only immediate problem as they saw it was his teachings of a new doctrine called Holiness.

This move to Jackson, Mississippi was also a timely move for Jones. For little did Jones know that a new Baptist Convention was being formed. For which he was in time to be a forming delegate of such, the name chosen for the new convention was the National Baptist Convention.

During this the first convention of the National Baptist. Jones became dissatisfied with the convention's complete resolution to cause a change on racism in America.

This position of the National Baptist focused on two main areas to cause improvements for blacks in America. The two main areas of concentration of this position were to address: (1) the political disfranchisement of blacks and (2) the dehumanization of blacks.

These were indeed great concerns that needed to be addressed but the groups focus was not on the spiritual solution, but rather the worldly secular nature of these events and their solutions addressing these important issues as was stated in the resolution.

The main resolve was addressing these solutions in the area of education, social and political change for the black man. This as Jones saw it had little or rather no focus on a religious solution.

These views by the Convention caused Jones to be disenfranchised with the National Baptist Convention. The newfound doctrine and teaching of holiness by Jones and Mason was also causing a small but noticeable change in the mindset of some of the National Baptist Convention delegates.

Jones and Mason were not the only one's disenfranchised by what they witnessed. The cause of this dis-enfranchisement could be called a more secular view of a problem that should be solved with a more spiritual slanted solution.

The following were the group of men looking for a more excellent way: W.S. Pleasant of Hazelhurst, Mississippi, C.P. Jones of Jackson, Mississippi and C.H. Mason of Lexington, Mississippi. These men would soon be described as "Militant Gospel Holiness Preachers"

It is now 1896, C.P. Jones and C.H. Mason made a call to all those that were disenfranchised to hold the first holiness convention and revival in the city of Jackson, Mississippi.

This meeting was said to have had such an impact on the city, (*due in most part to the holiness/sanctification preaching of Jones and Mason*); that many of the once open doors to Jones and Mason had now become closed.

Also during this time a request was made for C.P. Jones to come and preach in Natchez, Mississippi at the Asia Baptist Church that was pastored by J.L. Young. Jones took with him on this trip his new found teaching and revelations on sanctification and holiness.

Jones with power and effectiveness preached these new holiness doctrines and the effect of his preaching was a great stir in the church that caused a split between those that had accepted these new teachings and those that didn't.

This split caused Pastor Young to put in another call in to Jones to return and amend the doctrines he taught. This request was made due to the fact that most leaders were not subscribing to these doctrines at that time. Most believe that it was impossible to live a life that was not controlled by sin.

This was a request that Jones could not fulfill, due to a conflict of scheduling. He was already committed to fulfill a prior scheduled engagement. His friend C. H. Mason who agreed to go and run a revival meeting to address these issues was the solution to the request made by Pastor Young.

This revival lasted one week, during this time of Mason's sanctification and holiness preaching there was only one person that would come and receive the message to the point of conversion. This one new convert was Charles Pleas and he received sanctification by the word in 1896.

Charles Pleas would follow Bishop Mason until his transition. (*Bishop Mason would appoint him as Prelate of Kansas. A position he held for 55 years.*)

1896, was also the year that Jones had two great publishing accomplishments, one was a Holiness magazine called the *"Truth"* and a pamphlet *"The Work of the Holy Spirit in the Churches"*

1897, would become a year known as the year that the south would experience the burning of black churches. This occurrence would cause those that suffered these great losses to have to worship under brush abhors. When this persistent pioneering preacher Mason returned to Jackson, Mississippi; his first message back in the city was delivered from the south entrance of the courthouse, a location that he was force to accept due to these acts of terror.

At this time of such a hardship it was a common occurrence for these faithful worshippers that accepted this new doctrine to become deprived from their families, homes and church. This disenfranchisement caused many to wonder what could be done, because thousands throughout the south were being given the cold shoulder for their beliefs in these new doctrines. This treatment was not just limited to individuals, but also to groups.

It was reported that in Mississippi the State Convention, dis-fellowshipped a complete Baptist Association from the convention because of their acceptance of these doctrines. This attempt at assimilation was not limited to those without the circle. But some that witnessed these events first hand even tried to convert Mt. Helms into a holiness church, but their attempt was rebuffed.

By June of 1897, Jones would call others that were in the Baptist Church, but were shifting toward Holiness to a conference. Jones was active in the holiness movement but was still an active member of the Jackson Missionary Baptist Association (his membership in the Association would continue until 1900).

These hardships were stumbling blocks for the new movement, but not a cause to stop the new fledging group. A Mr. John Lee was so touched by the ministry of Mason that he allowed Mason to use his living room to become the meeting place for this new group of believers. This was a suitable location for only a short period of time. This new teaching was in great demand and drew a large crowd, so much and so until Mr. Lee's living room could not contain those in attendance.

This new problem of outgrowth was soon solved by an owner of a cotton gin house no longer in use in Lexington, Mississippi.

This gin house set just off the bank of a little creek. With the consent of its owner this site would become the new meeting place of these seekers and worshippers.

This great outpour of these new teachings in Holiness/Sanctification would of course cause the devil to rear his ugly head. He did so in such a manner that it would (*in today's terms*) be considered a drive by shooting.

Someone filled with great indignation for the success of these meetings shot into this group a pistol five times and two shots from a double barrel shotgun. God's hand was at work during this condemnable act, while the saints shouted and prayed some were injured by this act, but were not killed.

This meeting was so successful that organizing the people into a recognized organization, a church that would cause those that believed to become a part of was necessary.

This new organization would teach the doctrine of entire sanctification and a life style of true Holiness. There was a need to call those that believed together to form this new organization. Elder Jones, Elder Mason and Elder Pleasant made this formulation call jointly.

This call yielded a total of sixty charter members in response. This new holiness body was known as the "Church of God"

The next thing to be done was to purchase a piece of land that the new organization could call their own.

This new need was met a short time later with the purchase of a parcel of land on Gazoo Street, which was located just beyond the corporate line. The land was purchased from a Mr. John Ashcraft. With the purchase of this land, the next need was a facility where the people could worship.

This task was accomplished with the building of a small but permanent building of which size was 60 x 40.

The next major task before the group was that they needed a new name. In 1896, there were many organizations using the name the "*Church of God*" and so the leaders began to seek God for a name that would mark them different from those of like name. God answered the urgent task through its cofounder C.H. Mason. While he was walking down a certain street in Little Rock Arkansas. God revealed a name to him that would forever set this group apart from those of similar name.

The name that God revealed to Mason had a promise attached to it. The promise was simple, *"If you take this name there will not be a building built large enough to hold those that would follow."* This name was the CHURCH OF GOD IN CHRIST. This revelatory name was supported by I Thessalonians 2:14. When Mason presented this name to the brethren it was agreed upon by all. Once the brethren agreed to change the name, Mason made it legal by incorporating it in Memphis, Tennessee.

The next phase of change to the church was reorganization. The brethren agreed upon a new structure and Elder C.P. Jones was chosen as the General Overseer. Elder Mason was then chosen as the Overseer of Tennessee and Elder J.A. Jeter was chosen as the Overseer of Arkansas.

This original call of the 1896, group of men to hold the first holiness convention and revival in the city of Jackson, Mississippi was by 1898 an annual holiness convention of the Church of God in Christ (Holiness) that C.P. Jones the General Overseer was now hosting at the Mt. Helm Baptist Church.

Even though a large number of Mt. Helm members found these new doctrines unsettling.

To add logs to the fire Jones along with a few members proposed something that caused a lawsuit to be pursued by members of the Mt. Helm Baptist Church. This proposal was that the name of the Church be changed to Church of Christ, Holiness. This proposal would cause the church to split into two separate congregations.

A lawsuit was filed against Jones and those that wanted to change the name of the church. The court would issue an order that would rule against Jones and those that agreed with him, the ruling noted that: *"the land that the church was built on was donated for the express purpose of establishing a Baptist Church and neither Jones nor anyone else had the power to neither change its original purpose, nor its name, nor change its original doctrinal teachings or beliefs".*

There was a prevailing view between Baptist of the day that this new doctrine of holiness could not find a sound place in scripture. It was further believed that it would change what it meant to be a Baptist, if this new teaching was left unchallenged.

By 1899, E.C. Morris the president of the Arkansas Baptist State Convention and cofounder of the Arkansas Baptist College used his annual address to stop what he saw as an erosion of the Baptist belief by these new outside doctrines *(Morris was the mentor of both Jones and Mason)*.

The following was Morris' address, of which proclaims his official view as a Baptist on the subject of perfection and he stated: *"That there is such a doctrine as sanctification taught in the Scriptures must be admitted. And that this doctrine has been wantonly perverted and misunderstood must also be admitted. But I am Charitable enough to say that many who have misunderstood and misinterpreted this doctrine have done so from honest convictions which had formed in their hearts on account of incompetent teachers."*

Morris taught and believed that the only time one would become holy would be upon one's death. This teaching is evident by the following excerpt from the same address: *"Having received the sanctifying influence of the Holy Spirit in our hearts, we set about a cultivation of it with an anxious desire that we may become more like Christ each day. The deformity which sin has brought on us will only be lost in the regeneration of the world"*

To hear ones mentor dissent your view or beliefs would cause some to be so disheartened to a point that it would cause some to have a crisis of faith. This was not the attitude of Jones and Mason, but rather they both felt that their one time trusted wise counselor was just misinformed and just not clearly understanding the true holiness/sanctification message.

Later on Jones put on record addressing his mentor and others that questioned his belief in these doctrines with the following statement: *"Having reached my decision to follow my convictions and my Lord, I was looked upon as a fanatic by some, by other as of weak brain; by yet others as a sharper trying to distinguish myself by being different, by nearly all as a heretic."*

This dissenting and critical view of these two persistent pioneering preachers did not stop their teaching and living these doctrines.

These militant preachers continued to preach these new doctrines as the organization that they cofounded began to grow and take hold on the Baptist and other religious communities.

Jones and Mason would find themselves dis-fellowshipped from both the State and the National Baptist Conventions. This explosion and effect thereof was not just on a State and National level but also on a local level.

Jones would soon find himself removed as Pastor of Mt. Helm (this action was a forced action initiated by the Jackson Baptist Association).

After his forced outing of Mt. Helm Baptist Church. C.P. Jones founded the Christ Temple Church which was a full participating church now joined into the Church of God in Christ.

The founding of the Church of God in Christ gave those then African American Holiness Baptist and Methodist a new denomination from which to base their strength as a religious group.

The year is now 1906, and the revival that was sweeping through the west coast had reached the earshot of Mason and Jones. This revival would be a turning point in the life of Mason.

On the other hand upon getting the news of the revival and its happenings, Jones was almost against it from his first hearing of it.

Jones did not believe that receiving the Holy Ghost required the evidence of speaking in tongues.

He would write the following concerning receiving the Holy Ghost: *"Now Christ and the Holy Spirit are one; and the Holy Ghost is the Spirit of Christ, and when one who has asked and received the Holy Ghost lets some sort of Spirit cause him to deny the witness of the Spirit that he has received in order to get that other spirit, I ask you what has he done.*

Seymour the conductor of this revival in Los Angeles was no stranger to either Mason or Jones. For they were familiar with him due to the revivals he conducted in Mississippi.

This revival being ran by Pastor Seymour had peaked the attention of Mason and by March of 1907 caused him to want to go and see for himself its happenings.

Mason asked Jones to accompany him to Los Angeles to visit the Azusa Street Revival, but this request fell on deaf ears. Mason would make this journey to California to attend this great Pentecostal revival with two of his other closest companions; that of Elder D.J. Young and Elder J.A. Jeter.

Mason, Young and Jeter would enjoy the fellowship of the saints while there in Los Angeles for this Revival. Upon arriving there they heard the message of Elder William Joseph Seymour taken from Luke 24:49, *"And behold I send the promise of my father upon you; but tarry ye in the city of Jerusalem until ye be endued with power from on high."* This Pentecostal message would convince Mason of his need to experience this great outpouring.

The following is some of the testimony of his experience of this great outpouring:

"The first day in the meeting I sat to myself, away from those that went with me. I began to thank God in my heart for all things, for when I heard some speak in tongues, I knew it was right though I did not understand it. Nevertheless, it was sweet to me I also thanked God for Elder Seymour who came and preached a wonderful sermon. His words were sweet and powerful and it seems that I hear them now while writing. When he closed his sermon he said. "All of those that want to be sanctified or baptized with the Holy Ghost, go to the upper room; and all those that want to be justified, come to the alter." I said that is the place for me, for it may be that I am not converted and if not, God knows it and can convert me." "Glory!" The second night of prayer I saw a vision. I saw myself standing alone and had a dry roll of paper in my mouth trying to swallow it. Looking up towards the heavens, there appeared a man at my side. I turned my eyes at once, then I awoke and the interpretation came. God and Him only, he would baptize me. I said yes to Him, and at once in the morning when I arose, I could hear a voice in me saying, "I see...." I got a place at the alter and began to thank God. After that, I said Lord if I could only baptize myself, I would do so; for I wanted the baptism so bad that I did not know what to do. I said, Lord, you will have to do the work for me; so I turned it over into His hands..." Then, I began to seek for the baptism of the Holy Ghost according to Acts 2:41 which readeth thus: "Then they that gladly received His word were baptized. "Then I saw I had a right to be glad and not sad." The enemy said to me, there may be something wrong with you. Then a voice spoke to me saying, if there is anything wrong with you, Christ will find it and take it away and will marry you... Some said, let us sing. "I arose and the first song that came to me was "He brought me out of the Miry Clay." The Spirit came upon the saints and upon me ... Then I gave up for the Lord to have His way within me. So there came a wave of Glory into me and all of my being was filled with the Glory of the Lord. So when He had gotten me straight on my feet, there came a light which enveloped my entire being above the brightness of the sun. When I opened my mouth to say Glory a flame touched my tongue which ran down to me. My language changed and no word could I speak in my own tongue. Oh! I was filled with the Glory of the Lord My soul was then satisfied.

This Baptism of the Holy Ghost was the power of God in a great outpouring. These three would take back with them to their Holiness/Sanctification brothers a new experience, that of Pentecostalism.

This new Pentecostal experience which Elder Mason found for himself, he began to proclaim to others upon his return home to Memphis, Tennessee as a New Testament doctrine.

This new Pentecostal experience was not widely accepted among those that Elder Mason was in fellowship with. The then General Overseer of the Church Of God In Christ (Holiness), Elder C.P. Jones didn't agree to the idea of incorporating this new doctrine in with the Holiness doctrine.

This division between Mason and Jones was not the only division that would arise as of a result of this new Pentecostal experience, this division was also felt between Young and Jeter those that traveled with Mason to California.

Even though Jeter witnessed for himself the outpouring at the Azusa Revival he and others sided with Overseer Jones to disregard this new outpouring as an addition to the Holiness message. This difference in the teaching of this new addition to the holiness message went on from May of 1907 to August of 1907.

By August of 1907, there was a call for the General Assembly to meet for a doctrine discussing convention of the Church Of God In Christ (*Holiness*) in Jackson, Mississippi. This convention was called to discuss and present a resolution of the Church Of God In Christ's (*Holiness*) official position on this new doctrine of Pentecostalism.

At this meeting of the General Assembly of the Church Of God In Christ (*Holiness*); Jones, Jeter and others brought the matter before the general assembly.

Jones and his group held the view that this new Holy Ghost experience of speaking in tongues was simply a delusion and believed that this new doctrine and/or experience of Pentecostalism should not be added as an official part of the Holiness doctrine.

Much like Holiness was to the Baptist way, so was Pentecostalism to the Holiness way. After a vote on the matter the general assembly decided to terminate Mason's membership and all those that believed as he did.

This was done by the general assembly with the simple act of withdrawing *"the right hand of fellowship"* from those of that held Mason's belief on Pentecostalism.

The emergence of the Pentecostal COGIC

This decision by the general assembly caused C.H. Mason to leave and take with him ten (*10*) of the congregations of the Church Of God In Christ (*Holiness*). C.H. Mason called a special meeting in Memphis, Tennessee. The ministers that attended this meeting were E.R. Driver, J. Bowe, R.R. Booker, R.E. Hart, W. Welsh, A.A. Blackwell, E.M. Page, R.H.I. Clark, D.J. Young, James Brewer, Daniel Spearman and J.H. Boone.

This group of godly men made-up and organized the first Pentecostal General Assembly of the Church Of God In Christ. This new group of the Church Of God In Christ decided to keep the name. This new assembly of the (*Pentecostal*) Church Of God In Christ chose as their new leader Elder C. H. Mason.

Mason now bore the title of General Overseer and Chief Apostle of the Church Of God In Christ. This decision of the assembly in keeping the name the Church Of God In Christ was a decision that would again cause some contention between Jones and Mason.

Jones felt that he and his group should be able to keep the name of the organization that he served as the original General Overseer. As Mason and his group saw it they should be able to keep the name because God had given the name to Mason and also made the promise to him.

This disagreement between the two groups caused this case to ultimately be decided by a Tennessee Court in which the court decided that the name would be exclusively used by Mason and his group.

Jones would reorganize those that stayed with his group into a new Holiness denomination called the Church of Christ (*Holiness*) USA. Jones would remain the leader of this group until his death on January 19, 1949.

Jones was met with a great emotional loss in 1916 at the death of Fannie his first wife he would later remarry Pearl E. Reed 2 years later in 1918. At the start of his new denomination he was elected the president; this was changed to the office of Senior Bishop by 1927.

Bishop Jones was known for his song writing ability and he composed over a thousand songs. These songs were later immortalized with their inclusion in the Church of Christ (*Holiness*) Official Hymnal titled "Jesus Only, Songs and Hymnals".

The Church that Jones would pastor from 1917, until his death in 1949, would be the Christ Temple Church in which he founded in Los Angeles, Ca.

Bishop Mason as the Chief Apostle of the (*Pentecostal*) Church Of God In Christ was give the authority by the general assembly to organize auxiliaries for the church, completely establish doctrine for the church and to appoint Overseers (*Bishops*).

The first appointments he made to the office of State Overseer (*Bishop*) were as follows: Dr. Hart for Tennessee; Elder J. Bowe for Arkansas and sometime later he appointed another, the Elder J.A. Lewis for the state of Mississippi.

After more growth came to the church and more leadership was needed in other regions. Bishop Mason made other appointments and they were follows: Elder E.M. Page as Overseer of Texas; the Elder R.R. Booker as Overseer of Missouri; Elder E.R. Driver as Overseer of California and as the National Field Secretary W.B. Holt, who was an Elder of the Church Of God In Christ (*Pentecostal*).

Bishop C.H. Mason as the Chief Apostle made an immediate decision about the time of year for the National Meeting of the Church which would be called the *"Holy Convocation"*. This name of the meeting was chosen based on scripture such as Leviticus 23:1&2.

The timing of the meeting each year would be crucial to the success of the meeting. The time of the year that Bishop Mason chose and dedicated was twenty days, and these dates were from November 25th through December 14th.

This time of the year was chosen so that these saints could fellowship and conduct all the business of the Church.

This time of the year was easy for the saints who were mostly farmers and by this time of the year they would have gathered in their crops which would allow them to support the meeting in two ways; with their time and have resources that would allow them to financially support the Convocation.

The site of the first of these *"Holy Convocations"* was at 392 South Wellington Street, Memphis, Tennessee. The success of these first meetings led to the Church Of God In Christ building its first National Temple on 958 South Fifth Street, in Memphis, Tennessee this first Tabernacle was completed in 1925.

The Church Of God In Christ during this time proved to be an important organization to the then newly developing Pentecostal movement to both Black and White preachers. Although many were members of the Church Of God In Christ, many were not, but were given ministerial credentials or were even ordained by Bishop Mason between the times of 1907 to 1919.

During this time the Church Of God In Christ was one of the few Pentecostal denomination in the United States that was incorporated and charted as a religious organization with this status.

This legal designation of the Church Of God In Christ allowed those with credentials even though they may have been independent ministers could legally operate as Pastors.

It was also customary for ordained and licensed ministers to receive certain benefits such as half priced train tickets. These credentials were also used when these ministers came before the draft board during World War II.

Many of these independent ministers both Black and White were not a part of a recognized religious body with the power to give them bonefide credentials.

Which would allow them to perform legally recognized ministerial functions such as marriages and ministerial duties that required such credentials by law.

So Bishop Mason and the Church Of God In Christ ordained them.

To address segregationist laws of the time for those ministers that were white there was an agreement between Bishop Mason and the white ministers called a *"Gentlemen Agreement"*.

This agreement allowed the white ministers with credentials from the Church Of God In Christ the ability to issue to those ministers that would come in under their ministries to be also issued credentials from one of the first legally recognized Pentecostal organizations.

It is noteworthy to recognize that the first National Field Secretary, Elder W.B. Holt of the Church Of God In Christ was a "white pastor" of a *"white"* Church Of God In Christ that was organized in Memphis, Tennessee at 930 Louisiana Street. Elder Holt was later appointed as Superintendent in California.

By 1913, a line that had been washed away at the American Jerusalem was starting to reappear, because of the Southern Segregation laws and practices. A call was made to *"all Pentecostal Saints and Church Of God In Christ followers"* to meet in Hot Springs, Arkansas in April of 1914.

This invitational call made on December 20, 1913, by Elder E.N. Bell and Elder H.A. Goss. This call to convene a General Council went out only to the white saints.

In 1914, an organizing convention was being held in Hot Springs, Arkansas this organizing convention was organized by White Pentecostal ministers many of which were licensed and ordained by Bishop Mason and held credentials of the Church Of God In Christ.

These were the men establishing and organized the General Council of the Assemblies of God. The council established doctrines that didn't put emphasis on Sanctification and Holiness as required to receive the baptism of the Holy Ghost.

This was not a complete break from the Church Of God In Christ the fellowship was still there. The Assemblies of God council invited Bishop Mason to preach at the organizing convention in which he would address 400 white Pentecostal Ministers many of which held credentials with his name on them. This is a cordial relationship that exists between the two denominations even today.

Most blacks that had a religious experience under the auspices of Christianity had this experience by the way of the Methodist or Baptist Church. The Holiness and Pentecostal movements of which the Church Of God In Christ would lead the charge would change this religious landscape.

Bishop Mason would plant the seeds of Pentecostalism on the east coast and in the north that would grow when blacks would migrate to these regions.

These seeds were watered when Church Of God In Christ Evangelist would travel to these locations preaching the Holiness/Pentecostal message.

The growth of the Church Of God In Christ was evident in the North by 1917, with churches in Philly, Brooklyn and Pittsburgh

The General Assembly to the Annual Convocation Delegates and Officers at the National Tabernacle

In 1936, the National Organization was visited by a tragic fire that left the Church Of God In Christ without a National Temple. Bishop Mason the General Overseer and Chief Apostle of the church provided the local church that he pastored as the temporary site for the National meeting place which was located at 672 South Lauderdale. This site was used from 1936 to 1945.

By 1945, Bishop Mason and the Church Of God In Christ was able to see a dream and project that seemed impossible at the time come to full fruition. 1945, saw the completion and dedication of what was then the largest black owned religious facility of its day that of Mason Temple Church Of God In Christ.

Mason Temple was built during World War II. This was amazing because it was wartime and a national steel ration was in place. But in spite of this rationing God, saw Bishop Mason and the Church through this time with no problem in acquiring enough steel to complete this large facility, which was built for less than $400,000.00.

Mason Temple upon completion became the largest church or hall that was black owned and operated in the country. Mason Temple has three levels which is estimated to seat a total of 9,000.This seating capacity is as following 5,000 main seating, 2,000 balcony seating and a 2,000 capacity in the assembly room.

When Mason Temple was opened it was a one stop shop state of the art facility for its day. It had located between its walls a state of the art sound system for sound both inside and outside. A complete air condition and heating system, a post office, a nursery, both male, female showers and bath. Male and female restrooms, beauty salon and barber shop. A shoe shine parlor, baggage-check and registration room. First aid and emergency ward, picture booth, 2 professional kitchens, 2 cafeterias, concessions and in the business area 36 admin offices.

Mason Temple over the years has seen many historical and cultural events unfold between its walls. It is not widely known but Dr. King actually spoke twice at Mason Temple. His first speech at Mason Temple was a "get out the vote" rally held on July 31, 1959. The last public speech of Dr. King ("I've Been to the Mountain Top") which was in support of sanitation workers that were striking for a living wage was given on April 3, 1968.

Many gospel stars have performed at Mason Temple such as Mahalia Jackson, Richard White, The Clark Sisters and many others.

Because of the grace of God the (Pentecostal) Church Of God In Christ grew from a few congregations in 1907, to the largest Pentecostal Organization in America which was due in large part to the obedience of one of his servants that of Bishop Mason. Bishop Charles Harrison Mason's leadership and direction was both spiritual and apostolic.

From 1951, until his transition in 1961, Bishop Mason knew that his health was declining and knew that he alone would not be able to adequately see to the ecclesiastical and secular matters of the Church and after much prayer he appointed a special committee to assist him with these and other jurisdictional matters. The official name later chosen for this commission was the Executive Commission. This Commission was given complete authority to conduct and execute apostolic business formerly performed by Bishop Mason.

At the God blessed age of 95 in Detroit, Michigan Bishop Charles Harrison Mason closed his eyes for the last time on November 17, 1961, at the Harper's Hospital.

At Bishop Charles Harrison Mason's home going there were an estimated 10,000 people in attendance at Mason Temple. He was first entombed in the entrance of Mason Temple. He was later relocated on the second level.

The estimated membership of the Church Of God In Christ is currently over six million. There are currently estimated a total of Fifteen Thousand Five Hundred (15,000) churches under the parent body of the Church Of God In Christ headquartered in Memphis, Tennessee.

These churches can be found in the United States, in 52 countries, and on the islands in the seas.

SIDE NOTE:

Bishop Mason's first marriage was to Alice Saxton. They were married in 1891, **after only two years**, she divorced him in 1893. After he received his license to preach. No children were born of this union. He would remain unmarried until after her death.

His second marriage was to Sister Lelia Washington sometime in 1905. **They would enjoy 31 years** of marriage until her death in 1936. (*Lelia Washington Mason would be the bearer of the eight Mason children*).

Bishop Mason would remarry for the third and final time to Miss. Elise Washington in 1944, until his transition in 1961. (***They would enjoy 17 years*** *of marriage, no children were born of this union.*)

SIDE NOTE:

Born to the union of Bishop C.H. Mason and Sister Lelia (Washington) Mason would be a total of eight children. **Six daughters**: *Deborah Mason Patterson, Julia Mason Atkins, Lelia Mason Byas, Ruth Mason Lewis, Alice Mason Amos, Mary Ester Mason.* **Two sons**: *Arthur Mason aka skeets and Robert Mason aka Bob.*

THE TEXAS CONNECTION
International Leadership of COGIC (Mason)

The Mason Family
Bishop C.H. Mason, Mrs. Lelia Mason, her mother and 7 of their 8 children.

Mason Family extended
Bishop C. H. Mason his children their spouses and children

There is no known photo of Alice Saxton. Bishop Mason first wife. They were married in 1891, and she would divorce him in 1893. He would not marry until after Alice passed away. (12 years later).

Lelia (Washington) Mason
Bishop Mason's second wife Mother of their 8 children. They would wed in 1905 and would enjoy 31 yrs. of marriage until her transition in 1936.

Bishop C. H. Mason and wife Mrs. Elsie W. Mason would wed in 1944. They would enjoy 17 yrs. of marriage until his transition in 1961.

Elise (Washington) Mason
Bishop Mason's third wife, no children were born of this union. Mother would serve the church 45 yrs. after his transition, she would transition in January of 2006

Final Resting place of Bishop Mason
on the Second floor in Mason Temple

First resting place of Bishop Mason on the first floor in the foyer of Mason Temple

Bishop Mason and Ruth (Mason) Lewis
Daughter of Bishop Mason

Bishop Mason and son Bob
at the Page School in Texas

Mother Ruth Mason Lewis
Daughter of Bishop Mason
September 16, 1920 – November 28, 2015

Bishop O.T. Jones, Sr.

Bishop Ozro Thurston Jones, Sr.
Second Senior Bishop 1961-1968
Second Chief Apostle

It was on March 26, 1891, in Fort Smith, Arkansas, that Revered Merion Jones and Mrs. Mary Jones welcomed into this world their seventh child of eight children. This bouncing baby boy was named Ozro Thurston Jones. This new addition to the Jones family was welcomed into this Baptist home where Christ was the center of attention and the Word of God was seen as the final authority on every matter.

This esteem of God's word lead to the Jones family creed of living a life that was dedicated to serving God and lending aide to your fellow man. This creed further extended to the world of academic training; be it college or vocational training to better ones personal economic status and training for ones chosen occupation.

This family creed encouraged the young Jones to complete his elementary and secondary education there in Fort Smith. He furthers his education by graduating from the Lincoln High School in Fort Smith. He would graduate as valedictorian of his class and as a Latin Scholar.

In search of greater economic opportunity O.T. Jones moved to Philadelphia. He would carry this creed to Philly with him and would attend Temple University for a while.

It was at the young age of 21-years-old that he would experience Salvation and being filled with the Holy Ghost. This experience was a direct cause of the evangelist Justus Bowe, a Church Of God In Christ Evangelist.

His furtherance of a secular education was cut short by his pursuit of a higher calling. The higher calling was a calling to preach the Word of God.

This acceptance of his calling would benefit the Church Of God In Christ and the young people. After he embarked on his ministry, a series of *"new"* programs and ministers were born through his ministerial endeavors.

Jones lived a life that was such an example, that soon his older sister and brother would follow him and join as members of the Church Of God In Christ.

This evangelistic team of siblings would be the beacon for Northwest Arkansas and surrounding areas.

The faithfulness of Jones was recognized by Bishop C.H. Mason. In 1917, Bishop Mason appointed Jones to the office of the President of the National Y.P.W.W. of the Church Of God In Christ.

During this time he authored and edited the Young People Willing Worker (YPWW) Quarterly Topics, which grew under his leadership to one of the largest Pentecostal publications addressing itself To Christian Education.

In 1919, Elder O.T. Jones attended the 13th Annual Holy Convocation and during this meeting he met Miss. Neanza Zelma.

The then National Y.P.W.W. President *"Brother Ozro"* as he was called, got acquainted with her.

They were married in 1921, and resided in Fort Smith, Arkansas the next four years where the couple became the parents of their first two children: O.T. Jr., and Walter B.

In 1925, Senior Bishop C.H. Mason requested the young Elder Jones to go to Philadelphia to become pastor of a small band of saints that eventually became Holy Temple COGIC. The family established a home, and four more children were born: William V., Jean (Anderson), Elma Harriet (Freeman), and Marion Elizabeth (Ellison).

In 1929, he founded the International Youth Congress of the Church Of God In Christ, which grew under his leadership, to become one of the largest annual gatherings of Christian youth and youth workers in the nation. In 1941, he organized the youth Department of the Church Of God In Christ and became its appointed President

Under Bishop Jones' leadership as President of the Youth Department, *(which continued for more than forty years)*. Bishop Jones made his most distinguishing contribution as a Christian minister.

Nearly thirty auxiliaries engaged in church sponsored youth programs which were organized for youth work throughout the jurisdictions and local works of the Church Of God In Christ. He gave leadership, spiritual inspiration and Christian training to virtually all of the next generation of church leaders through the training programs which he inspired or sponsored.

From 1951, until his transition in 1961, Bishop Mason knew that his health was declining and knew that he alone would not be able to adequately see to the ecclesiastical and secular matters of the church. After much prayer he appointed a special commission to assist him with these and other church matters.

The official name later chosen for this commission was the Executive Commission. This commission was given complete authority to conduct and execute apostolic business formerly performed by Bishop Mason.

These activities of the commission included but were not limited to making all appointments. The following were the initial appointments to this commission by Bishop Mason: On June 5, 1951, three men were appointed and they were Bishop A.B. McEwen, Bishop J.S. Bailey and Bishop O.M. Kelley. On May 19, 1952, one man was appointed to the commission in the person of Bishop J.O. Patterson, Sr., and on October 12, 1955, three men were added Bishop U.E. Miller, Bishop S.M. Crouch and Bishop O.T. Jones, Sr.

Bishop C.H. Mason's transition was on November 17, 1961, at the God blessed age of 95. The Constitution of the Church of God in Christ stipulated that at his transition the leadership and supervision of the International Church would be reverted to the Board of Bishops with a directive to the General Assembly to elect, by a two-third vote of those present, two or more Bishops who shall hold office, during good behavior and shall have general supervision of the church.

The General Assembly, in keeping with the Constitutional provision, retained the seven men, and elected five more members making a total of twelve men. This twelve man Commission later changed its name to the Executive Board. Subsequent appointees were Bishops: Wyoming Wells, L.H. Ford, C.E. Bennett, John White, and W.G. Shipman. Bishop B.S. Lyles was honored as a member emeritus of this board.

Bishop A.B. McEwen was elected as the Chairman, Bishop J.S. Bailey, Vice-Chairman and Bishop J.O. Patterson, Sr. the General Secretary of the church and to the Executive Board. Bishop O.T. Jones, Sr., was honored because of his seniority by the Executive Board and the General Assembly with the title of *"Senior Bishop."*

A dispute arose in the 1964, National Convocation as to the authority and power of the "Senior Bishop", and the authority and power of the Executive Board. On October 10, 1967, in a Consent Decree entered in the Chancery Court, in Memphis, Shelby County, Tennessee, the Parties to the controversy acknowledged that the ultimate solution and all related ancillary questions should be determined by the General Assembly of the Church Of God In Christ in a Constitutional Convention called for that purpose.

The first Constitutional Convention of the Church Of God In Christ convened at its Memphis, Tennessee Headquarters, January 30th Through February 2, 1968. This historic Constitutional Convention adopted the Following by-laws:

1. The Abolishment of the Office of Senior Bishop, and Executive Board of Bishops.

2. To form a General Board of Twelve (12) Bishops to serve for a term of four (4) years, with a Presiding Bishop, and First and Second Assistant Presiding Bishop. The Presiding Bishop is to be Chief Executive Officer, and is to be empowered to conduct the executive affairs of the Church Of God In Christ during and between meetings of the General Assembly and the General Board, with the limitation that the action of the Presiding Bishop would be subject to the approval of a majority of the General Board and the General Assembly.

3. The General Assembly would continue to be the only doctrine-expressing and law-making authority of the Church.

4. Civil officers of the corporation, known as the Church Of God In Christ, were to be elected by a majority vote of the members of the General Assembly present and voting.

5. Ecclesiastically, the heads of departments were to be appointed by the General Board, for a term of four years, provided such appointments were approved by a majority of the General Assembly.

To maintain an uninterrupted and smooth operation of the administrative affairs, a Resolution was submitted and adopted to defer until a specific time during the election of the General Board, and the Presiding Bishop

It was further resolved that the Board of Bishops be empowered to appoint a Board of seven men to negotiate the administrative functions of the church until the November 1968 Convocation. Those appointed to this "Board were Bishops J.S. Bailey, Chairman; A.B. McEwen, J.O. Patterson, Sr., S.M. Crouch, O.M. Kelly, Wyoming Wells, and L.H. Ford.

THE TEXAS CONNECTION
International Leadership of COGIC (Jones, Sr.)

At the sixty-second International Convocation, November 5-15, 1968, the First General Election was held. The following Bishops were elected to the General Board. Bishops – J.O. Patterson, Sr., J.S. Bailey, S.M. Crouch, Wyoming Wells, L.H. Ford, O.M. Kelly, C.E. Bennett, J.A. Blake, Sr., John White, F.D. Washington, D. Lawrence Williams, J.D. Husband.

In the second phase of the election Bishop J.O. Patterson, Sr., was elected Presiding Bishop; Bishop J.S. Bailey was elected First Assistant Presiding Bishop; and Bishop S. M. Crouch, Second Assistant Presiding Bishop.

1961 – 1968 in Church Of God In Christ History is regarded as the '***DARK PERIOD***". This Dark Period was evidenced by a polarization of deep-seated opinions, broken spiritual fellowships and friendships, and questionable Christian conduct.

It is worthy of noting that Bishop O.T. Jones, Sr., didn't want to cause a split in the Church Of God In Christ and his love for the church caused him to step aside and vow to always be a part of the Church Of God In Christ.

(The elected executive Board along with Mother Coffey.)

Back Row: Bishops (D.L. Lawrence not a member of this board), J.W. White, L.H. Ford, W.G. Shipman, C.E. Bennett
Standing: Bishops (W.R. Nesbit not a member of this board) J.S. Bailey, S.M. Crouch, O.T. Jones, Sr., Mother Coffey, A.B. McEwen, J.O. Patterson, Sr.,

Bishop O.T. Jones, Sr. Taking care of YPWW business

W. Roberts, C.H. Mason, O.T. Jones, Sr.,

*Bishop O.T. Jones, Sr., (standing)
Bishop C.H. Mason, (siting)*

Some of the first Bishops of COGIC with the Mayor of Memphis
Bishop E.M. Page (Dallas, TX) Bishop R.F. Williams (Cleveland, OH)
Senior Bishop C.H. Mason (Memphis, TN) Mayor Walter Chandler
Bishop Wm Roberts (Chicago, IL) Bishop O.T. Jones, Sr., (Phil, PA)
Bishop A.B. McEwen (Memphis, TN)

Bishop J.O. Patterson, Sr.

Bishop James Oglethrope Patterson, Sr.
First Presiding Bishop 1968-1989
Third Chief Apostle

Bishop James Oglethrope Patterson, Sr., was born in Derma, Calhoun County, Mississippi, on July 21, 1912, to William Marion Patterson and Mollie Edwards Patterson. When he was eleven, the family moved to Memphis, Tennessee the headquarters of their church, the Church Of God In Christ, the second largest Pentecostal body in the United States.

His parents would give him spiritual guidance and would train him in these godly precepts.

The greatest loss of his young life came on June 24, 1924, at the demise of his mother. In spite of this loss, his ambition to be a man was not weakened. He was reared by his two older sisters and brother in law (*Alice, Lillian and John Terry.*) He received his public school education in school systems in Mississippi and Tennessee.

He was saved in the Church Of God In Christ and was trained thoroughly at the Howe School of Religion (*presently a part of the Lemoine-Owen College*).

Bishop Patterson, Sr., was brought up in the Church Of God In Christ. Bishop Patterson married Bishop Mason's beautiful daughter Deborah Mason July 4, 1934. He and Deborah had two children. J.O. Patterson, Jr. (*later Bishop J.O. Patterson, Jr., now transitioned*) and the late Janet Laverne Patterson. Bishop J.O. Patterson, Sr., and Deborah Mason-Patterson would enjoy almost 51 years of marriage (*which was ended at her transitioned on June 2, 1985.*)

After some time in the Dry cleaning and Coal sales business. Patterson decided to pursue his ministerial career and attended the House school of Religion in Memphis, Tennessee and in 1936, he was ordained by Bishop A.B. McEwen and was assigned his first pastoral charge to a eight member church in nearby Gates, Tennessee.

This would not be his only assignment as pastor. He would serve as pastor at Gates Tennessee; Brownsville, Tennessee, at the Homeland Church Of God In Christ, Reid Temple Church Of God In Christ and an additional church (*this church's name is not recorded.*)

His service as Pastor of Pentecostal Temple Church Of God In Christ started in 1941, with less than twenty members.

He was appointed to the Executive Commission by Bishop C.H. Mason. In 1953 he was appointed the jurisdictional prelate of the Second Jurisdiction of Tennessee. When the then General Secretary, Bishop E.U. Miller, became ill (*and needed a loyal friend to assist him*) he asked Bishop Mason to appoint Bishop Patterson as his assistant. At the transition of Bishop Miller, the Elders Council and General Assembly elected Bishop Patterson as his successor. He also served as the manager of the Church Of God In Christ Publishing House.

From 1951 until his transition in 1961, Bishop Mason knew that his health was declining and knew that he alone would not be able to adequately see to the ecclesiastical and secular matters of the Church and after much prayer, he appointed a special seven man commission to assist him with these and other jurisdictional matters. The official name later chosen for this commission was the Executive Commission, this commission was given complete authority to conduct and execute apostolic business formerly performed by Bishop Mason.

These activities of the commission included but were not limited to making all appointments. The following were the initial appointments to this Commission by Bishop Mason: On June 5, 1951, three men were appointed and they were Bishop A.B. McEwen, Bishop J.S. Bailey and Bishop O.M. Kelley. On May 19, 1952, one man was appointed to the commission in the person of Bishop J.O. Patterson, Sr., and on October 12, 1955, three men were added Bishop U.E. Miller, Bishop S.M Crouch and Bishop O.T. Jones, Sr.

Bishop C.H. Mason would close his eyes for the last time on November 17, 1961, at the God blessed age of 95.

At the transition of Bishop Mason, The Constitution of the Church Of God In Christ stipulated that at his transition the leadership and supervision of the International Church would be reverted to the Board of Bishops with a directive to the General Assembly to elect, by a two-third vote of those present, two or more Bishops who shall hold office, during good behavior and shall have general supervision of the church.

The General Assembly, in keeping with the Constitutional provision, retained the seven men, and elected five more members making a total of twelve men. This twelve man Commission later changed its name to the Executive Board. Subsequent appointees were Bishop Wyoming Wells, Bishop L.H. Ford, Bishop C.E. Bennett, Bishop John White and Bishop W.G. Shipman and Bishop B.S. Lyles was honored as an emeritus member.

Bishop A.B. McEwen was elected as the Chairman, Bishop J.S. Bailey, Vice-Chairman and Bishop J.O. Patterson, Sr. the General Secretary of the church and to the Executive Board. Bishop O.T. Jones, Sr., was honored because of his seniority by the Executive Board and the General Assembly with the title of *"Senior Bishop."*

A dispute arose in the 1964, National Convocation as to the authority and power of the *"Senior Bishop"*, and the authority and power of the Executive Board. On October 10, 1967, in a Consent Decree entered in the Chancery Court, in Memphis, Shelby County, Tennessee, the Parties to the controversy acknowledged that the ultimate solution and all related ancillary questions should be determined by the General Assembly of the Church Of God In Christ in a Constitutional Convention called for that purpose.

The first Constitutional Convention of the Church Of God In Christ convened at its Memphis, Tennessee Headquarters, January 30th Through February 2, 1968. This historic Constitutional Convention adopted the Following by-laws:

1. The Abolishment of the Office of Senior Bishop, and the Executive Board of Bishops.

2. To form a General Board of Twelve (12) Bishops to serve for a term of four (4) years, with a Presiding Bishop, and First and Second Assistant Presiding Bishop. The

THE TEXAS CONNECTION   *International Leadership of COGIC (Patterson, Sr.)*

Presiding Bishop is to be Chief Executive Officer, and is to be empowered to conduct the executive affairs of the Church Of God In Christ during and between meetings of the General Assembly and the General Board, with the limitation that the action of the Presiding Bishop would be subject to the approval of a majority of the General Board and the General Assembly.

3. The General Assembly would continue to be the only doctrine-expressing and law-making authority of the Church.

4. Civil officers of the corporation, known as the Church Of God In Christ, were to be elected by a majority vote of the members of the General Assembly present and voting.

5. Ecclesiastically, the heads of departments were to be appointed by the General Board, for a term of four years, provided such appointments were approved by a majority of the General Assembly.

To maintain an uninterrupted and smooth operation of the administrative affairs, a Resolution was submitted and adopted to defer until a specific time during the election of the General Board, and the Presiding Bishop

It was further resolved that the Board of Bishops be empowered to appoint a Board of seven men to negotiate the administrative functions of the church until the November 1968 Convocation. Those appointed to this Board were Bishops J.S. Bailey, Chairman; A.B. McEwen, J.O. Patterson, Sr., S.M. Crouch, O.M. Kelly, Wyoming Wells, and L.H. Ford.

At the sixty-second International Convocation, November 5-15, 1968, the First General Election was held. The following Bishops were elected to the General Board. Bishops – J.O. Patterson, Sr., J.S. Bailey, S.M. Crouch, Wyoming Wells, L.H. Ford, O.M. Kelly, C.E. Bennett, J.A. Blake, Sr., John White, F.D. Washington, D. Lawrence Williams, and J.D. Husband.

In the second phase of the election Bishop J.O. Patterson, Sr., was elected Presiding Bishop; Bishop J.S. Bailey was elected First Assistant Presiding Bishop; and Bishop S. M. Crouch, Second Assistant Presiding Bishop.

1961 – 1968, in Church Of God In Christ History is regarded as the 'DARK PERIOD". This Dark Period was evidenced by a polarization of deep-seated opinions, broken spiritual fellowships and friendships, and questionable Christian conduct.

As the newly elected Presiding Bishop. Bishop Patterson having "*come to the kingdom for such a time as this*" he tended the seeds of discord and reconciled dissident jurisdictional factions.

During the 1960's Bishop Patterson had gained the respect of the younger generation in the Church Of God In Christ by being one of the few Pentecostal leaders willing to support the civil rights movement. While others felt that the preachers should avoid political action, Bishop Patterson was a leader in the Memphis Ministers and Citizens League and supported sit in demonstrations.

As the first elected Presiding Bishop in the Church Of God In Christ, he brought with him to this office the discipline and technology of the business world and the pastoral and executive dexterity of the ecclesiastical world.

The first four years (*1968 to 1972*) of Bishop Patterson's term of Office were marked with accelerated growth and programs of unparalleled new dimensions. The accomplishments of his first four years were documented as follows:

(1) The proposed financial goals for 1969, resulted in the greatest income the Church Of God In Christ had ever received at that time.

(2) The establishment of a Department of Research and Survey to ascertain the numerical strength of the COGIC world-wide.

(3) The institutionalization of the Charles Harrison Mason Memorial Scholarship Fund to aid students in need of financial educational assistance.

(4) The involvement and encouragement of the Church Of God In Christ youth and adults to utilize their secular skills and professions within the framework of the Church.

(5) The establishment of a Church Of God In Christ Hospital Plan.

(6) A modification in August 1970, from the varitype system of printing to the IBM System, the Installation of a photographic laboratory and purchase of other modern equipment and machinery revolutionized and increased the potentials of production and quality for the Publishing House.

(7) A new Constitution to meet growing ecclesiastical demands and innovations.

(8) A new Doctrine and Discipline Handbook which would include information for ecclesiastical and liturgical requisites, the Constitution tenets of Faith and the Church's position on Social Concerns.

(9) The establishment in 1970, of the Charles Harrison Mason Theological Seminary in Atlanta, Georgia offering a Master's of Divinity and Masters in Religious Education Degree.

(10) A system of Bible Colleges throughout the Church.

(11) The gift of the Chisca Hotel of Memphis, Tennessee by Mr. Robert Snowden February of 1972, valued at three million dollars.

In 1969 following the transition of Bishop A.B. McEwen, Sr., (*who was the Jurisdictional Bishop of the Headquarters Jurisdiction in Memphis, Tennessee,*) a rift began in the Patterson family.

Many of the Pastors of West Tennessee wanted Bishop W.A. Patterson, Sr. (*the father of G.E. Patterson and Brother of J.O. Patterson, Sr.*) to return from Detroit to fulltime service in Memphis as the Bishop of West Tennessee.

Presiding Bishop J.O. Patterson, Sr., refused using the Catholic Church as his example. He felt that the Presiding Bishop of the Church Of God In Christ should be the Bishop of Memphis just as the Pope is the Bishop of Rome.

During this time there were many drastic changes initiated by this God-Sent man Bishop J.O. Patterson that provoked undue criticism, it was the general consensus of opinion that at the close of his first elected term in office God had given him the reign and vision for the Church. As a result many regarded his re-election as a mandate so that other significant areas of his platform could be acted upon.

At the 1972, November Convocation in Memphis, Tennessee, Bishop J.O. Patterson, Sr., was re-elected to his second term office (*1972-1976*)

After the election, this celebrated Presiding Bishop immediately set out to implement unfinished goals and reveal new goals. Some of them are as follows:

To move the Publishing House residence, its staff and machinery to the lower levels of what was formerly known as the Chisca Hotel to enable a greater expansion, efficiency and production.

To remove all tenants from the Chisca Hotel and to use it exclusively for Church purposes.

To departmentalize the General Board into Commissions, such as, the Judicial Commission, the Commission on Education, the Ministerial Health and Welfare Commission. The Church Extension Commission, the Commission on Finance, the Commission on Evangelism and the Commission on Communications.

In 1984, Ebony magazine named him one of the hundred most influential Black Americans. In his last years he dreamed of establishing a World Outreach Center, and All Saints University, and a multilingual publishing house. His wife Deborah transitioned on June 2, 1985. He married Mary Peat in April 1989, he was diagnosed with pancreatic cancer. Instead of treatment he opted to just trust God. *(He served five full terms and two years into his sixth term as the first elected Presiding Prelate.)*

There shall be forthcoming other aspirations and goals for the Church Of God In Christ.

Other Churchmen will be chosen in the future to the position of the Office of the Presiding Bishop, but Bishop James Oglethorpe Patterson, Sr., the first elected Presiding Bishop of the Church Of God In Christ will never be regarded as one who fitted into any of the neat little categories of the clergy.

He served faithfully, heroically, and courageously proving to be the man of the hour. On December 29, 1989, he finished his course and went from labor to reward.

Mother D.I. Patterson a graduate of CH Mason on November 13, 1979

Bishop Patterson Mother Patterson and Dr. A.J. Hines

Bishop J.O. Patterson, Sr., at the 64th Holy Convocation 1970

THE TEXAS CONNECTION *International Leadership of COGIC (Patterson, Sr.)*

2nd GENERAL BOARD MEMBERS
1972 to 1976

J.O. Patterson, Sr.

Bishop J.O. Patterson, Sr.
Bishop F.O. White

Back row: J.A. Blake, F.D. Washington, J. Cohen, J.W. White, J.D. Husband, C.L. Anderson
Front row: W. Wells, O.M. Kelly, L.H. Ford, J.O. Patterson, Sr., S.M. Crouch, J.S. Bailey (not pictured)

Four Generations
of Servant Leaders

1st Generation

Bishop C.H. Mason
Father-in-Law, Grandfather, and Great-Grandfather

2nd Generation

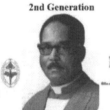

Bishop J.O. Patterson, Sr.
Son-in-Law, Father, and Grandfather

3rd Generation

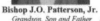

Bishop J.O. Patterson, Jr.
Grandson, Son and Father

4th Generation

Bishop C.H. Mason Patterson
Great-Grandson, Grandson and Son

Bishop L.H. Ford

Bishop Louis Henry Ford
Second Presiding Bishop 1989-1994
Fourth Chief Apostle

Bishop Louis Henry Ford, a churchman with a vision, was born May 23, 1914, in Clarksdale, Mississippi. In 1926, he was called to the ministry and service of Christ and in 1927, he attended Saints Junior College. In the early 1930's he moved to Chicago, Illinois, where he served as Assistant Pastor in Evanston, Illinois.

It was at Hovland Court Church Of God In Christ in Evanston, Illinois that Louis Henry Ford would meet, fall in love with and later married Margaret "Babe" Little on December 12, 1934.

He was ordained an Elder by Bishop William Roberts in 1935 and founded St. Paul Church Of God In Christ in 1936, where upon he purchased Chicago's oldest house and grounds for a new church.

In the late 1930's, he became an outstanding Chicago radio minister, and moved to a larger church located at 51st and Michigan.

From 1940 to 1948, Elder Ford conducted the first of many tent revivals; was appointed Superintendent of the South Shore District; was appointed State Chairman of Illinois; laid the cornerstone for St. Paul Church Of God In Christ, 4526 South Wabash Avenue; was appointed National Public Relations Director; and also Chairman of the National Founders Day Program.

The 1950's brought forth the following; His appointment as State Overseer of Iowa; the dedication of *"Ford's Temple"* in De Moines, Iowa; his receiving the *"The Most Outstanding Alumna Award"* from Saints College.

In 1954, he was consecrated to the National Bishopric staff and also selected as a member of the Board of Education – Saints College. He was appointed Bishop for Central Illinois and was the foremost minister in the *"Emmitt Till Case"* in 1955.

In 1956, he was given the keys to Memphis, Tennessee. He went on to chair the Golden Jubilee Anniversary and received the *"Charles Harrison Mason"* Award. He promoted the naming of Mason Street; was appointed Vice Chairman for the publishing Board; hosted the International Sunday School Convention and founded the C.H. Mason Institute.

In the 1960's he was a leader in enterprises helping fire victims; stirred Chicago in a great Soul Saving Revival; received the Leadership Award by the Church Federation, and was an Advisor on Chicago School Problems. He was elected to the Executive Board of Twelve Bishops. He co-chaired the *"Committee to Fulfill Rights"* and received a Doctor of Divinity Degree from Saints Junior College. The Phase I remodeling of St. Paul Church Of God In Christ, was also began and he promoted the State Treasury in its assistance of local churches.

He was selected as an Executive Committee member of the NAACP; was chosen as a consultant on Urban Opportunities, and served as Race Relations Advisor to the Mayor of Chicago. In 1967, he was named Prelate over Minnesota, and selected as a member of the Church Governing Board of Seven Bishops.

He was elected as one of the 12 original Bishops in 1968, to the General Board of the Church Of God In Christ, Inc.

In 1968 and 1969, he launched the Phase II, $125,000 remodeling and expansion program for St. Paul Church Of God In Christ, and helped motivate New Projections and New Horizons for administrations of the general church.

In the early 1970's, he was appointed Special Advisor to Chicago's mayor Richard J. Daley; was guest speaker at twelve State Convocations, and elected a second time to the General Board. He dedicated five new churches and was the guest speaker at twenty-four banquets around the country in 1975.

In 1976, he was appointed Second Assistant International Presiding Bishop. In the late 1970's, he projected new additions for St. Paul and plans for a Senior Citizen Home Complex, and dedicated the Chaney Ford Day Care Center.

In 1980, he was elevated to the office of the First Assistant Presiding Bishop; also receiving the Banner Jurisdiction for Financial Report in the National Spring Meeting. In 1981, he hosted the International U.N.A.C. (United National Auxiliaries Convention).

In 1985, he celebrated his *"50th Golden Anniversary"* as founding Pastor of St. Paul Church Of God In Christ. The plans for the new addition for St. Paul were completed in 1986, and the Phase III construction of a 15,000 square feet addition began in 1987.

In 1988, Bishop Ford was re-elected to the General Board for a sixth term; and was re-appointed the First Assistant Presiding Bishop. In 1989, he celebrated his 75th birthday.

Upon the transition of Presiding Bishop J.O. Patterson, Sr., on December 29, 1989, Bishop L.H. Ford was elevated to Interim Presiding Bishop and the $1 million addition to St. Paul was completed. In 1990, Bishop Ford was elected the second Presiding Bishop of the Church Of God In Christ

Bishop Ford gave over sixty years of valued, faithful, inspired leadership, with unselfish service, rendering immeasurable contributions to mankind and the progress of the Church Of God In Christ.

The most important accomplishment took place when he revived and built a multi-million dollar structure at Saints Academy in Lexington, Mississippi, during his four year tenure. Bishop Louis Henry Ford went from labor to reward on March 31, 1995.

Mamie Till after seeing the arrival of her son Emmitt Till's remains in Chicago on September 2, 1955 after he was beaten, lynched (*murdered*) and sunk in the river while visiting family in Mississippi.

Bishop Isaiah L. Roberts, Gene Mabley and Bishop Louis Henry Ford supporting Mamie Till.

The resting place of Bishop L. H. Ford

Bishop C.D. Owens

Bishop Chandler David Owens, Sr.
Third Presiding Bishop 1995-2000
Fifth Chief Apostle

Bishop Chandler David Owens, Sr., was born in Birmingham, Alabama, on October 2, 1931, to the union of the late Elder William Owens and Mrs. Martha Owens. He was the fifth child of eight children born to this union.

Bishop Owens' father the Elder Williams Owens was a Church Of God In Christ minister in Birmingham, Alabama. Bishop Owens was saved when he was five years old at Smithfield Church Of God In Christ pastored by Elder Shepard Skanes.

Bishop Owens almost immediately started preaching and became known as the *"Boy Preacher"* this young lad was prayed for and especially anointed for the ministry in Alabama by Bishop Charles Harrison Mason.

The Church Of God In Christ became his exalted family and from that moment, men such as Riley F. Williams, Bishop L.C. Page, Bishop J.O. Patterson, Sr., Bishop John Seth Bailey, and Bishop L.H. Ford contributed greatly in shaping and molding him for the task of Presiding Bishop.

In spite of his early beginning into the ministry, he enjoyed a normal childhood, participating in sport activities such as boxing and football. He was known as one of the smartest students to matriculate through the Birmingham Public School System.

Bishop Owens often talked about how at the age of seventeen, Bishop L.H. Ford, gave him some of his first evangelism opportunities, which in turn helped introduce him to the national Church Of God In Christ.

Elder C.D. Owens served as the junior pastor of Power View Church Of God In Christ (*his father's church.*) He would also serve as an adjutant to Bishop C.H. Mason.

Elder Owens would spend a lot of his time after graduation in the library educating himself by reading up on various subjects covered in many books; toning up his word study with thesauruses, dictionaries and the latest world events by studying encyclopedias. The effort of self-education was due in large part because his parents could not afford college for their eager to learn son.

Shortly after high school Elder Chandler David Owens would move to Detroit, Michigan to find work at the Henry Ford Auto Plant.

After landing the job, he would also find the hand of the love of his life Shirley Jeannett Hardy.

By this time his service to the church would be recognized when he would be appointed to pastor the church in Newark, New Jersey (*the Wells Cathedral Church Of God In Christ.*) This appointment was made by Bishop John Seth Bailey.

Elder Chandler David and Shirley Owens would move twice first to Orange, New Jersey and then to Newark, New Jersey.

This union of Elder C.D. Owens and Shirley Jeannett Owens would see three children born to this young couple two daughters and one son: (*Chandra Stephanie, Chandler David, Jr., and a deceased daughter Shirlitha Shirae*).

His unusual oratorical gift has made him one of the most sought after speakers in the Church Of God In Christ for more than thirty years. He has served in almost every area of responsibility including serving as the Chairman of the Commission for the Constitution of the Church.

He has held lead responsibilities in the Department of Evangelism and Youth. Thousands would fill Pentecostal Temple during the Holy Convocation, to hear him preside over the National Musicals.

He would travel much as an evangelist. He would travel and cover much ground in the United States and foreign fields such as Caribbean Islands, India and Europe.

Elder Owens was consecrated Bishop of New Jersey Third Ecclesiastical Jurisdiction of the Church Of God In Christ, Inc., while he was pastoring the Wells Cathedral Church Of God In Christ.

In 1976, Bishop Owens made history in the Church Of God In Christ by being the youngest Bishop ever elected to the General Board of the church. He was known as the *Man with the Golden Voice*.

Bishop Owens served as First Assistant Presiding Bishop under Bishop L.H. Ford and when Bishop Ford transitioned on March 31, 1995, one of the church's most popular and gifted leaders had already been groomed to continue this great legacy of Leadership. At the transition of Bishop Ford, Bishop Owens was elevated to Interim Presiding Bishop. Bishop Owens was later elected as the Third Presiding Bishop and the Fifth Chief Apostle to lead the Church Of God In Christ.

It was no surprise that the Church Of God In Christ received him with such a warming confidence. Bishop Owens program for the Church was titled "*Vision 2000 and Beyond*"

He especially targeted concerns such as Evangelism, Church growth, financial solvency, national auxiliaries, women in ministry, Christian education and C.H. Mason Bible College, as his priority during his tenure.

Bishop Owens was a *"warrior for his principles"* as noted by Dr. David Hall. It was under his administration in April 1997, that Mother Rivers was appointed as Supervisor of the Women's Department of the Church Of God In Christ.

It was also under Bishop Owens administration that AIM (*Auxiliaries In Ministry*) was established. This is the summer convention of the Church Of God In Christ that replaced UNAC-5.

Bishop Owens was challenged by Bishop G.E. Patterson for the election as Presiding Prelate of the Church Of God In Christ. Bishop Owens would defeat Bishop Patterson by one (1) vote.

Bishop C.D. Owens was defeated in the election held in November 2000 by Bishop Gilbert Earl Patterson. But Bishop Owens will be remembered as one of the most popular presiding officers the Church Of God In Christ has had. He remained a member of the General Board of Bishops.

Bishop CD Owens went from labor to reward early Sunday morning on March 6, 2011, after a short hospital stay.

Bishop G.E. Patterson

Bishop Gilbert Earl Patterson
Fourth Presiding Bishop 2000-2007
Sixth Chief Apostle

Gilbert Earl Patterson was born September 22, 1939, in the parsonage next door to the Church Of God In Christ in Humboldt, Tennessee. He is the son of the late Bishop William Archie Patterson, Sr. and the late Mrs. Mary Louise Patterson. Bishop William Patterson, Sr., was the brother of Presiding Bishop J.O. Patterson, Sr.

The siblings of Gilbert Earl are the late Elder William Archie Patterson, Jr., Evangelist Mary Alice Patterson Hawkins, Assistant Supervisor Lee Ella Patterson Smith and Evanglist Barbara Patterson Davis.

In November of 1939, the Patterson family moved from Humboldt, Tennessee to Memphis, Tennessee.

In May of 1951, a revival was being conducted by Elder Johnny Brown at the Holy Temple Church Of God In Christ, 1254 Wilson Street, Memphis, Tennessee where Elder William Archie Patterson, Sr., was pastor. It was during this revival that the young 11-year-old Gilbert Earl Patterson was saved.

Since Memphis, Tennessee is the home of the Church Of God In Christ, many of the early leaders of the Church stayed or ate dinner at the Patterson's home. From childhood Gilbert knew Bishop Mason and many of the early leaders. He attended the Lincoln Elementary School that was directly across the street from his home at 1567 South Orleans Street. In May of 1952, the Patterson family moved to 1695 Chicago Blvd in Detroit, Michigan.

While in Detroit at the age of 16 Gilbert Earl received the precious gift of the Baptism of the Holy Ghost, on Sunday night September 16, 1956, at New Jerusalem Church Of God In Christ pastored by Elder W.A. Patterson, Sr., located at 7361 Linwood Avenue.

In the month of October of 1956 the Lord called him into the gospel ministry. He preached his first sermon on Tuesday night, January 22, 1957. The sermon text was Isaiah 59:9; his subject was *"We Wait For Light, But We Walk In Darkness."*

Gilbert Patterson was licensed by his father in March of 1957 and was ordained by Bishop J.S. Bailey on August 28, 1958.

In Detroit he attended and graduated from Hutchins Intermediate and Central High School. He also attended the Detroit Bible Institute. As a teenager, he worked diligently as a choir member, lead singer in the New Jerusalem Ensemble and as a part-time national evangelist.

While yet a teenager, he was privileged to speak in the National Holy Convocation of the Church Of God In Christ and in the International Youth Congress. On two occasions, he was privileged to preach in the presence of Bishop C. H. Mason.

In December 1961, Gilbert Patterson returned to Memphis to serve as Co-Pastor of Holy Temple Church Of God In Christ and to attend Lemoyne College. At that time Holy Temple Church Of God In Christ had 80 adult members and a few children.

From December 1961 thru June 1964, Holy Temple experienced no growth. However something happened in June of 1964 that turned the church around. Elder Gilbert Patterson led the congregation in 3 days and nights of total abstinence fasting and prayer. This was followed in July with a 30-day tent revival which was held two blocks from the church on the corner of Wilson and McLemore. During the revival, 55 new members were added to the church. From that time on. God blessed Gilbert Patterson to bring together large crowds, seemingly at will.

In 1965, Elder Gilbert Patterson became known as God's young Apostle because of his gift to gather large crowds and lead so many to Jesus Christ. At that time he was also talking about establishing missions and organizing churches. He continued as Co-Pastor of Holy Temple and the church experienced tremendous growth between July 1964 and December 1974.

Elder G.E. Patterson was one of the nine person team that invited Dr. Martin Luther King, Jr., to the sanitation workers strike, striking for a living wage.

Dr. King would deliver his famous last public speech (*I've Been to the Mountain Top"*) on April 3, 1968, at this strike.

This speech was given at Mason Temple Church Of God In Christ (*not a Masonic Temple as some reports have named the location*).

In 1969, following the transition of Tennessee Bishop A.B. McEwen, Sr., a rift began in the Patterson family. Many of the Pastors of West Tennessee wanted Gilbert Patterson's father, Bishop W.A. Patterson, Sr., to return from Detroit to fulltime service in Memphis as the Bishop of West Tennessee.

Presiding Bishop J.O. Patterson, Sr., refused, using the Catholic Church as his example. He felt that the Presiding Bishop of the Church Of God In Christ should be the Bishop of Memphis just as the Pope is the Bishop of Rome.

Gilbert Patterson attempted to champion the cause for his father, but failed. During the Convocation of 1974, the General Board supported the Presiding Bishop and was preparing to move against Bishop W.A. Patterson, Sr., and Gilbert Earl to remove them from Holy Temple. In an effort to end the feud and stop any further efforts against his father, Gilbert Patterson resigned from Holy Temple with an effective date of February 23, 1975.

In the meantime, Gilbert Patterson purchased and remodeled the old Mt. Veron Baptist Church building at 547 Mississippi Boulevard. At that location he opened Temple of Deliverance, the Cathedral of Bountiful Blessings on March 2, 1975. On that day 436 people became members of the church.

They came from every denomination and religious organization in Memphis. The church was too small from the first day. In less than three years the membership grew to over 2,000, therefore, immediate plans were made to build a larger sanctuary. On October 8, 1978, 3 years and 7 months from the opening, Temple of Deliverance entered its new sanctuary.

At a cost of $1.2 million dollars, it was the first church built by blacks in Memphis at a cost more than a million dollars.

It was noted in the December 7, 1978, issue of the Jet magazine.

After adding chairs in the aisles, the crowd frequently overflowed into the fellowship hall downstairs where the worship could be viewed on a closed circuit T.V. screen. On July 5, 1987, Bishop C. D. Owens dedicated the new wing that seated approximately 600.

In September of 1986, during a telephone conversation with his uncle, the Presiding Bishop J.O. Patterson, Sr., the Presiding Bishop expressed his desire to see his nephew back as an active member of the Church Of God In Christ, Inc. As a result of that conversation, Bishop J.O. Patterson, Sr., had Gilbert Patterson's name added to the General Board's agenda during the Convocation of 1986.

Many of the Board members had waited for this day and had often spoken of Gilbert Patterson's return. Board members such as Bishop O.T. Jones, Jr., Bishop F.D. Washington, Bishop J.D. Husband, Bishop LeRoy Anderson and Bishop C. D. Owens were very ardent in their support.

The most vocal was Gilbert Patterson's lifelong friend, Bishop Chandler D. Owens. He refused to break his friendship with Gilbert Paterson although he was frequently under great pressure to do so.

During the November 1986, General Board meeting, the General Board voted 11 to 0 to invite Gilbert Patterson to come back in the active ministry of the Church Of God In Christ as a Jurisdictional Bishop with jurisdiction in Memphis.

This meeting was chaired by Bishop L.H. Ford in the absence of Presiding Bishop J.O. Patterson, Sr. This action of the General Board in November of 1986, was not executed by Bishop J.O. Patterson, Sr., until January 29, 1988, at the Bishop's Conference in Jacksonville, Florida.

Bishop G.E. Patterson was elected to the General Board for the first time starting in 1992. At the transition of Bishop L.H. Ford in 1995, Bishop C.D. Owens who was the First Assistant Presiding Prelate became the interim Presiding Prelate.

The election for the office of Presiding Prelate was to be held in November of 1996 and Bishop Owens was expected to be elected to the office to a four year term without any formable opposition, but for the first time in the history of the election for Presiding Prelate of the Church Of God In Christ, the seated Prelate was challenged.

The general assembly had two choices between the seated Presiding Prelate Bishop C. D. Owens and Bishop G. E. Patterson. They received the most votes in the election for General Board. Because of the results a runoff was needed, in the runoff vote Bishop C.D. Owens won by one vote.

Bishop G.E. Patterson graciously conceded the election to Bishop C.D. Owens not wanting a rift to arise in the church due to the election.

In the election of 2000, Bishop G.E. Patterson and Presiding Bishop C.D. Owens, Sr., were once again in a face off for the office of Presiding Prelate. This time though Bishop G.E. Patterson would receive 59 percent of the vote, which gave the election to Bishop Patterson.

This made history because it made Bishop Patterson the sixth leader of the Church Of God In Christ (4th elected Presiding Prelate) and it also marked, for the first time in the

THE TEXAS CONNECTION
International Leadership of COGIC (G.E. Patterson)

history of the Church God In Christ, a Presiding Prelate was unseated.

This wasn't the end of the two friends meeting in the election for the office of Presiding Prelate.

Bishop Patterson and Bishop Owens would face off again in the election of 2004, but this election was unanimously Bishop Patterson's, when Bishop Owens withdrew from the ballot.

Bishop Patterson built an almost five thousand seat church auditorium to try and accommodate his large following. As Presiding Bishop. Bishop Paterson's television programs viewing audience grew to the largest audience of any minister in the Church Of God In Christ.

He is also credited with redefining the Office of Presiding Prelate. He would state that the office was *"mired in bureaucracy and isolation far above the people it was created to serve."*

Bishop Patterson was hospitalized in January of 2006 for a hematoma. Previously he had surgery, but returned quickly to work. Bishop Patterson's ministry was a global empire that included television, radio, internet and publishing. Bishop G.E. Patterson went from labor to reward on March 20, 2007 at the age of 67.

Charles E. Blake and Gilbert E. Patterson

Evangelist L. Patterson and Bishop G.E. Patterson

Bishop F.O. White and Bishop G.E. Patterson

Presiding Bishop Patterson entering the Holy Convocation In Memphis, TN

resting place of Bishop G.E. Patterson

Presiding Bishop Patterson at the Holy Convocation In Memphis, TN

Bishop W.A. Patterson, Sr.
Father of Bishop G.E. Patterson and elder brother of Bishop J.O. Pastterson, Sr.

Bishop C.E. Blake, I

Bishop Charles Edward Blake, I
Fifth Presiding Bishop 2007-Present
Seventh Chief Apostle

Charles Edward Blake was born on August 5, 1940, in North Little Rock, Arkansas. He is the son of the late Bishop Junious Augustus Blake, Sr., and the late Mrs. Lula Champion Blake.

He was licensed in 1959 and ordained in 1962. He received his Bachelor of Arts from California Western University (*now known as United States International University*). He received his Master of Divinity degrees from the Interdenominational Theological Center in 1965 and from the Fuller Theological Seminary in Pasadena, California.

Elder C.E. Blake would start his pastoral career as the co-pastor of the Greater Jackson Memorial Church Of God In Christ, located in San Diego, California a position he would hold from 1959 to 1963.

In 1963, he would further his pastoral experience as the Pastor of the Marietta Church Of God In Christ, in Marietta, Georgia. He pastored there until sometime in 1964.

On July 11, 1964, Pastor Charles Edward Blake and Miss Mae Lawrence were united in holy matrimony his father, Bishop Junious Augustus Blake, Sr., would officiate the ceremonies.

Three children were born of this union *Kimberly (Blake) Ludlow, Charles E. Blake, Jr., and Lawrence Blake.*

Elder C.E. Blake, Sr., was an active member of the Church Of God In Christ, during what has been described as the "*Dark Days*" of the Church. That period in time immediately following the transition of Bishop Mason, until the resolution of this dispute circa 1951 to 1968.

During these days Pastor Blake was very active serving in various positions such as the Vice Chair and the President of the Publishing Board. He served as the Chair of the Christian Education Board and with the Youth Department during the years of 1965 to 1970. Also during the same time he was editor of the YPWW (*Young Peoples Willing Worker*) topic from 1966 to 1971.

Another note worthy event during this time in his life was in 1969. Elder Charles Edward Blake, Sr., would be appointed the Pastor of the West Angeles Church Of God In Christ, located on Crenshaw Blvd, in Los Angeles, California.

Also, from 1971 to 1993, Pastor Blake was a trustee of the Interdenominational Theological Center and a trustee for the Charles Harrison Mason Theological Seminary in Atlanta, Georgia.

In 1973, he was consecrated by Bishop J.O. Patterson, Sr., as the Jurisdictional Prelate of the Southern California Jurisdiction of the Church Of God In Christ. Inc.

Bishop C.E. Blake, Sr., earned his Doctorate of Divinity degree from the California Graduate School of Theology in 1982, and is an Honorary Doctorate recipient of the Oral Roberts University.

From 1988 to 2000, he served with distinction and honor as a General Board member of the Church Of God In Christ.

From 2000 to 2007, he served with distinction and loyalty as the First Assistant Presiding Bishop to the late Presiding Bishop Gilbert Earl Patterson.

He also has served as the Jurisdictional Prelate of the First Jurisdiction of Southern California since 1973, which is comprised of more than 250 churches.

He is the pastor of West Angeles Church Of God In Christ, with a membership of over 24,000. West Angeles is deeply involved in providing not only for the spiritual life of its people, but also it provides more than 80 programs for the psychological, social and economic entrancement of the community.

As founder and CEO of Save Africa's Children, Bishop Blake oversees the support of more than 200 thousand children, in 400 orphan care programs, throughout more than 23 nations on the continent of Africa.

He has served as Chairman of the Executive Committee of the Board of Directors of Oral Roberts University.

He has served as a member of the Board of Directors of the International Charismatic Bible Ministers.

In 2006, he served on the Los Angeles Board of the Azusa Centennial Celebration. He has also formerly served as an Advisory Committee Member of the Pentecostal World Conference. He serves as the Chairman and Founder of the Los Angeles Ecumenical Congress (*LAEC*), an interdenominational coalition of religious leaders and pastors.

He is also a member of the Council on Foreign Relations, Religions Advisory Committee.

He has received numerous awards, commendations and accolades. A few are:

In the year 2000, he was the designated recipient of the L.A. Urban Leagues' Whitney M. Young Award.

In 2003, he was awarded the Harvard Foundation Humanitarian Medal for his work with Save Africa's Children and its mission to support orphanages throughout that continent.

February 5, 2004, was designated a "*Bishop Charles E. Blake Day*" by the Los Angeles County Board of Supervisors.

The 2006, Trumpet Award, the Salvation Army's William Booth Award, the Greenling Institute's Big Heart Award.

The Distinguished Leadership Award presented by the African Presidential Archives and Research Center at Boston University in April 2007.

Also in April, 2007, Bishop Blake moved swiftly to fill the void of leadership left by the beloved Bishop Gilbert Patterson, who transitioned on March 20, 2007.

In April 2007, Bishop Blake instituted measures to secure and centralize the financial systems of the Church Of God In Christ, National.

In May of 2008, a summit of the Church Of God In Christ, leadership convened in Los Angeles, Detroit, and Memphis to encourage an inclusive environment through which the Church might begin forecasting the direction the Church ought to take for the next 25 years.

During this very busy time. In the midst of a flurry of business activity, he found time to visit three nations outside of the United States, meeting with well over 100 denomination pastors in South America, Malawi, and South Africa.

It was a first, ever, visit by a Presiding Bishop of the Church Of God In Christ, to the nation of Belize, South America and for Malawi, Africa.

As a member of the White House Advisory Council the Presiding Bishop of the Church of God in Christ, Bishop Charles E Blake, I was chosen as one of the 25 member advisors by President Barack Obama.

As a member of this board Bishop Blake was chosen on April 6, 2009, to be an advisor on Neighborhood and Faith-Based Partnerships.

Bishop C.E. Blake, I, serves as the Seventh Chief Apostle and the 5th Elected Presiding Prelate of the Church Of God In Christ, Inc. He has been elected to serve as Presiding Prelate since 2008 to present.

Wedding Pic: *Bishop & Mrs. J.A. Blake and Elder Charles E. Blake at his wedding*

Charles E. Blake and Gilbert E. Patterson

Lady Mae L. Blake
Wife of Bishop C.E, Blake, Sr.

Blake Wedding July 11, 1964
(left to right) Bishop Elton A. Lawrence & Mrs. Myrtle Lawrence & Lady Mae (Lawrence) Blake & Elder Charles E. Blake Bishop & Mrs. J.A. Blake

THE TEXAS CONNECTION
International Leadership of COGIC (Blake, Sr.)

__Back row:__ C.E. Blake, Sr., P.A. Brooks, Unknown, C. Brewer __Front row:__ W.L. Porter, R.L.H. Winbush, L.T. Walker, W. James, C.D. Owens, unknown, J.N. Haynes, unknown, Unknown (__6 future General Board members, 2 future Presiding Bishops, 2 future First Assistant Presiding Bishops and many other national departmental leaders__)

Bishop C.E. Blake, Sr., Bishop F.O. White

Bishop P.A. Brooks, II., Elder C.E. Blake, II., Bishop J.W. Macklin, Elder L. Blake, Bishop C.E. Blake, I

Father and Mother of Bishop C.E. Blake, Sr. in Little Rock during the 1940's Elder J.A. Blake, Sr. and Mrs. L.C. Blake

Bishop J.A. Blake, Sr. and Mother L.C. Blake

The General Board
Church of God in Christ, Inc.

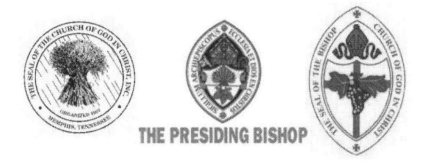

The Presidium of the
Church of God in Christ, Inc.

The Presidium of the Church Of God In Christ, Inc., is the 12 member board that is formally named the General Board of the Church Of God In Christ, Inc. To become a member of this board, the candidate must be elected by the General Assembly. In order to qualify, the Bishop-candidate must be a member of the board of Bishops in good standing and in good behavior.

There are only 12 positions on this board. The leading position for this board is that of Presiding Bishop. The Presiding Bishop is elected in the second phase of the election to this board. The Presiding Bishop is the one who received the most votes. There is also a first and second assistant Presiding Bishop. There are other positions also filled by the members of this board. The term of election to this board is for a period of 4 years (Quadrennial.)

(The predecessor of the General Board was the Executive Board, which started out as the Executive Commission. The Executive Commission was put in place at the failing health of Bishop C.H. Mason on June 5, 1951.)

It is the responsibility of this board to establish and execute policies for the Church of God in Christ and its membership, while sustaining and perpetuating spiritual order in the body. The decisions of this board are final and can only be over turned or modified by the General Assembly.

The General Board meets officially three times a year at the April Call meeting, at the International Holy Convocation and at the necessary call of the presiding bishop.

The General Board
Church of God in Christ, Inc.

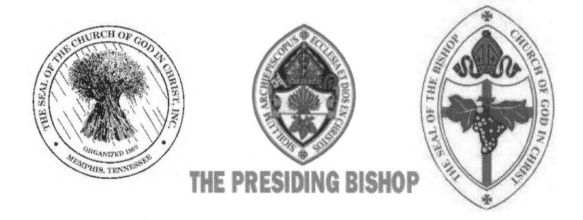

The Presidium of the
Church of God in Christ, Inc.

THE TEXAS CONNECTION　　　　　　　The General Board *(The Commission)*

The Presidium of the Church of God in Christ, Inc.
The Senior Bishop & the Constitutional Board of December 10, 1922
The Executive Commission ♦ The Executive Board
The 1968 Administration Board ♦ The Elected General Boards

*Bishop Charles Harrison Mason
Founder & First Senior Bishop

Members of the 1922 Constitutional Board

*R.R. Booker	D. Bostic	Mack E. Jonas
*E.R. Driver	*J. Bowie	*V.M. Baker
*W. Curtis	R.H.I. Clark	*C.C. Frederick
*D.J. Young	*W.M. Page	

(The above Overseers comprised the Constitutional General Assembly of the church.)
(* The General Board of the Church Of God In Christ of America.)

The Executive Commission
The initial appointment of (3) to the Executive Commission by Bishop CH Mason on June 5, 1951 are below:

Bishop A.B. McEwen　　**Bishop J.S. Bailey**　　**Bishop O.M. Kelly**
Appointed on June 5, 1951　Appointed on June 5, 1951　Appointed on June 5, 1951

The single appointment of (1) to the Executive Commission by Bishop CH Mason on May 19, 1952 are below:

Bishop J.O. Patterson, Sr.
appointed on May 19, 1952

The Third appointment of (3) to the Executive Commission by Bishop CH Mason on October 12, 1955 are below:

Bishop E.U. Miller
appointed on
October 12, 1955

Bishop S.M. Crouch
appointed on
October 12, 1955

Bishop O.T. Jones, Sr.
appointed on
October 12, 1955

At the transition of Bishop Mason on November 17, 1961, the Board of Bishops which became the governing body of the Church Of God In Christ by stipulation of the 1922 Constitution of the Church Of God In Christ. The General Assembly was given a directive to elect by a two-thirds vote of those present two or more Bishops who shall hold office, during good behavior and shall have general supervision of the church. The General Assembly retained the seven men that were already members of the Executive Commission and elected five more members making those on the commission a total of twelve members.

The Fourth appointment of (5) to the Executive Commission by the General Assembly in November of 1961 are below:
(also honored as a member emeritus was Bishop B. S. Lyles)

Bishop Wyoming Wells
appointed in
November of 1961

Bishop L.H. Ford
appointed in
November of 1961

Bishop C.E. Bennett
appointed in
November of 1961

Bishop J.W. White
appointed in
November of 1961

Bishop W.G. Shipman
appointed in
November of 1961

Bishop B.S. Lyles
honored as
Member emeritus

THE TEXAS CONNECTION — The General Board (Executive Board)

The Executive Board

Because of the seniority of Bishop O.T. Jones, Sr., the Executive Board and the General Assembly honored him with the title of "Senior Bishop". This Board was the governing arm of the Church from 1961 until 1968. The Executive Board and the Office of Senior Bishop were abolished in 1968.

Bishop A.B. McEwen — Chairman
Bishop J.S. Bailey — Vice Chairman
Bishop J.O. Patterson, Sr. — Exe. Sect. Board & Church
Bishop O.T. Jones, Sr. — Member

Bishop S.M. Crouch — Member
Bishop O.M. Kelly — Member
Bishop Wyoming Wells — Member
Bishop L.H. Ford — Member

Bishop J.W. White — Member
Bishop C.E. Bennett — Member
Bishop E.U. Miller — Member
Bishop W.G. Shipman — Member

Mother Coffey congratulates 10 Members of the newly elected Executive Board

(2 bishops in the picture were not a part of the Executive Board.)

This board would be empowered from 1961 to 1964. *(In the 1964 Holy Convocation, a dispute would arise concerning the authority and power of the office of Senior Bishop and the Executive Board.*

THE TEXAS CONNECTION — The General Board *(Administrative Board)*

The Executive Board was replaced by the General Board. This 12 member board was to serve a four year term with a Presiding Bishop and a 1st and 2nd assistant Presiding Bishop. The Office of Presiding Bishop was empowered to conduct the executive affairs of the Church. This was accomplished by a vote of the general assembly, but a General Board would not be chosen until the election held at the 62nd National Holy Convocation held in November of 1968.

The Interim Administrative board was empowered to negotiate the administrative function of the Church until the November Holy Convocation. The following are members of that board:

The 1968 Administrative Board

This board was empowered to serve to negotiate the administrative affairs of the church. The board was appointed by the board of Bishops with a resolution of the General Assembly at the First Constitutional Convention of the Church Of God In Christ which was held from January 30 thru Feb 2, 1968.

Their service as the Administrative Board would only last from their appointment after the Constitutional Convention from Feb 2, 1968 to the 62nd National Holy Convocation which was held November 5-15, 1968. The following were the appointments to this board:

Bishop J.S. Bailey *Chairman*

Bishop A.B. McEwen Member

Bishop J.O. Patterson, Sr. Member

Bishop S.M. Crouch Member

Bishop O.M. Kelly Member

Bishop W.W. Wells, Sr. Member

Bishop L.H. Ford Member

After the General Assembly voted during the general elections of the Church Of God In Christ in November of 1968 the first General Board of the Church Of God In Christ was elected.

General Board of the Church Of God In Christ, Inc.
The Year Book 1968 to 2017

The international leadership of the church was changed by a directive to the general assembly that at the adoption of the constitutional amendments of 1922. Which stated, at the failing health and transition of Bishop C.H. Mason the leadership would transfer to the board of bishops. The founder and first Senior Bishop of the Church Of God In Christ, Inc, would transition on September 17, 1961 and entered the church triumphantly. His transition would bring to an end, fifty four (54) years of faithful, foundational and formative leadership from 1907 until 1961.

- Upon Bishop Mason's transition at the God blessed age of 95 years old, a new Senior Bishop would be selected from the church's senior leadership in the person of Bishop O.T. Jones, Sr. Bishop Jones would serve as the second Senior Bishop and second international leader of the church in succession for seven (7) years from 1961 until 1968. Due to a question of his authority as Senior Bishop.

The first Elected General Board of the Church Of God In Christ, Inc., would be elected at the 62nd Holy Convocation in November of 1968. As of the printing of this volume (the *quadrennial term of 2016 to 2020*), there has been a total of Eighteen (18) General Boards of the Church Of God In Christ, Inc.

Of the eighteen boards, thirteen (13) were elected, three (3) were interim, one (1) was a replacement board and one (1) was a vacancy board. The table below lists the Board's Number, the Election Year, and the Convocation's Number. The Board's Term and any notable changes to the board or changes during its board term are listed in the notes. The term of each elected board starts at the time of election. The term starts November of that same year and is for a period of four years (*quadrennial term*). (*) by bd# indicates an elected board.

Board #	Election Yr.	Convocation	Board Term	Notes
1st*	1968	62nd	1968 to 1972	This is the first elected quadrennial 12 member General Board of the Church Of God In Christ, Inc. Bishop J.O. Patterson, Sr., was elected as the First Presiding Bishop, Chief Apostle and the third international leader of the church in succession. Bishop J.S. Bailey would be elevated as the First Assistant Presiding Bishop and Bishop S.M. Crouch, Sr., would be elevated as the Second Assistant Presiding Bishop. The other nine Bishops to make up the first twelve member General Board were Bishops O.M. Kelly, L.H. Ford, Wyoming Wells, C.E. Bennett,

Board#	Election Yr.	Convocation	Board Term	Notes
2nd*	1972	66th	1972 to 1976	J.A. Blake, Sr., J.W. White, F.D. Washington, D.L. Williams and J.D. Husband. This Board served out its full quadrennial term. (*See Yearbook*) This is the second elected quadrennial 12 member General Board of the Church Of God In Christ, Inc. Bishop J.O. Patterson, Sr., is re-elected for his second quadrennial term as the Presiding Bishop and the Chief Apostle. Bishop S.M. Crouch, Sr. is elevated to First Assistant Presiding Bishop. Bishop J.A. Blake, Sr., is elevated to Second Assistant Presiding Bishop. Returning members were Bishops J.S. Bailey, O.M. Kelly, Wyoming Wells, L.H. Ford, J.W. White, F.D. Washington, J.D. Husband. New members to this board are Bishops J. Cohen and C.L. Anderson. This board served out its quadrennial term. (*See Yearbook*)
3rd*	1976	70th	1976 to 1980	This is the third elected quadrennial 12 member General Board of the Church Of God In Christ, Inc. Bishop J.O. Patterson, Sr., is re-elected for his third quadrennial term as the Presiding Bishop and the Chief Apostle. Bishop S.M. Crouch, Sr., transitions on August 14, 1976 and enters the church triumphantly. Bishop O.M. Kelly is elevated to First Assistant Presiding Bishop. Bishop L.H. Ford is elevated to the office of second Assistant Presiding Bishop. Returning members were Bishops J.S. Bailey, J.A. Blake, J.W. White, F.D. Washington, Wyoming Wells, J.D. Husband, J. Cohen and C.L. Anderson, C.D. Owens, Sr., is elevated as the youngest member to the General Board. (*See pictorial yearbook*)
4th*	1980	74th	1980 to 1984	This is the fourth elected quadrennial 12 member General Board of the Church Of God In Christ, Inc. Bishop J.O. Patterson, Sr., is re-elected for his fourth quadrennial term as the Presiding Bishop and the Chief Apostle. Bishop L.H. Ford would be elevated as the First Assistant Presiding Bishop and Bishop F.D. Washington would be elevated as the Second Assistant Presiding Bishop. Returning members were Bishops J.A. Blake, Sr., J.W. White, C.L. Anderson, Jr., J. Cohen, J.D. Husband, and C.D. Owens, Sr. New addition to this board was Bishops L. R. Anderson. Bishop J.A. Blake, Sr., transitioned on November 13, 1984 and enters the church triumphantly. Bishops J.N. Haynes was elevated at the transition of Bishop Blake. Bishop J.W. White, transitions and enters the

Board#	Election Yr.	Convocation	Board Term	Notes
				church triumphantly. D.A. Burton is elevated. Bishop Burton also served as the general secretary of the church. (See Yearbook,)
5th*	1984	78th	1984 to 1988	This is the fifth elected quadrennial 12 member General Board of the Church Of God In Christ, Inc. Bishop J.O. Patterson, Sr., is re-elected for his fifth quadrennial term as the Presiding Bishop and the Chief Apostle. Bishop L.H. Ford would remain as the First Assistant Presiding Bishop and Bishop F.D. Washington would remain as the Second Assistant Presiding Bishop. Returning members were Bishops C.L. Anderson, Jr., J. Cohen, C.D Owens, Sr., J.N. Haynes and J.D. Husband. New additions to this board were Bishops L. R. Anderson, P.A. Brooks, II, O.T. Jones, Jr. and S.L. Green, Jr. Bishop F.D. Washington transitioned on January 12, 1988 and enters the church triumphantly. Bishop C.D. Owens, Sr. is elevated as the Second Assistant Presiding Bishop. (See Yearbook
			Bishop J.S. Bailey transitions in 1985	
6th*	1988	82nd	1988 to 1992	This is the sixth elected quadrennial 12 member General Board of the Church Of God In Christ, Inc. Bishop J.O. Patterson, Sr., is re-elected for his sixth quadrennial term as the Presiding Bishop and the Chief Apostle. Bishop L.H. Ford would remain as the First Assistant Presiding Bishop and Bishop C.D. Owens, Sr., would remain as the Second Assistant Presiding Bishop. Returning members were Bishops C.L. Anderson, Jr., L.R. Anderson, P.A. Brooks, II, O.T. Jones, Jr., J.N. Haynes, Sr., R.H.L Winbush, L.E. Willis, Sr. Bishop J.O. Patterson, Sr., transitioned on December 29, 1989 and enters the church triumphantly. (See Yearbook
7th	Until 1992	1st Interim General Board	1989 to 1992	Upon the transition of Bishop J.O. Patterson, Sr., the first Interim General Board is put in place. Bishop L.H. Ford, the first Assistant Bishop would serve as the Interim Presiding Bishop, Chief Apostle and the fourth international leader of the church in succession. Bishop C.D. Owens, Sr., would be elevated as the First Assistant Presiding Bishop and Bishop C.L. Anderson, Jr., would be elevated as

Board#	Election Yr.	Convocation	Board Term	Notes
				the Second Assistant Presiding Bishop. Bishop Ford would be affirmed as the Second Elected Presiding Bishop, Chief Apostle and the fourth international leader of the church in succession, in a special election by the general assembly. This board's members would remain in place from the election of 1988, they were Bishops, J. Cohen, L. R. Anderson, P.A. Brooks, II, O.T. Jones, Jr., J.N. Haynes, C.E. Blake, Sr., R.H.L Winbush, L.E. Willis, Sr. and J.D. Husband. Due to his conduct not becoming, Bishop J.D. Husband is removed in 1991, from the office of bishop and was relegated to an Elder without a charge. Later that same year, Elder Husband would transition. Bishop S.L. Green, Sr., is added to the board. This board would serve until the election of 1992. *(See Yearbook)*
8th*	1992	86th	1992 to 1996	This is the seventh elected quadrennial 12 member General Board of the Church Of God In Christ, Inc. Bishop L.H. Ford is re-elected to a second term as the Second Presiding Bishop and the Chief Apostle. *(This is his first quadrennial term as the elected Presiding Bishop)*. Bishop C.D. Owens, Sr., would remain as the First Assistant Presiding Bishop and Bishop C.L. Anderson, Jr., would remain as the Second Assistant Presiding Bishop. Returning members were L. R. Anderson, P.A. Brooks, II, O.T. Jones, Jr., J.N. Haynes, C.E. Blake, Sr., R.H.L Winbush, L.E. Willis, Sr. New additions to this board were Bishops I. Clemmons and G. E. Patterson. Bishop Ford would only serve four months into his third term as Presiding Bishop. Bishop L. H. Ford Transitions on March 31, 1995 and enters the church triumphantly. *(See Yearbook)*
9th	Until 1996	2nd Interim General Board	1995 to 1996	Upon the transition of Bishop L.H. Ford, the second Interim General Board is put in place. Bishop C.D. Owens, Sr., the first Assistant Bishop would serve as the Interim Presiding Bishop, the fifth international leader of the church in succession. Bishop Owens would be affirmed in a special election by the general assembly as the Third Elected Presiding Bishop, Chief Apostle and the fifth international leader of the church in succession. Bishop C.L. Anderson, Jr., would be elevated as the First Assistant Presiding Bishop and Bishop J.N. Haynes, would be elevated as the Second Assistant Presiding Bishop. Remaining elected members were Bishops L. R. Anderson, P.A. Brooks, II, O.T. Jones, Jr., C.E. Blake, Sr., R.H.L Winbush, L.E. Willis, Sr., I. Clemmons and G. E. Patterson. Bishop S.L. Green, Jr., would again be added to the board. This board would

THE TEXAS CONNECTION — The General Board (Notes)

Board#	Election Yr.	Convocation	Board Term	Notes
10th*	1996	90th	1996 to 2000	serve out the term of the 7th elected board, elected November of 1992. (*See Yearbook*) This is the eighth elected quadrennial 12 member General Board of the Church Of God In Christ, Inc. Bishop C. D. Owens, Sr., is re-elected to a second term as the Presiding Bishop and the Chief Apostle. (*This is his first quadrennial term*). Bishop J.N. Haynes would be elevated as the First Assistant Presiding Bishop and Bishop O.T. Jones, Jr., would be elevated as the Second Assistant Presiding Bishop. Returning members were Bishops L. R. Anderson, P.A. Brooks, II, S.L. Green, Jr., C.E. Blake, Sr., R.H.L Winbush, L.E. Willis, Sr., I. Clemmons, G. E. Patterson. This board would see two of its members enter the church triumphant both in the same year of 1999. Bishop I. Clemmons would transition on January 9, 1999 and enter the church triumphantly. Bishop C. L. Anderson, Jr., would transition on September 15, 1999 and enter the church triumphantly. (*During the election of 1996, for the first time a seated Presiding Bishop is challenged for the office of Presiding Bishop. Bishop G.E. Patterson's bid to become presiding bishop would fall short by only one vote. To continue the unity of the brotherhood, Bishop Patterson would refuse a recount of the votes.*) (*See Yearbook*)
11th	Until 2000	1st Replacement Board	Served Until Election of 2000	Bishops W. J. Porter, H.J. Bell and William Morgan James were elevated to General Board members to fill vacancies at the change from active to emeritus member and the transitions of General members. (*See Yearbook*)
12th*	2000	94th	2000 to 2004	This is the ninth elected quadrennial 12 member General Board of the Church Of God In Christ, Inc. During this regular quadrennial election of 2000, for the first time a seated Presiding Bishop is unseated. Bishop G.E. Patterson was elected for his first term as the fourth Presiding Bishop, Chief Apostle and the sixth international leader of the church in succession. (*This is his first quadrennial term*) Bishop C.E. Blake, Sr., would be elevated as the First Assistant Presiding Bishop and Bishop J.N. Haynes would serve as the Second Assistant Presiding Bishop. Returning members were Former Presiding Bishop C.D. Owens, Sr. and Bishops L. R. Anderson, P.A. Brooks, II, S.L. Green, Jr., R.H.L Winbush, L.E. Willis, Sr., New additions to this board were Bishops W.W.

THE TEXAS CONNECTION — The General Board (Notes)

Board#	Election Yr.	Convocation	Board Term	Notes
				Hamilton, G.D. McKinney, N.W. Wells, Jr. For the first time this board has an Elected Presiding Bishop and a Former Elected Presiding Bishop (*See Yearbook*)
13th*	2004	98th	2004 to 2008	This is the tenth elected quadrennial 12 member General Board of the Church Of God In Christ, Inc. Bishop G.E. Patterson, was re-elected to his second term as the Presiding Bishop and the Chief Apostle. (*This is his second quadrennial term*) Bishop C.E. Blake would remain as the First Assistant Presiding Bishop and Bishop J.N. Haynes would remain as the Second Assistant Presiding Bishop. Returning members are Former Presiding Bishop C.D. Owens, Sr. Bishops W.W. Hamilton, R.H.L Winbush, P.A. Brooks, II, L. R. Anderson, S.L. Green, Jr., G.D. McKinney, N.W. Wells, Jr. L.E. Willis, Sr. A new addition to this board was Bishop J.W. Macklin. Bishop G.E. Patterson, transitions on March 20, 2007 and enters the church triumphantly. (*See Yearbook*)
14th	Until 2008	3rd Interim General Board	2007 to 2008	Upon the transition of Bishop G.E. Patterson. The third Interim General Board is put in place. Bishop C.E. Blake, Sr., the first Assistant Bishop would serve as the Interim Presiding Bishop, Chief Apostle and the seventh international leader of the church in succession. Bishop J.N. Haynes, would be elevated as the First Assistant Presiding Bishop and Bishop P.A. Brooks, II, would be elevated as the Second Assistant Presiding Bishop. Bishop Blake would be affirmed in a special election on November 12, 2007, by the general assembly as the fifth Elected Presiding Bishop, Chief Apostle and the seventh international leader of the church in succession. Elected members remaining are Former Presiding Bishop C.D. Owens, Sr. Bishops W.W. Hamilton, R.H.L Winbush, L. R. Anderson, S.L. Green, Jr., G.D. McKinney, N.W. Wells, Jr. A new addition to this board was Bishop E.J. Wright, Jr. and Bishop L.E. Willis, Sr. is again added to the board. This board would serve during the historic 100th Year celebration of the Church Of God In Christ, Inc. (*See Yearbook*)
15th*	2008	101st	2008 to 2012	This is the eleventh elected quadrennial 12 member General Board of the Church Of God In Christ, Inc. Bishop C.E. Blake, Sr., was re-elected to his second term as the Presiding Bishop and the Chief Apostle. (*This is his first quadrennial term*). Bishop P.A. Brooks, II would remain as the First Assistant Presiding Bishop

THE TEXAS CONNECTION — The General Board (Notes)

Board#	Election Yr.	Convocation	Board Term	Notes
				and Bishop J.W. Macklin would remain as the Second Assistant Presiding Bishop. Members returning are Former Presiding Bishop C.D. Owens, Sr. Bishops W.W. Hamilton, R.H.L Winbush, J.N. Haynes, S.L. Green, Jr., G.D. McKinney, N.W. Wells, Jr. New additions to this board were Bishops F.O. White and S. Daniel. For the first time in its 106th year history the Annual Holy Convocation of the Church Of God In Christ was moved from Memphis, Tennessee to St. Louis, Missouri (*See Yearbook*)
16th	Until 2012	Board Vacancy	2011 to 2012	Former Presiding Bishop and then current board member Bishop C.D. Owens, Sr., transitions on March 6, 2011 and enters the church triumphantly. At his request Bishop Haynes was made members emeritus (*See Yearbook*)
17th*	2012	105th	2012 to 2016	This is the twelfth elected quadrennial 12 member General Board of the Church Of God In Christ, Inc. Bishop C.E. Blake, Sr., was re-elected to his third term as the Presiding Bishop and the Chief Apostle. (*This is his second quadrennial term*). Bishop P.A. Brooks, II would remain as the First Assistant Presiding Bishop and Bishop J.W. Macklin would remain as the Second Assistant Presiding Bishop. Members returning are R.H.L Winbush, G.D. McKinney, N.W. Wells, Jr., S. Daniels, F.O. White. New additions were Bishops J.D. Sheard, B.B. Porter, T.G. Thomas, Sr., and L.M. Wooten, Sr. At his request Bishop J.N Haynes was made a board member emeritus. Former Board member emeritus Bishop J.N Haynes, transitions on March 9, 2015 and enters the church triumphantly. At their request Bishops R.L.H. Winbush and F.O. White were made members emeritus during end of 2016. (*See Yearbook*)
18th*	2016	109th	2016 to 2020	This is the thirteenth elected quadrennial 12 member General Board of the Church Of God In Christ, Inc. Bishop C.E. Blake, Sr., was re-elected to his fourth term as the Presiding Bishop and the Chief Apostle. (*This is his third quadrennial term*). Bishop P.A. Brooks, II would remain as the First Assistant Presiding Bishop and Bishop J.W. Macklin would remain as the Second Assistant Presiding Bishop. Members returning are G.D. McKinney, N.W. Wells, Jr., S. Daniels, J.D. Sheard, B.B. Porter, T.G. Thomas, Sr., and L.M. Wooten, Sr. New additions were Bishops D. Hines and M. Williams. Former Board member emeritus Bishop F.O. White, transitions on January 20, 2017 and enters the church triumphantly. In a letter

THE TEXAS CONNECTION — The General Board (Notes)

Board#	Election Yr.	Convocation	Board Term	Notes
				dated February 8, 2017, the Presiding Bishop and the Chief Apostle would make known his new appointments for his third quadrennial term. In one of his most notable appointments, Bishop Blake would appoint Mother Barbara McCoo Lewis the Eighth General Supervisor and seventh President of the International Women's Convention. Mother Lewis served as the first assistant supervisor to Mother Rivers. Mother Rivers would be the first General Supervisor to not be reappointed as the seated general supervisor. Mother Rivers is the first General Supervisor Emeritus. (See Yearbook)

First Elected Quadrennial Term General Board
Church Of God In Christ, Inc.
1968 - 1972

The Year Book

The General Board
Church of God in Christ, Inc.

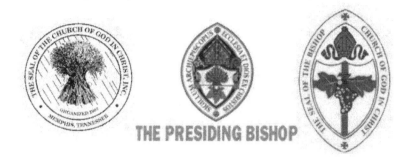

The Presidium of the
Church of God in Christ, Inc.

Following this cover page you will find the Year Book pages of each General Board. The year book pages gives the reader: The election year, the convocation election number, term of service, the Presiding Prelate, the First and Second Assistant Presiding Prelate and each members of that General Board of the Church Of God In Christ, which covers from 1968 to Present.

The General Board
Church of God in Christ, Inc.

The Presidium of the
Church of God in Christ, Inc.

THE TEXAS CONNECTION					The General Board *(The Year Book)*

The Presidium of the Church of God in Christ, Inc.

The 1st General Board
(Elected at 62nd Convocation 1968)

Term of Service
1968 thru 1972

Bishop J.O. Patterson, Sr.

Presiding Prelate
Chief Apostle

Bishop J.S. Bailey

1st Assistant Presiding Prelate

Bishop S.M. Crouch, Sr.

2nd Assistant Presiding Prelate

Bishop O.M. Kelly

Member

Bishop L.H. Ford

Member

Bishop W.W. Wells

Member

Bishop J.A. Blake, Sr.

Member

Bishop J.W. White

Member

Bishop C.E. Bennett

Member

Bishop F.D. Washington

Member

Bishop D.L. Williams

Member

Bishop J.D. Husband

Member

The General Board
Church of God in Christ, Inc.

The Presidium of the
Church of God in Christ, Inc.

THE TEXAS CONNECTION   The General Board *(The Year Book)*

The Presidium of the Church of God in Christ, Inc.

The 2nd General Board
(Elected at 66th Convocation 1972)

Term of Service
1972 thru 1976

Bishop J.O. Patterson, Sr.

Presiding Prelate
Chief Apostle

Bishop S.M. Crouch, Sr.

1st Assistant Presiding Prelate

Bishop J.A. Blake, Sr.

2nd Assistant Presiding Prelate

Bishop O.M. Kelly

Member

Bishop J.S. Bailey

Member

Bishop W.W. Wells

Member

Bishop J.A. Blake, Sr.

Member

Bishop J.W. White

Member

Bishop F.D. Washington

Member

Bishop J.D. Husband

Member

Bishop C.L. Anderson, Jr.

Member

Bishop J. Cohen

Member

The General Board
Church of God in Christ, Inc.

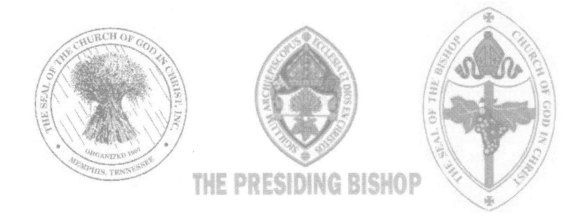

The Presidium of the
Church of God in Christ, Inc.

THE TEXAS CONNECTION	The General Board *(The Year Book)*

The Presidium of the Church of God in Christ, Inc.

The 3rd General Board
(Elected at 70th Convocation 1976)

Term of Service
1976 thru 1980

Bishop J.O. Patterson, Sr.

Presiding Prelate
Chief Apostle

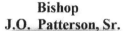

Bishop O.M. Kelly

1st Assistant Presiding Prelate

Bishop L.H. Ford

2nd Assistant Presiding Prelate

Bishop J.S. Bailey

Member

Bishop W.W. Wells

Member

Bishop J.A. Blake, Sr.

Member

Bishop J.W. White

Member

Bishop F.D. Washington

Member

Bishop J.D. Husband

Member

Bishop C.L. Anderson, Jr.

Member

Bishop J. Cohen

Member

Bishop C.D. Owens

Member

The General Board
Church of God in Christ, Inc.

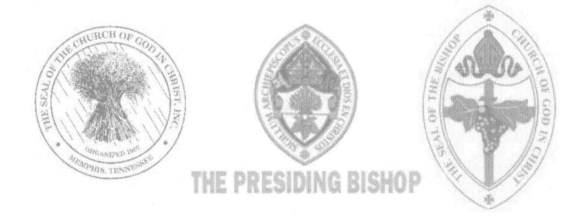

The Presidium of the
Church of God in Christ, Inc.

THE TEXAS CONNECTION   The General Board *(The Year Book)*

The Presidium of the Church of God in Christ, Inc.

The 4th General Board
(Elected at 74th Convocation 1980)

Term of Service
1980 thru 1984

Bishop
J.O. Patterson, Sr.

Presiding Prelate
Chief Apostle

Bishop
L.H. Ford

1st Assistant Presiding Prelate

Bishop
F.D. Washington

2nd Assistant Presiding Prelate

Bishop
J.A. Blake, Sr.

Member

Bishop
J.W. White

Member

Bishop
C.L. Anderson, Jr.

Member

Bishop
J. Cohen

Member

Bishop
J.D. Husband

Member

Bishop
C.D. Owens, Sr.

Member

Bishop
L.R. Anderson

Member

Bishop
J.N. Haynes

Member

Bishop
D.A. Burton

General Secretary

The General Board
Church of God in Christ, Inc.

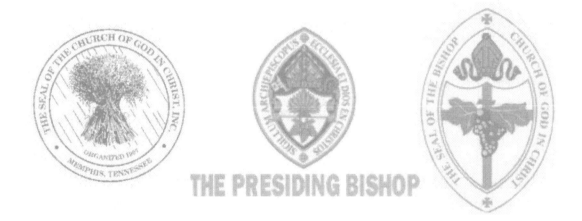

The Presidium of the
Church of God in Christ, Inc.

The Presidium of the Church of God in Christ, Inc.

The 5th General Board
(Elected at 78th Convocation 1984)

Term of Service
1984 thru 1988

Bishop J.O. Patterson, Sr.

Presiding Prelate Chief Apostle

Bishop L.H. Ford

1st Assistant Presiding Prelate

Bishop F.D. Washington

2nd Assistant Presiding Prelate

Bishop C.L. Anderson, Jr.

Member

Bishop J. Cohen

Member

Bishop J.D. Husband

Member

Bishop L.R. Anderson,

Member

Bishop C.D. Owens, Sr.

Member

Bishop J.N. Haynes

Member

Bishop S.L. Green, Jr.

Member

Bishop O.T. Jones, Jr.

Member

Bishop P.A. Brooks, II

Member

The General Board
Church of God in Christ, Inc.

The Presidium of the
Church of God in Christ, Inc.

THE TEXAS CONNECTION — The General Board *(The Year Book)*

The Presidium of the Church of God in Christ, Inc.

The 6th General Board
(Elected at 82nd Convocation 1988)

Term of Service
1988 thru 1992

Bishop J.O. Patterson, Sr.

Presiding Prelate
Chief Apostle

Bishop L.H. Ford

1st Assistant Presiding Prelate

Bishop C.D. Owens, Sr.

2nd Assistant Presiding Prelate

Bishop C.L. Anderson, Jr.

Member

Bishop J.D. Husband

Member

Bishop L.R. Anderson

Member

Bishop P.A. Brooks, II

Member

Bishop O.T. Jones, II

Member

Bishop J.N. Haynes

Member

Bishop R.H.L. Winbush

Member

Bishop I.E. Willis, Sr.

Member

Bishop C.E. Blake, Sr.

Member

The General Board
Church of God in Christ, Inc.

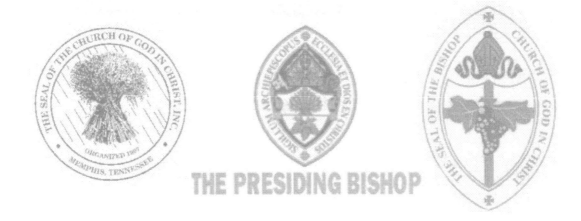

The Presidium of the
Church of God in Christ, Inc.

THE TEXAS CONNECTION | The General Board *(The Year Book)*

The Presidium of the Church of God in Christ, Inc.

First Interim (7th) General Board
(Elected at 82nd Convocation 1988)

Term of Service
1989 thru 1992

Bishop
L.H. Ford

Presiding Prelate
Chief Apostle

Bishop
C.D. Owens, Sr.

1st Assistant Presiding Prelate

Bishop
C.L. Anderson, Jr.

2nd Assistant Presiding Prelate

Bishop
J.D. Husband

Member

Bishop
L.R. Anderson

Member

Bishop
P.A. Brooks, II

Member

Bishop
O.T. Jones, Jr.

Member

Bishop
J.N. Haynes

Member

Bishop
R.H.L. Winbush

Member

Bishop
L.E. Willis, Sr.

Member

Bishop
C.E. Blake, Sr.

Member

Bishop
S.L. Green, Sr.

Member

The General Board
Church of God in Christ, Inc.

The Presidium of the
Church of God in Christ, Inc.

THE TEXAS CONNECTION   The General Board *(The Year Book)*

The Presidium of the Church of God in Christ, Inc.

The 8th General Board
(Elected at 86th Convocation 1992)

Term of Service
1992 thru 1996

Bishop L.H. Ford

*Presiding Prelate
Chief Apostle*

Bishop C.D. Owens, Sr.

1st Assistant Presiding Prelate

Bishop C.L. Anderson, Jr.

2nd Assistant Presiding Prelate

Bishop L.R. Anderson

Member

Bishop P.A. Brooks, II

Member

Bishop O.T. Jones, Jr.

Member

Bishop J.N. Haynes

Member

Bishop R.H.I. Winbush

Member

Bishop L.E. Willis, Sr.

Member

Bishop C.E. Blake, Sr.

Member

Bishop I. Clemmons

Member

Bishop G.E. Patterson

Member

The General Board
Church of God in Christ, Inc.

The Presidium of the
Church of God in Christ, Inc.

THE TEXAS CONNECTION   The General Board *(The Year Book)*

The Presidium of the Church of God in Christ, Inc.

Second Interim (9th) General Board   **Term of Service**
(served until the 1996 elections)   1995 thru 1996

Bishop C.D. Owens, Sr.

Presiding Prelate Chief Apostle

Bishop C.L. Anderson, Jr.

1st Assistant Presiding Prelate

Bishop J.N. Haynes

2nd Assistant Presiding Prelate

Bishop L.R. Anderson

Member

Bishop P.A. Brooks, II

Member

Bishop O.T. Jones, Jr.

Member

Bishop R.H.I. Winbush

Member

Bishop L.E. Willis, Sr.

Member

Bishop C.E. Blake, Sr.

Member

Bishop I. Clemmons

Member

Bishop G.E. Patterson

Member

Bishop S.L. Green, Jr.

Member

The General Board
Church of God in Christ, Inc.

The Presidium of the
Church of God in Christ, Inc.

The Presidium of the Church of God in Christ, Inc.

10th General Board
(Elected at the 90th Convocation 1996)

Term of Service
1996 thru 2000

Bishop C.D. Owens, Sr.

Presiding Prelate
Chief Apostle

Bishop J.N. Haynes

1st Assistant Presiding Prelate

Bishop O.T. Jones, Jr.

2nd Assistant Presiding Prelate

Bishop P.A. Brooks, II

Member Sect

Bishop S.L. Green, Jr.

Member Asst. Sect

Bishop C.L. Anderson, Jr.

Member/Emeritus Former Assist Presiding Prelate

Bishop C.E. Black, Sr.

Member

Bishop G.E. Patterson

Member

Bishop R.H.I. Winbush

Member

Bishop I. Clemmons

Member

Bishop L.E. Willis, Sr.

Member

Bishop L.R. Anderson

Member

The General Board
Church of God in Christ, Inc.

The Presidium of the
Church of God in Christ, Inc.

THE TEXAS CONNECTION   The General Board *(The Year Book)*

The Presidium of the Church of God in Christ, Inc.

11th General Board
(replacements at episcopal transitions and emeritus)

Term of Service
(until the 2000 elections)

Bishop
C.D. Owens, Sr.

Presiding Prelate
Chief Apostle

Bishop
J.N. Haynes

1st Assistant Presiding Prelate

Bishop
O.T. Jones, Jr.

2nd Assistant Presiding Prelate Emeritus

Bishop
P.A. Brooks, II

Member
Secretary to the Board

Bishop
S.L. Green, Jr.

Member
Asst. Secretary to the Board

Bishop
C.E. Blake, Sr.

Member

Bishop
G.E. Patterson

Member

Bishop
L.R. Anderson

Member

Bishop
R.H.L. Winbush

Member

Bishop
L.E. Willis, Sr.

Member

Bishop
W.J. Porter

Member

Bishop
H.J. Bell

Member

Bishop
W.M. James

Member

The General Board
Church of God in Christ, Inc.

The Presidium of the
Church of God in Christ, Inc.

THE TEXAS CONNECTION   The General Board *(The Year Book)*

The Presidium of the Church of God in Christ, Inc.

12th General Board
(Elected at the 94th Convocation 2000)

Term of Service
(2000 thru 2004)

Bishop G.E. Patterson

Presiding Prelate
Chief Apostle

Bishop C.E. Blake, Sr.

1st Assistant Presiding Prelate

Bishop J.N. Haynes

2nd Assistant Presiding Prelate

Bishop C.D. Owens, Sr.

Member
Former Presiding Prelate

Bishop W.W. Hamilton

Member
Secretary to the Board

Bishop R.H.L. Winbush

Member
Asst. Secretary to the Board

Bishop P.A. Brooks, II

Member
Former Secretary

Bishop L.R. Anderson

Member

Bishop L.E. Willis, Sr.

Member
Member

Bishop S.L. Green, Jr.

Member

Bishop G.D. McKinney

Member

Bishop N.W. Wells, Jr.

Member

Bishop O.T. Jones, Jr.

Member
(Emeritus)

The General Board
Church of God in Christ, Inc.

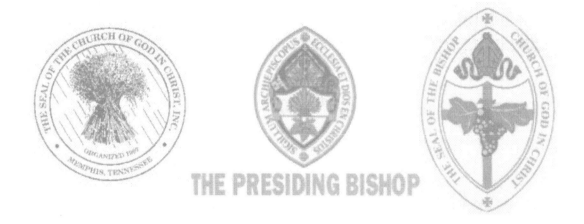

The Presidium of the
Church of God in Christ, Inc.

THE TEXAS CONNECTION   The General Board *(The Year Book)*

The Presidium of the Church of God in Christ, Inc.

13th General Board
(Elected at the 98th Convocation 2004)

Term of Service
(2004 thru 2008)

Bishop G.E. Patterson

Presiding Prelate
Chief Apostle

Bishop C.E. Blake, Sr.

1st Assistant Presiding Prelate

Bishop J.N. Haynes

2nd Assistant Presiding Prelate

Bishop C.D. Owens, Sr.

Member
Former Presiding Prelate

Bishop W.W. Hamilton

Member
Secretary to the Board

Bishop R.H.L. Winbush

Member
Asst. Secretary to the Board

Bishop P.A. Brooks, II

Member
Former Secretary

Bishop L.R. Anderson

Member

Bishop S.L. Green, Jr.

Member

Bishop G.D. McKinney

Member

Bishop N.W. Wells, Jr.

Member

Bishop J.W. Macklin

Member

The General Board
Church of God in Christ, Inc.

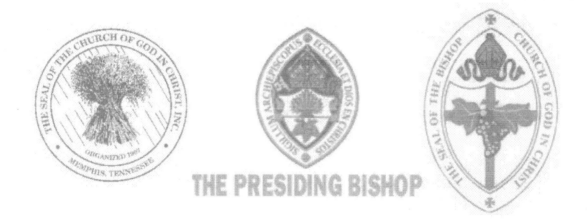

The Presidium of the
Church of God in Christ, Inc.

THE TEXAS CONNECTION	The General Board *(The Year Book)*

The Presidium of the Church of God in Christ, Inc.

The Third Interim (14th) General Board
(served until the 2008 elections)

Term of Service
(2007 thru 2008)

Bishop C.E. Blake, Sr.

Presiding Prelate
Chief Apostle

Bishop J.N. Haynes

1st Assistant Presiding Prelate

Bishop P.A. Brooks, II

2nd Assistant Presiding Prelate

Bishop C.D. Owens, Sr.

Member
Former Presiding Prelate

Bishop W.W. Hamilton

Member
Secretary to the Board

Bishop R.H.L. Winbush

Member
Asst. Secretary to the Board

Bishop S.L. Green, Jr.

Member

Bishop G.D. McKinney

Member

Bishop N.W. Wells, Jr.

Member

Bishop J.W. Macklin

Member

Bishop L.E. Willis, Sr.

Member

Bishop E.J. Wright, Jr.

Member

The General Board
Church of God in Christ, Inc.

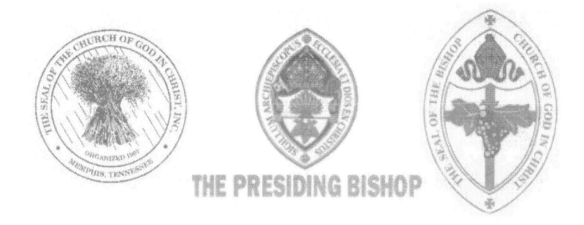

The Presidium of the
Church of God in Christ, Inc.

THE TEXAS CONNECTION The General Board *(The Year Book)*

The Presidium of the Church of God in Christ, Inc.

15th General Board
(Elected at the 101st Convocation 2008)

Term of Service
(2008 thru 2012)

Bishop C.E. Blake, Sr.

Presiding Prelate
Chief Apostle

Bishop P.A. Brooks, II

1st Assistant Presiding Prelate

Bishop J.W. Macklin

2nd Assistant Presiding Prelate

Bishop C.D. Owens, Sr.

Member
Former Presiding Prelate

Bishop J.N. Haynes

Member
Past Asst. Presiding Prelate

Bishop W.W. Hamilton

Member
Secretary to the Board

Bishop R.H.I. Winbush

Member
Asst. Secretary to the Board

Bishop S.L. Green, Jr.

Member

Bishop G.D. McKinney

Member

Bishop N.W. Wells, Jr.

Member

Bishop S. Daniels

Member

Bishop F.O. White

Member

The General Board
Church of God in Christ, Inc.

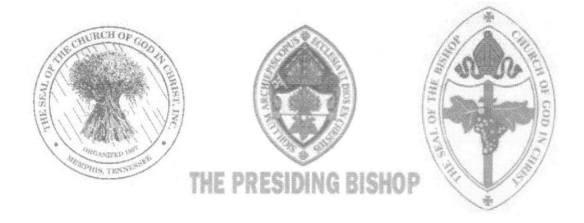

The Presidium of the
Church of God in Christ, Inc.

THE TEXAS CONNECTION   The General Board *(The Year Book)*

The Presidium of the Church of God in Christ, Inc.

16th General Board vacancy
Transition/Emeritus of Bishops Owens/Haynes)

Term of Service
(2011 thru 2012)

Bishop C.E. Blake, Sr.

Presiding Prelate
Chief Apostle

Bishop P.A. Brooks, II

1st Assistant Presiding Prelate

Bishop J.W. Macklin

2nd Assistant Presiding Prelate

Bishop C.D. Owens, Sr.

Member
Former Presiding Prelate

Bishop J.N. Haynes

Member
Past Asst. Presiding Prelate

Bishop W.W. Hamilton

Member
Secretary to the Board

Bishop R.H.I. Winbush

Member
Asst. Secretary to the Board

Bishop S.L. Green, Jr.

Member

Bishop G.D. McKinney

Member

Bishop N.W. Wells, Jr.

Member

Bishop S. Daniels

Member

Bishop F.O. White

Member

The General Board
Church of God in Christ, Inc.

The Presidium of the
Church of God in Christ, Inc.

THE TEXAS CONNECTION | The General Board *(The Year Book)*

The Presidium of the Church of God in Christ, Inc.

17th General Board
Elected at the 105th Convocation 2012)

Term of Service
(2012 thru 2016)

Bishop C.E. Blake, Sr.

Presiding Prelate
Chief Apostle

Bishop P.A. Brooks, II

1st Assistant Presiding Prelate

Bishop J.W. Macklin

2nd Assistant Presiding Prelate

Bishop R.H.I, Winbush

Member
Asst. Secretary to the Board

Bishop G.D. McKinney

Member

Bishop N.W. Wells

Member

Bishop S. Daniels

Member

Bishop F.O. White

Member

Bishop J.D. Sheard

Member

Bishop B.B. Porter

Member

Bishop T.G. Thomas, Sr.

Member

Bishop L.M. Wooten, Sr.

Member

The General Board
Church of God in Christ, Inc.

The Presidium of the
Church of God in Christ, Inc.

THE TEXAS CONNECTION   The General Board *(The Year Book)*

The Presidium of the Church of God in Christ, Inc.

18th General Board
Elected at the 109th Convocation 2016

Term of Service
(2016 thru 2020)

Bishop C.E. Blake, Sr.

Presiding Prelate
Chief Apostle

Bishop P.A. Brooks, II

1st Assistant Presiding Prelate

Bishop J.W. Macklin

2nd Assistant Presiding Prelate

Bishop G.D. McKinney

Member

Bishop N.W. Wells, Jr.

Member

Bishop S. Daniels

Member

Bishop J.D. Sheard

Member

Bishop B.B. Porter

Member

Bishop T.G. Thomas, Sr.

Member

Bishop L.M. Wooten, Sr.

Member

Bishop D. Hines

Member

Bishop M. Williams

Member

The Gallery

Early Leaders & The General Board

Early leaders · The First Overseers · State Overseers Meetings · The Two remaining original five Bishops appointed by Bishop Mason· The Executive Board
The Official General Board Photos

(Following this page the reader will find the meaning of the Bishop's Shield. The reader will also find group photos of all the above mentioned leaders and *where available those leaders are listed.)*

The General Board
Church of God in Christ, Inc.

The Presidium of the
Church of God in Christ, Inc.

The Meaning of the Shield of the Bishop

1.) The Mitre
2.) The Tippet
3.) The Cross
4.) The Grapes and
5.) The Shield

1.) The Mitre – The MITRE is a crown which symbolizes authority and glory. It is the connecting of collegiality with the Presiding Bishop of the Church. All bishops are the inheritors of the same authority given to Peter by Christ.

2.) The Tippet – This symbol is that of a slave. It is the yoke that binds the bishop to his church. On that tippet, is the seal of the Church of God in Christ and the seal of the Bishop. It is the symbol of Jurisdiction or Assignment. The tippet says that the bishop is also under authority.

3.) The Cross – This is always our Message. The Cross of Christ is always the message of the bishop and all preaching servants who serve with the bishop in the jurisdiction.

4.) The Grapes and Leaves – The grapes remind the bishop of his own personal inconvenience for service – suffering. The bishop, must as did his savior, treads the winepress of sorrow for the good of the Church. The leaves represent "healing". Therefore, while the bishop makes himself inconvenient for the mission of the Church, his very presence and office should also bring healing for these who are left out or rejected. He is also to be the healer of the breach within the Body of Christ.

5.) The Shield – A symbol of faith. A bishop is more than an administrator; he is a believer on Christ Jesus and of the doctrine and tenets of our Church. He is called upon to be an example of faith to his people.

Thus, the bishop must be a man of faith in Him who died to save us a preacher of the Cross, willing to suffer the indignity of Christ and serving as a healer among all people. He is under the authority of the Church. He is man of authority himself, he remembers that his authority comes from the Chief Apostle who consecrates him to the sacred Office of bishop.

Early Leadership of the Church of God in Christ

Some Early Leaders of the Church of God in Christ
Bishop E.R. Driver, Bishop E.M. Wilson, Bishop S.M. Crouch
Bishop C.H. Mason and others ....Circa 1916

Some of the first Bishops of COGIC with the Mayor of Memphis
Bishop E.M. Page (Dallas, TX) Bishop R.F. Williams (Cleveland, OH)
Senior Bishop C.H. Mason (Memphis, TN) Mayor Walter Chandler
Bishop Wm Roberts (Chicago, IL) Bishop O.T. Jones, Sr., (Phil, PA)
Bishop A.B. McEwen (Memphis, TN) ....Circa 1941

Bishops Roberts and O.T. Jones, Sr., were among the original five (5) State Overseers appointed by Bishop Mason. The other bishops pictured (below) were consecrated in 1951 and 1952

Bishop C.H. Mason with some of the State Overseers. The state bishops were call State Overseers as the work grew their title changed to State Bishops and the Jurisdictional Prelate. Bishop Mason's original title in 1907 was that of General Overseer.

Bishop Mason is seated in the center third from the left.

Two of the original five State Overseers appointed by Bishop Mason are pictured here.

<u>Seated:</u> Bishops O.M. Kelley, O.T. Jones, Sr., C.H. Mason, R.F. Williams, V.M. Barker, J.H. Boone
<u>Standing:</u> Bishops W.M. Roberts, J.S. Bailey, C.E. Bennett, A.B. McEwen, S.M. Crouch C. Pleas, D. Bostic

State Overseers Meeting with Bishop Mason
<u>Seated:</u> Bishops J.H. Boone, Charles Pleas, C.H. Mason, W.M. Roberts, O.T, Jones, Sr., S.M. Crouch
<u>Standing:</u> Bishops Taylor, C.E. Bennett, J.S. Bailey A.B. McEwen, O.M. Kelley, V.M. Barker, D. Bostic

Bishop Mason with the last 2 original 5 Overseers appointed by him
Bishops W.M. Roberts, C.H. Mason, O.T. Jones, Sr.

The General Board
Church of God in Christ, Inc.

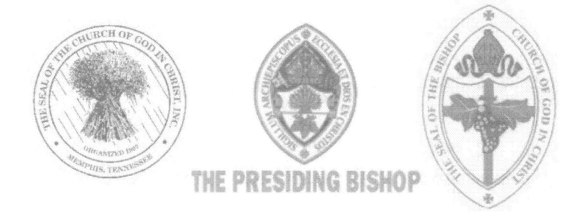

The Presidium of the
Church of God in Christ, Inc.

Early Leadership of the Church of God in Christ

THE EXECUTIVE BOIARD

Mother Lillian Brooks Coffey congratulating 10 of the 12 members of the newly elected Executive Board and others.

This board was put in place at the transition of Bishop Mason.

This board would serve from 1961 to 1968 and was replaced by the Quadrennial elected General Board.

Mother Coffey served as the second General Supervisor of the department of Women.

Circa 1961

Back Row: Bishops (D.L. Lawrence, not a member of this board), J.W. White, L.H. Ford, W.G. Shipman, C.E. Bennett **Standing:** (W.R. Nesbit, not a member of this board), J.S. Bailey, S.M. Crouch, O.T. Jones, Sr., Mother Coffey, Bishops A.B. McEwen, J.O. Patterson, Sr., (seated in the foreground is Bishop J.E. Bryant, not a member of this board)

The Executive Board
A meeting of 7 members of the 12 member board
Circa 1961

(left to Right) Bishops O.T. Jones, Sr., Samuel Crouch, J.O. Patterson, Sr., A.B. McEwen, O.M. Kelly, J.S. Bailey
U.E. Miller

The Executive Board
4 members of the the 12 member Executive Board with two others.
Circa 1961

Seated: (not identified), Bishop O.T. Jones, Sr., A.B. McEwen, C.D. Owens, Sr. (Owens was not a member of this board), J.O. Patterson, Sr. and L.H. Ford

The General Board
Church of God in Christ, Inc.

The Presidium of the
Church of God in Christ, Inc.

THE TEXAS CONNECTION — The General Board *(The Year Book)*

First Elected General Board
of the Church Of God In Christ, Inc. circa 1968

STANDING: Bishop L. H. Ford, Bishop J. A. Blake, Bishop J. D. Husband, Bishop D. L. Williams, Bishop J. W. White, Bishop W. Wells.
SEATED: Bishop O. M. Kelly, Bishop J. S. Bailey, Bishop S. M. Crouch, Bishop J. O. Patterson, Bishop F. D. Washington.

BISHOP C. E. BENNETT
Member of the General Board

The General Board

Church of God in Christ

This board was the first quadrennial elected General Board of the Church Of God In Christ. It was elected in the year 1968, during the 62nd Annual Convocation in Memphis, TN. This board replaces the prior National Ecclesiastical Leadership structure of the church.

This 12 member board would be elected to hold a Quadrennial term of service *(1968 to 1972)*. The board was elected by the general assembly of the church. The Genera Board was authorized to conduct the affairs of the church.

Side Note: *Upon the transition of Bishop C.H. Mason the beloved Founder and Senior Bishop of the Church Of God In Christ, in 1961. The Executive Board was elected as the next leadership structure to head the church. From 1961 to 1968 and Bishop O.T. Jones, Sr., was honored with title of Senior Bishop. Bishop Jones would serve as the second Senior Bishop and second leader of the church in succession. The present leadership structure, the 12 member Quadrennial term elected General Board of the Church Of God In Christ would be put in place in a first of its kind quadrennial election of 1968.*

The General Board
Church of God in Christ, Inc.

The Presidium of the
Church of God in Christ, Inc.

THE TEXAS CONNECTION — The General Board (The Year Book)

Second Elected General Board
of the Church Of God In Christ, Inc. circa 1972

Bishop J.S. Bailey
Member of the General Board

STANDING: Bishops J.A. Blake, Sr., F.D. Washington, J. Cohen, J.W. White, J.D. Husband, C.L. Anderson, Jr.   **SEATED:** Bishops W. Wells, O.M. Kelly, L.H. Ford, J.O. Patterson Sr., S.M. Crouch

The General Board

Church of God in Christ

This board was the second quadrennial elected General Board of the Church Of God In Christ. It was elected in the year 1972, during the 66th Annual Convocation in Memphis, TN.

10 members of the first board would be re-elected along with two new members to a Quadrennial term of service *(1972 to 1976)*.

The Genera Board is authorized to conduct the affairs of the church. This board meets officially three times a year.

Side Note: Bishop J.O. Patterson, Sr. and the General Board would put many things in place that would change the church in both uniform and structure. New attire would be required for the clergy on the local, district, state and national levels. In the area of structure the local church would mimic the district. The district would mimic that state and the state would mimic the national church. These structural level models are not required, but are traditionally the models followed. Each structural level model is left to the discretion of its leader of that level.

The General Board
Church of God in Christ, Inc.

The Presidium of the
Church of God in Christ, Inc.

THE TEXAS CONNECTION — The General Board (The Year Book)

The General Boards of 1985 & 1989
Church Of God In Christ, Inc.

Top Row: Bishops C.L. Anderson, Jr., J. Cohen, L.H. Ford, J.O. Patterson, Sr., F.D. Washington, J.D. Husband, L.R. Anderson **Bottom Row:** Bishops C.D. Owens, J.N. Haynes, P.A. Brooks, II, S.L. Green, Jr., O.T. Jones, Jr.

Top Row: Bishops C.L. Anderson, Jr., J. N. Haynes, , L.H. Ford, J.O. Patterson, Sr., C.D. Owens, J.D. Husband, O.T. Jones, Jr. **Bottom Row:** Bishops P.A. Brooks, II, L.E. Willis, Sr., R.H.I. Winbush, C.E. Blake, Sr., S.L. Green, Jr.

Top Row: Bishops P.A. Brooks, II, J. N. Haynes, C.D. Owens, Sr. , L.H. Ford, C.L. Anderson, Jr. , J.D. Husband, O.T. Jones, Jr. **Bottom Row:** Bishops P.A. Brooks, II, L.E. Willis, Sr., R.H.I. Winbush, L.R. Anderson, C.E. Blake, Sr., S. L. Green, Jr.

The 1985 & 1989 elected quadrennial General Board would be the last 2 boards that Bishop J.O. Patterson, Sr., the first elected Presiding Prelate would serve on before his transition.

The 1990 board would be the first interim General Board, after the transition of Bishop J.O. Patterson, Sr., December 29, 1989.

This first interim board was headed by Bishop L.H. Ford the Second Presiding Prelate and fourth leader in succession.

The General Board
Church of God in Christ, Inc.

The Presidium of the
Church of God in Christ, Inc.

The General Boards of 1996 & 2000
Church Of God In Christ, Inc.

Top & Left: Bishops C.D. Owens, J. N. Haynes, W.M. James, L.R. Anderson, C.E. Blake, Sr., G.E. Patterson **Right:** O.T. Jones, Jr., P.A. Brooks, II, S. L. Green, Jr., R.H.I. Winbush, L.E. Willis,,Sr. H.J. Bell(not pictured) **Bottom (L t R):** Bishops W.W. Hamilton(Sect), C.L. Anderson, Jr. (*Deceased*)

Top & Left: Bishops G.E. Patterson, C.E. Blake, Sr., C.D. Owens, Sr., S.L. Green, Jr., L.R. Anderson, N.W. Wells, Jr. **Right:** J. N. Haynes, W.W. Hamilton, R.H.I. Winbush, P.A. Brooks, II, G.D. McKinney, L.E. Willis, Sr. **Bottom (L t R):** Elder A.Z. Hall (Gen. Sect), Bishop O.T. Jones, Jr. (*2nd Asst. Presiding Bishop Emeritus*)

The General Board

Church of God in Christ

The 1995 General Board would be the first replacement board. This board was headed by Bishop Owens, the Third Presiding Prelate and fifth leader in succession.

The 2000 elected quadrennial General board headed by Bishop G.E. Patterson the Fourth Presiding Prelate and sixth leader in succession. This board is the first time a Presiding Prelate is unseated in a election.

The General Board
Church of God in Christ, Inc.

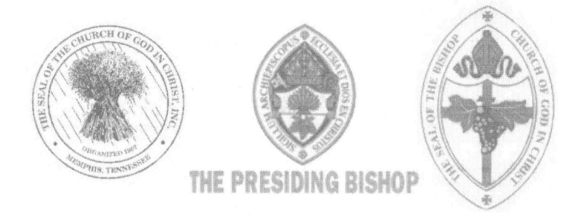

The Presidium of the
Church of God in Christ, Inc.

The General Board 2008, 2012 & 2016
Church Of God In Christ, Inc.

The General Board Members of the Church of God In Christ, Inc.
2008 to 2011

Standing: Bishops F.O. White, S. Daniels, R.H.I. Winbush, N.W. Wells, Jr., J. N. Haynes, G.D. McKinney, S.L. Green, Jr. **Seated:** W.W. Hamilton, P.A. Brooks, II, C.E. Blake, Sr., J.W. Macklin, C.D. Owens, Sr. *(transited March 6, 2011)*

The General Board Members of the Church of God In Christ, Inc.
2012 to 2016

Back Row: Bishops B.B. Porter, J.D. Sheared, L. Wooten **Middle Row:** Bishops F.O. White, G.D. McKinney, S. Daniels, N.W. Wells, Jr., T.G. Thomas R.H.I. Winbush, **Front Row:** Bishops P.A. Brooks, II, C.E. Blake, Sr., J.W. Macklin

The General Board Members of the Church of God In Christ, Inc.
2016 to 2020

Back Row: Bishops, T.G. Thomas, D. Hines, M. Williams **Middle Row:** Bishops B.B. Porter, L. Wooten, J.D. Sheared, S. Daniels, G.D. McKinney, N.W. Wells, Jr. **Front Row:** Bishops P.A. Brooks, II, C.E. Blake, Sr., J.W. Macklin

The General Board
Church of God in Christ, Inc.

THE PRESIDING BISHOP

The Presidium of the Church of God in Christ, Inc.
The Seals

COGIC SEAL: This seal represents the general assembly of the Church Of God In Christ and all its members **PRESIDING BISHOP:** This seal represents the Office of the Presiding Bishop, the Chief Apostle of the Church Of God In Christ. **BISHOP's SEAL:** This seal represents the office of the Bishop.

Side Note: *The General Board would see from its ranks the transition of Former Presiding Prelate member, Bishop Chandler David Owens, Sr., enter the church triumphantly on March 6, 2011. This board would serve from 2008 to March of 2011. The Interim board would serve out its time until the election of 2012.*

Also during this same time at his request Bishop Haynes would be made board member emeritus. In November of 2016 Bishop F.O. White and Bishop R.H.I. Winbush would be made board member emeritus at their request.

The General Board
Church of God in Christ, Inc.

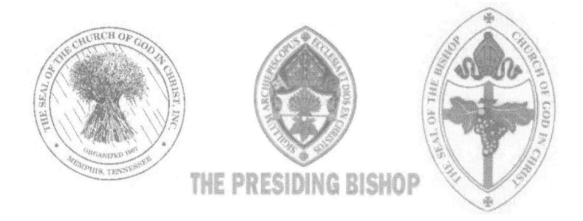

The Presidium of the
Church of God in Christ, Inc.

General Supervisor

established 1911

The Department of Women of the Church Of God In Christ has been a thriving and valuable entity of the Church Of God In Christ since its inception. When the beloved founder of the Church Of God In Christ, Bishop Charles Harrison Mason selected Mother Lizzie Woods Robinson as the General Mother, she immediately began to organize and create a structure that would be beneficial to the development of the church. Every leader of the Department of Women since Mother Robinson has continued to build on the firm foundation which has been established and perpetuated through the process of time. The Department of Women has had to-date a total of seven General Supervisors also called General Mother of the Department of Women. Among these, six have served as President of the Women's International Convention, which was founded in 1951 by the Second Supervisor, Mother Lillian Brooks Coffey.

In this section we will present brief profiles of all seven of the General Supervisors of the Church of God in Christ. Also included in this section are other outstanding/notable personalities of the Department of Women of the Church of God in Christ.

"*Profiles of Pioneering Women*" Church of God in Christ 1897-1997 (100) Centennial Historical Perspective Department of Women Mother Willie Mae Rivers General Supervisor

THE TEXAS CONNECTION *General Supervisors*

Senior Pioneer State Supervisors Honored

Front Row (L to R) Maydie Payton-NY, Anne L. Bailey-NJ, Bertha Polk-TX, Mable Maylor-RI, J.V. Hearne-OK **Second Row (L to R)** D.M. Matthews - CT, Sarah Drake – CO, Liza Hollins– LA, **L.A. Henderson**-AZ, Carrie Buchannan-MS **Third Row (L to R)** Bobbie Buffkins –WN, L.O. Hale –CA, Jessie B. Washington-AR

Steering Committee 1966 Intl Women's Convention

Front Row (L to R) **Mother Cora Berry**-*Asst. State Supervisor*, **Mother L.O. Hale**-*State Supervisor and Hostess*, **Bishop S.M. Crouch**-*Jurisdictional Prelate and Host*, **Mother Luella White**-*Chair of the Intl Hospitality Committee*, **Bishop J.A. Blake, Sr.,** - *Asst. Jurisdictional Prelate*, **Second Row (L to R)** **Mother Hunt Wilson**-*Member*, **Sis. Clemmie Dorsey**-*Member* **Third Row (L to R)** **Mother Freddie Bell**-*State Supervisor, California SW*, **Sister Lillian Morris**-*Member*, **Elder Benjamin Crouch**-*Member*, **Mother Jessie Wilson**-*Former State Mother California SW*, **Sister Price**-*Member* **Fourth Row (L to R)** **Sister Lillie Williams**-*Chair Local housing committee*, **Sister Jamie Dickey**-*Chair California Information Committee*

Profiles of the General Supervisors

Following this page you will find a cover which profiles all of the general supervisors'. The Supervisor's profile gives the reader: The accomplishments of that supervisor, her positions held, her term of service and her service as President of the Annual Women's Convention.

General Supervisors Department of Women of the Church of God in Christ, Inc.

* Tenure as Department Leader

Mother Lizzie Woods Robinson
First General Supervisor
*1911-1945

Dr. Lillian Brooks Coffey
Second General Supervisor
First President Women's Convention
*1945-1964

Dr. Anne L. Bailey
Third General Supervisor
2nd President Women's Convention
*1965-1975

Dr. Mattie McGlothen
Fourth General Supervisor
3rd President Women's Convention
*1976-1994

Mother Emma Frances Crouch
Fifth General Supervisor
4th President Women's Convention
*1995-1996

Dr. Willie Mae Smalls Rivers
Sixth General Supervisor
5th President Women's Convention
*1997-2017

Dr. Barbara McCoo Lewis
Seventh General Supervisor
6th President Women's Convention
*2017-Present

THE TEXAS CONNECTION — General Supervisors

Mother Robinson and Bishop Mason

Mother Robinson and daughter Ida Baker

Dr. Mattie McGlothen escorting Mother Coffey at the 1st Women's Convention

Home of Mother Lizzie Woods Robinson Omaha, Nebraska

Mason Temple Sign purchased by Mother Robinson hours before transition

Letter written by Mother Robinson to Bishop Williams on her personal Letterhead dated November 10, 1945

Mother Lizzie Woods Robinson

Mother Lizzie Woods Robinson
First General Supervisor 1911-1945

On April 5, 1860, a little baby girl was born to Mose Smith and Elizabeth Jackson in Phillips County, Arkansas.

She was named Elizabeth Isabelle who later would became known as *"Lizzie."* We are not given much information about Lizzie's early childhood.

We are informed that her father was a solider during the civil war. During this time when Lizzie was still a baby, he died leaving the young mother with five children.

Her mother supported this young family as a washer woman. She was not able to read and write, but she was determined to make certain that her children could. The only book she had to accomplish this with was the Bible, the very word of God.

Lizzie's history *(HER-story)* picks up with her first marriage which was a short one, to Mr. Henry Holt. They were joined in holy matrimony in 1881, but it was ended at his death. Her second marriage was to William H. Woods and that union produced one child, a daughter, whom she named Ida Florence Woods.

After the birth of her daughter, she experienced the saving grace of God and joined the Baptist Church in Pine Bluff, Arkansas in 1892.

1901, a book had fallen into the hands of Lizzie Woods. This book had a great impact on her life. This book was called *"Hope"* written by Joanna P. Moore, who was a White Baptist missionary.

Hope emphasized the spiritual duties of the women in the church. It also included within its pages, biblical training for such areas as childcare, household duties of the women and it included Sunday school lessons.

It is also noted that Moore was influenced by the holiness movement. This influence caused Moore to enlist her readers to become a part of this movement by being sanctified.

This was a resounding call that resonated with Robinson and her seeing the need for what she would later identify as a *"deeper life"* and so in 1901, she became sanctified.

After this experience Robinson wrote to Sister Moore, about what she was now experiencing as a direct cause of her reading the "Hope" which at this time had become a monthly Bible study guide that was the product of Joanna P. Moore.

Mother Robinson would express in her correspondence that her earnest desire was, that *"The Lord would take my hands out of the wash tubs and fill them with good books and bibles that I might go from house to house and teach God's people that were lost sheep, that didn't know the way"*

This communication touched something in Sis. Moore. This would cause Moore to use her influence with the Missionary Society of the American Baptist to further the spiritual training of Robinson. Robinson was soon able to enroll in the Baptist training academy located in Dermott, Arkansas.

Lizzie attended the School for two years. She completed her studies and evidently becoming the matron of the Academy.

Her duties were to pray and instruct the children from the bible. Her instructions to the children were simple and stated that *"when we read the bible, God is talking to us."*

This wasn't an easy task. She would experience such childhood moods as the children crying and not wanting to eat their breakfast.

While there in Dermott, Arkansas Lizzie Woods would meet a Church Of God In Christ, Elder who was preaching the Holiness Pentecostal message. The elder was Elder O.W. Welk. This was Sister Lizzie Woods' introduction to the Church Of God In Christ.

In the year of 1906, a great revival under the auspices of Elder W. J. Seymour started in Los Angeles, California and swept the western portion of the United States. The news of this revival reached Memphis, Tennessee, Bishop Mason and other ministers of this gospel that led to the baptism of the Holy Ghost.

After receiving this blessing, the Chief Apostle of the COGIC, Bishop Mason traveled sharing the Good News of Holiness and Pentecostalism. One of these missions of goodwill took him to Dermott, Arkansas. A place that was predestined by God, for there he would met Lizzie Woods, matron of the Baptist Academy.

Mrs. Woods a woman of very high standings had made quite an outstanding record in public service as a teacher of the word of God. Bishop Mason would explain to her the reason for their mission trip. She was interested in what he had to say and listened intently. Bishop Mason explained the scriptures so that she stated, *"I believe that Jesus Christ is the Son of God."* Then and there she received the baptism of the Holy Ghost.

This is her account of the meeting: *I was sanctified in the Baptist School but did not have the Baptism of the Holy Ghost. Elder Roach was pastoring the Church of God in Christ at Dermott at that time and Bishop Mason came there to preach and came to the school. There was a teacher in the school who would go where Brother Mason was when he would come. That time he came on a Saturday and it was the day I would always go down to pay my grocery bill, but I saw him coming and I didn't go, I sent an errand boy. When Brother Mason came in he asked me where was the other ladies. They were upstairs. Mrs. Crow, Mrs. Jones, and Mrs. Cora came downstairs and he began to teach us, I told him that I had been living right for six years, but I hadn't been baptized with the Holy Ghost. So, I received the baptism of the Holy Ghost that day, and Mrs. Jones, Mrs. Crow, and Mrs. Stewart looked on and were amazed.*

She visited the Jurisdictional Convocation which was in session in Pine Bluff, Arkansas, where Lillian Brooks, (later Mother Lillian Brooks Coffey), the singing evangelist, gave her the right hand of fellowship and insisted that she should come to the National Holy Convocation in Memphis, Tennessee in the fall.

The work among the women had been started, but lacked organization. God gave the right woman, at the right time. Lizzie Woods, who had accepted the Doctrine of Pentecost, was prepared more than ever to teach the unadulterated Word of God. Bishop Mason with his keen insight, saw that this woman was an organizer, able to inspire, and direct. With this insight and also upon the recommendation of Evangelist Lillian Brooks. Lizzie Woods would be chosen as the first General Mother of Women, to organize and create such work as would be beneficial to the development of the church.

On her first tour she would meet Elder Robinson, whom she later married. During this tour she would find, two groups of women in the church, one group praying, the other group studying and teaching the Word. One was known as the Prayer Band and the other, the Bible Band. She combined the two under the name of the Prayer and Bible Band.

Mother Robinson's consideration began with remembering Jer. 9:17-20. *"Thus said the Lord of Host, consider ye and call for the mourning women, that they may come; and send for the cunning women, that they may come. "And let them make haste and take up a wailing for us, that our eyes may run with tears, and our eyelids gush out with waters. "For a voice of wailing is heard out of Zion, how are we spoiled! We are greatly confounded, because we have forsaken the land, because our dwellings have cast us out. "Yet we heard the Word of the Lord, o ye women and let our ears receive the words of His mouth, and teach your daughters wailing and everyone her neighbor lamentation."*

She strengthened a small group of women, whom she found sewing, called the daughters of Zion, and organized them giving them the name of *"Sewing Circle."* For she remembered the great woman of Acts 9:36-40.

"Now there was in Joppa a certain disciple named Tabitha, which by interpretation is called Dorcas: this woman was full of good work and alms deeds, which she did."

In the year of 1926, during Mother Robinson's tour through the western states, she met Elder Searcy of Portland, Oregon, who was interested in Foreign Missions. She invited him to attend the Memphis meeting and meet the brethren.

This trip resulted in the formation of a Foreign Mission band of which Elder Searcy became Secretary/Treasurer. Mother Robinson went everywhere organizing the women into Home and Foreign Mission bands. Elder Searcy did not remain with the movement very long. Mother Robinson asked Bishop Mason to appoint Elder C.G Brown as Secretary of the Home and Foreign Mission Board.

During those days of travel, she and her husband worked as evangelist digging out and establishing churches underwent great suffering. Finance being most limited with very few doors open to receive them, at most times. They would travel by way of either foot or in wagons, yet they kept moving on.

Her daughter, Ida Baker, moved to Omaha, Nebraska, and later she and Elder Robinson followed, where they established a church and their own home. This took Elder Robinson from her side as a traveling companion.

She would then choose some of her daughters in the work to accompany her and train others; Fannie Jackson, Lucinda Bostick, Jessie Strickland, Nancy Gamble and Eliza Hollins. The work grew so rapidly that she began a state organization and these women where whom she had trained became the church's first state mothers.

Her daughter became her traveling companion. Mother taught the Word of God in power, against Lodges, exposing their rituals. She was imprisoned, rotten-egged and beaten for this. Her daughter Ida was a gifted singer and cheered the hearts of the people. In their hours made weary from hard traveling, Ida would break forth with songs like: *"I'm Climbing the Hills of Light, I'm Singing Along My Way, My Path is as Bright as Day, I'm Seeking a Better Home."*

Her tireless efforts to support the work enabled her to raise $168.50 in which she gave to Bishop Mason to open the first bank account for the Church Of God In Christ.

Elder Robinson's health began to fail and soon he was called from labor to reward. Mother's grief was great but she said, *"I cannot stop; I must work the work for him that sent me while it is day, for the night cometh and no man can work."*

No writer could do justice to the life work of this illustrious woman of God, nor of the numerous deeds of kindness done by her, nor the height of esteem in which she was held in by thousands of followers.

The day came when hard work and continued traveling took its toll and her weak frame gave way under it. And she was only able to attend the National Convocations. For five years she battled to regain her strength but kept her program going through her different State Mothers.

She was greatly interested in the building of the National Headquarters and with her very efficient daughter as her secretary, she kept her National Drives functioning until she knew the building was ready for dedication. She journeyed southward to the 1945, Convocation; she felt that her days were numbered and that she would not return home.

After reaching Memphis, she took new strength, walked through the building, looked at the work of her hands, sat in the assembly hall, which bears her name, held conference with the State Supervisors, revised her constitution, examined every phase of it for soundness, sat by her window and looked at the large electrical sign.

She allocated the balance of the funds needed to make possible its purchase. The sign which reads, *"National Headquarters of the Church Of God In Christ."* Her daughter had solicited funds, but the amount was not sufficient: thus she completed the sum.

Mother Robinson ably admonished her daughters on the Women's day of the Convocation to continue in the Faith. To stay out of lodges and not to engage in politics. She turned to her daughter Lillian Brooks Coffey (*whom she trained and who became her assistant*) to courageously lead the women on in the fear of the Lord. To stick to the bible. To not to depart from the law of the Lord. She went to her room tired and weary and in a few hours she drew the drapery of the couch about her and fell asleep and enters the church triumphantly, in November of 1945.

Headstone of Mother Robinson

Mother Robinson' transition notice

Mother Lillian Brooks Coffey

Dr. Lillian Brooks Coffey
Second General Supervisor 1945-1964
Organizer and First President of
the Women's Convention

Mother Coffey, Little Lillian as she was called, was a *"Dreamer."* She was a woman with a great vision. When she was a small child, Bishop Mason was invited to their home by her grandfather who was a Baptist minister.

When Bishop Mason started his church in Memphis, she and other neighborhood children were carried to Sunday School and services, which were held in a tent across the street from where she lived.

One Sunday morning he came and taught them about Jesus in a childlike manner. The Lord touched and saved little Lillian, beginning her life in the church under the Leadership of Bishop Mason, where she remained until her transition in 1964.

As she grew older, Bishop Mason continued to influence her life. She read the Bible through once every year, a practice she continued even after reading it eleven times.

She traveled with him reading and singing while he preached. When her parents died, he became her father. She worked as secretary in his office for twenty-one years and as assistant financial secretary until her appointment to General Supervisor in 1945.

Mother Coffey was one of the greatest leaders and organizers that ever lived. She continued to build the existing auxiliary programs and began to organize the units and helps for the Department of Women.

Some of the units that were organized during her administration were: **Missionary Circle, Hospitality, Executive Hospitality, Hulda Club, Wide Awake Band, Minister's Wives Circle, Deaconess, Deacon's Wives Circle, Prayer Warriors, Young Women's Christian Council, Usher Board, Educational Committee, Boy's League, Big Brothers, Cradle Roll, Women's Chorus, Board of Examiners, Public Relations, News Reports and the Burners** which was her pet project.

During the Women's Convention banner march, burners marched with lights symbolizing that lights were to lighten the darkened world of Africa.

She was the founder of the Lillian Brooks Coffey Rest Home in Detroit, Michigan. Mother Lillian Brooks Coffey is best remembered for her work in 1951, when she organized the **Women's International Convention** first held in Los Angeles, California hosted by Mother L.O. Hale and Bishop S.M. Crouch.

This convention was born through a dream she had of a better way to support missions. Her heart was burdened over the condition of suffering foreign Missionaries and their various fields. One hundred women who paid $100.00 each, the cost of the Red Card registration, rode the Coffey train to the convention in 1951, carrying their money, $10,000, in a brown paper bag. She presided over 14 conventions 1951-1964.

THE TEXAS CONNECTION
General Supervisors (Coffey)

Mother Coffey's memory still lives with us. **"Methods change, but principles remain the same."** And the table blessing is continually repeated at most meal functions, **"We make no excuse for the things, which we have, for that which we have, the Lord has provided and we are thankful."**

Above: *Mother Coffey being installed as the Second General Supervisor*

Above: *The LB Coffey Rest home for retired foreign Mission workers of the Church Of God In Christ.*

Mother Coffey and others arriving in California for the First Women's International Convention of the Church Of God In Christ.....circa 1951

Mother Coffey's Telegram from President Kennedy

Women's International Conventions presided over by Mother Coffey (14)

No.	Year	Location of Convention	Theme of Convention
1st	1951	Los Angeles, Ca.	Leadership Conference
2nd	1952	New York City, NY	Workers United Purpose
3rd	1953	Miami, Fl	Organization and Function
4th	1954	Chicago, Il	Solving Christian Problems
5th	1955	Boston, Ma	Action Campaign
6th	1956	Los Angeles, Ca	Dedication, Co-operation, Information
7th	1957	Detroit, MI	Understanding, Fellowship, Peace
8th	1958	Seattle, Wa	The Power of Faith in this Satellite Age.
9th	1959	Memphis, TN	Aiming At Excellence
10th	1960	Kansas City, Ka	Power of United Effort
11th	1961	Oakland, Ca	The Building of God
12th	1962	Washington, D.C.	Orbiting with Christ
13th	1963	Chicago, Il	Answering the Clarion Call
14th	1964	Albany, NY	A Christian Perspective of Peace

Mother Anne Bailey

Dr. Anne L. Bailey
Third General Supervisor 1964-1975
Second President of the Women's Convention

Mother Bailey, as she was affectionately called, started out as Anne L. Garrett on September 22, 1894, in Temple, Texas to Rev. and Mrs. Felix Garrett. She was converted at the age of 12 years old and embraced the Baptist faith. As a child she was trained to be faithful to the church.

This training as a child made her ardent and dedicated to Sunday School and a devoted youth worker which prepared her for the future work she would have in the Church Of God In Christ.

The year is now 1915 and Anne is now 21 years old. She heard of the gospel of Sanctification and the Baptism of the Holy Ghost. This she believed with all her heart. God for Christ's, sake forgave her and washed her from sin in his own blood, baptizing her with the Holy Ghost, speaking in tongues as the spirit gave utterance. Elder B.J Mitchell was her pastor.

Sometime in 1916, Elder J.E. Bryant became her pastor and also during this time she served God and her Church well. By 1919, she left the southland in the company of her pastor, Sister Hattie Robinson Fray and Sister M.M. Jackson, coming to Buffalo, New York.

She labored untiringly with a fire that burned in her heart. The fire of evangelism stirred up a pioneering spirit in her that would cause her to dig out churches in New Jersey, Connecticut, New York City, Springfield and Boston.

This street corner ministry of playing the guitar, singing, praying and teaching until souls were saved didn't just stop at those cities, but would later move to Maryland in 1927, to Delaware and Washington in 1927 and 1928, respectively.

She was a good friend to Bishop CH Mason and his family. This work of Mother Bailey was stopped for a short period of time when, at the illness of Bishop Mason, she attended to his needs from 1929 until May of 1930, when she returned to her labor of work.

In February of 1934, she would marry the love of her life, her faithful companion and escort the Elder John Seth Bailey (*later Bishop Bailey, a member of the General Board*). She was the mother of one child a daughter.

She was appointed as the Financial Secretary of the Jurisdiction of New Jersey. She was appointed by Mother Lizzie Woods Robinson as the Financial Secretary of the International Women's Department.

Mother Bailey was also Assistant International Supervisor to the International Supervisor of Women Dr. Lillian Brooks Coffey and as Vice-President of the Women's International Convention.

She served as governess to the Mason children for a number of years. She also traveled as an aid and secretary to Bishop Mason in his declining years. He spent many happy hours in the Bailey home in Detroit, Michigan.

She organized women everywhere, supported pastors and their wives and families and taught other women to do the same. She rightly earned the name she was fondly called by the brethren. *"Darling of the Brotherhood"* *"Sweetheart of the Church"*.

Under the supervision of Dr. Bailey the work that she loved continued to grow and prosper. The units that she added were the: **Business and Professional Women's Rescue Squad, Sunday School Representatives Unit, United Sisters of Charity, National Secretaries Unit, Jr. Missionaries, renewed the women's magazine (The COGIC Woman) and appointed the first National President of the Sewing Circle-Artistic Fingers.**

During her tenure she presided over eleven women's conventions, 1965-1975, several of which her daughter Clara attended with her. Mother Bailey was a woman of wisdom and left a great legacy.

Her words will never be forgotten. They are echoed across the general church: *"When you have done your best, the angels in heaven can't do any better;"*

"When you have done the best you can do, that's all the Lord requires."

Written in 1972, the following are excerpts from a letter that she addressed to the women as "Dearly Beloved" exhorting them to grow in spiritual maturity giving these life changing ideas: *"Broaden your vision: Win,*

don't repel: Communicate, Listen-Understand and Care; Be more ready to hear than to talk; Keep Learning; Be yourself; Give as you would get; Don't jump to conclusions; Take time to think: Pray, until you touch the source; Ponder this — in everything, give thanks; Above all my darlings, "Stand Fast" and hold the traditions we have been taught, so that our own work can praise us in the gates.

Mother Bailey went from Labor to Reward in December of 1975.

Women's International Conventions presided over by Mother Bailey

See Next Page

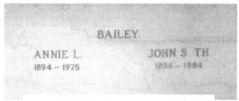

Final resting place of Bishop and Mother Bailey

Mother Anne L. Bailey speaking, Dr. McGlothen Standing in the background

Women's International Conventions presided over by Mother Bailey (10)

No.	Year	Location of Convention	Theme of Convention
15th	1965	Oklahoma City, Ok	Indebted – Involved-Inspired
16th	1966	Los Angeles, Ca	Becoming Acquainted
17th	1967	Denver, Colorado	Effective Leadership Among Women in This CRISIS
18th	1968	Miami, Fl	Take Another Look
19th	1969	Dallas, TX	Dimensions of Christian Activity Today
20th	1970	Oklahoma City, Ok	How shall Christian Women Meet the 1970 Changes
21st	1971	Detroit, Mi	Sound Out the Pentecostal Message
22nd	1972	New Orleans, La	Reality vs. Art
23rd	1973	Cleveland, Ohio	Christ for theCrisis
24th	1974	San Antonio, TX	Living for Others
25th	1975	San Francisco, Ca	From Needle Thin To Anchor Heavy

Mother Anne L. Bailey leading this sainted group of senior Mothers.

Bishop and Mother Bailey

Bishop J.S. Bailey

Mother A.L. Bailey

Mother A.L. Bailey

THE TEXAS CONNECTION *General Supervisors (Bailey)*

Mother Mattie McGlothen

Dr. Mattie McGlothen
Fourth General Supervisor 1976-1994
Third President of the Women's Convention

Mattie Mae Carter was born in Tehuacana, Texas near Mexia (*Me-Hare*). She was the eleventh of fifteen children. She attended public school in Sapulpa, Oklahoma and college at Quindaro College in Kansas City, Kansas.

In July 1921, she was saved, Holy Ghost filled and healed of tuberculosis the same night. She married Charles Wenzell McGlothen (later Bishop C.W. McGlothen) in September 1923. They founded and pastored churches in Hugo, Idabelle, Tulsa, Oklahoma, Des Moines, Iowa, Pittsburgh; Fresno, Los Angeles and Richmond, California.

Dr. Mattie McGlothen served as a Supervisor in California for sixty-one years (1933-1994), and as General Supervisor for the international Women's Department and Third President of the Women's International Women's Convention of the Church Of God In Christ for eighteen years (1976-1994).

At the transition of Mother Anne Bailey, Mother Mattie McGlothen was elevated to the office of General Supervisor by then Bishop J.O. Patterson, Sr.

She had founded, organized or reorganized the **International Hospitality; Education and Scholarship Fund; Bishop's Wives Scholarship Fund; Screening Committee for Jurisdictional Supervisors; McGlothen Foundation; Emergency Relief Fund; WE-12; Lavender Ladies; Leadership Conference for Jurisdictional Leaders and National Workers; and the Business and Professional Women's Federation.**

The Pavilion in Port-au-Prince, Haiti; a home for missionaries in the Bahamas Island, McGlothen House Annex, Women's Department Office and guest house and the Women's Convention Project, "*I Am Concerned,*" were a few of her humanitarian efforts.

Mother McGlothen would introduce to the Women's Department of the Church Of God In Christ, the black habit while ministering or civic service and the white habit as ceremonial attire. This would help to change the visibility of women in ministry.

Mother McGlothen transitioned on May 4, 1994, at her home in Richmond, California.

Women's International Conventions presided over by Mother McGlothen

See Next Page

THE TEXAS CONNECTION *General Supervisors (McGlothen)*

Women's International Conventions presided over by Mother McGlothen (19)

No.	Year	Location of Convention	Theme of Convention
26th	1976	Atlanta, Georgia	
27th	**1977**	**Miami Beach, Florida**	
28th	1978	Houston, Texas	
29th	1979	Chicago, Illinois	
30th	1980	Los Angeles, California	
31st	1981	Forth Worth, Texas	
32nd	1982	Detroit, Michigan	
33rd	1983	New Orleans, Louisiana	
34th	1984	Atlanta, Georgia	
35th	1985	Washington, D.C.	
36th	1986	Long Beach, California	
37th	1987	Kansas City, Missouri	
38th	1988	Miami Beach, Florida	
39th	1989	Portland, Oregon	
40th	1990	Cincinnati, Ohio	
41st	1991	Richmond, California	
42nd	1992	Milwaukee, Wisconsin	
43rd	1993	Nashville, Tennessee	*"Holy Women Upholding the Foundations & Landmarks of Our Faith"* Isaiah 28:16 Proverbs 22:2/8
44th	1994	San Diego, California	

Mother Emma Crouch

Mother Emma Frances Crouch
Fifth General Supervisor 1994-1997
Fourth President of the Women's Convention

Emma Frances Searcy was born on a Texas Homestead in 1911. She was born and shaped in humble beginnings, much like the start of the Church Of God In Christ.

This humble start would typify the challenges confronting her development and encouraged her longevity in Christian service.

The native Texan was saved, sanctified and filled with the Holy Ghost in 1930. She married Elder B.J. Crouch (*later Bishop*) and enjoyed family life in the church.

She proved to be an ardent worker for the Lord and her church. The quiet spirit she was, masked her dynamism in local ministry and helped her life as model for other aspiring missionaries. She started at the local and state level ministries and worked her way through the ranks.

She served as YPWW Chairlady, District Missionary, and became the first Supervisor of Women for the Texas Southwest Jurisdiction and remained until her transition. In 1956, she was appointed to that position by Bishop T.D. Iglehart and she served with honor.

She would serve on the National Board of Trustees. Her tenure as supervisor was accented in 1976 with her appointment as First Assistant General Supervisor.

At the transition of Mother McGlothen in 1994, Mother Crouch was elevated by Presiding Bishop Louis Henry Ford to the rank of General Supervisor of Women. Her time of service was brief as the General Supervisor by the standard of her predecessors, but nonetheless meaningful.

Mother Crouch exemplified holiness through her daily walk in life. By any standard, she proved to be a gifted and dedicated woman of service.

Some people speak about their focus of faith and labor. Mother Emma Crouch lived that focused life with distinction. She organized the **Christian Women's Council**.

Her labor was that of a worthy and prudent woman. She added to the rich heritage and tradition of the Church Of God In Christ, woman everywhere.

This historic observation is appropriate, but the reward that Christ has for her is what she truly deserves. Possibly, the women who remain can recognize through her life that in the Church Of God In Christ, a woman can have it all, family and ministry!

Mother Crouch now rest with those whom she labored so incessantly. She joined them in rank on January 6, 1997, in heavenly reward.

She will be remembered as one of the prominent figures in the Women's work and Church Of God In Christ history.

THE TEXAS CONNECTION
General Supervisors (Crouch)

We honor her memory and celebrate Mother Crouch's life, her work and her legacy.

Women's International Conventions presided over by Mother Crouch

(L to R) Madam Emily Bram Bibby, **Mother Mattie McGlothen** (4th Gen Sup),) **Mother Emma Frances Crouch**(5th Gen Sup) **and Mother Willie Mae Rivers**(6th Gen Sup).

Women's International Conventions presided over by Mother Crouch (2)

No.	Year	Location of Convention	Theme of Convention
45th	1995	Memphis, Tennessee	
46th	1996	New Orleans, Louisiana	*"Church of God In Christ Women Moving Forward together with Christ Into the Year 2000" Philippians 3:12-14*

Mother E.F. Crouch

Mother E.F. Crouch

Mother E.F. Crouch

(L to R) Mother E.F. Crouch, Bishop T.D. Iglehart and Mother D. Iglehart

Mother E.F. Crouch

Mother Willie Mae Rivers

Mother Willie Smalls Rivers
Sixth General Supervisor 1997-2017
Fifth President of the Women's Convention

Willie Mae Smalls Rivers has touched and continues to touch the lives of many people throughout this world. It was stated that she was born *"...to be different..."* on February 20, 1926, to the late Robert and Anna Mitchell Smalls.

As a child, Willie Mae exemplified great promise that she would one day contribute greatly to mankind. *"Willie Ray" (as she was affectionately called by her loving father)* was and still is concerned about the welfare of others.

Mother Rivers received her formal education in Berkeley and Charleston County School Systems.

Her Christian experience began as a child. She attended the Mt. Zion AME Church Sunday School. Because of her interest and dedication, she represented her church as a delegate to many conventions. The president Elder remarked *"...this child will one day be a great leader...she has a mark on her life."*

At the age of fifteen, June 26, 1941, the very lovely Willie Mae Smalls was united in holy matrimony to Mr. David Rivers. Their marriage lasted just short of 56 years until his demise on May 15, 1997. This union was blessed with twelve children; two sons and ten daughters.

In 1946, Mother Rivers attended a revival one night and after hearing the gospel preached (*by the husband and wife team, Supt. Jacob C. & Missionary Francena Dantzler*) she believed and was baptized in the Holy Ghost.

Mother Rivers became a member of the Calvary Church Of God In Christ. She was appointed Church Mother at the age of twenty (20). She continues to serve in that capacity.

Because of her dedication, Mother Rivers was chosen to serve as District Missionary and later Assistant Supervisor to the late Mother Alice Marie Saunders.

In 1968, she was appointed and is presently the Supervisor of the Department of Women for the South Carolina Jurisdiction. Her loyal dedication to God and her leaders is exemplified throughout the Church Of God In Christ, Inc.

Mother Rivers has served on the National level in the following capacities:
International Marshal – Women's Convention
Chairperson of the Board of Supervisors
Member, Executive Board
Member, Screening Committee
Member, Program Committee – Gen. Church
Coordinator – Leadership Conference
Instructor – District Missionaries Class
Member, Steering Committee – Women's Convention
Chairperson – Exhibits- Women's Convention
Third Assistant General Supervisor
Second Assistant General Supervisor

First Assistant General Supervisor

Upon the transition of Mother Crouch, Mother Rivers was appointed and installed as the International General Supervisor in April 1997, by Presiding Bishop C.D. Owens.

Since her appointment as General Supervisor, Mother Rivers has been featured in the May 1999, edition of Charisma and on February 3, 2000, she had her first appearance on the 700 Club. She made a special guest appearance on TBN in May of 2005.

She continues to minister to the needs of individuals in her community.

Mother Rivers has sponsored and spread the Gospel for several years through the "*Evangelist Speaks*" ministry on WTUA 106.1 FM (*St. Stephens, SC*) and WBBP 1480 AM (*Memphis, TN*) radio stations. The Evangelist Speaks radio ministry recently joined WJNI 106.3 FM (*North Charleston, SC*).

Mother Rivers is also the founder and president of the Community Christian Women & Men Fellowship, which was organized to reach people in all walks of life.

Giving all praises to God, this fellowship has been a blessing to many souls through spiritual enrichment. Aid is provided for those less fortunate and the bereaved receive love and comfort during their time of sorrow.

Mother Rivers is a true servant of God and she touched the life of her sons, the late Robert Lee Rivers and Samuel Rivers. She continues to touch the lives of her ten daughters, twenty grandchildren, thirty-six great-grandchildren, three great-great grand's, three sisters, uncles, aunts, many cousins, her community and the Grand Ole Church Of God In Christ Family.

Mother Rivers is replaced

As the newly re-elected Fifth Presiding Bishop and Seventh Chief Apostle in Succession, in his fourth term would in a letter dated February 8, 2017, make known his Quadrennial appointments (*2017 to 2020*).

Bishop Blake, I, would in a historic move after much prayer and counsel choose to not reappoint Mother River as the General Supervisor for the department of Women.

This would be the first time in the over 100 year history of the Church Of God In Christ that a Presiding Prelate has not reappointed a seated general supervisor.

Bishop Blake would appoint Mother Barbara McCoo Lewis Supervisor of the Southern California First Jurisdiction as the General Supervisor and Sixth President of the International Women's Convention.

Mother Rivers has the distinction as the second longest tenured General Supervisor and the longest tenured President of the Women's Convention. She has served under all five Presiding Bishops. She celebrated her 91st birthday in 2017.

Women's International Conventions presided over by Mother Rivers

See Next Page

THE TEXAS CONNECTION — General Supervisors (Rivers)

Mother Rivers awarded an Honorary Doctorate

Mother Rivers and Bishop GE Patterson

Mother Rivers Speaking

Women's International Conventions presided over by Mother Rivers (20)

No.	Year	Location of Convention	Theme of Convention
47th	1997	Philadelphia, Pennsylvania	
48th	1998	Kansas City, Missouri	
49th	1999	Detroit, Michigan	
50th	2000	Los Angeles, California	*"Holy Women Perpetuating Fifty Years of Historical Facts and Traditional Teaching"*
51st	2001	Birmingham, Alabama	
52nd	2002	Minneapolis/St. Paul, Minnesota	
53rd	2003	Tampa, Florida	
54th	2004	St. Louis, Missouri	
55th	2005	Atlanta, Georgia	
56th	2006	Dallas, Texas	
57th	2007	Orlando, Florida	
58th	2008	Kansas City, Missouri	
59th	2009	Denver, Colorado	
60th	2010	Los Angeles, California	*"Women of Wisdom Striving to accomplish great things for our Great God"*
61st	2011	Dallas, Texas	
62nd	2012	Atlanta, Georgia	
63rd	2013	Orlando, Florida	
64th	2014	Louisville, Kentucky	
65th	2015	Minneapolis, Minnesota	
66th	2016	Detroit, Michigan	

Mother Barbara McCoo Lewis

Mother Barbara McCoo Lewis
Seventh General Supervisor 2017-Present
Sixth President of the Women's Convention

The McCoo family who were members of the Emmanuel Church Of God In Christ. Pastored by Bishop Samuel M. Crouch; would welcome into this world a bouncing baby girl that they would name Barbara.

As the third generation of her family in the Church Of God In Christ, she was christened by her pastor Bishop Crouch and would grow up under his leadership and ministry at Emmanuel in Los Angeles, California.

At the tender age of only nine years of age she would be saved and filled with the Holy Ghost. She would get her primary education from the school system. She would receive the start of her training that would lead her to elevation in the church from Emmanuel.

She would meet and marry Elder James A. Lewis, Sr., on June 9, 1962. (*They would welcome two sons born of this union, James A. Lewis, Jr. and Jeffrey M. Lewis.*)

In February of 1970, Los Angeles would see the establishment of a new body of believers. This new church would apply be named New Antioch Church Of God In Christ. The founders of the church were Pastor James A. Lewis, Sr., and wife Missionary Barbara McCoo Lewis.

Even though these two faithful servants have been elevated to various positions on both the state and national levels (*Senior Administrative Assistant Dr. James A. Lewis, Sr. and Jurisdictional Supervisor Mother Barbara McCoo Lewis*). They remain faithful to the local work.

As the cofounder and first lady of New Antioch Church Of God In Christ, she has worn many hats. Her humble service has recently included serving as the President and Teacher of the local Prayer and Bible Band Unit.

Mother Lewis is well educated, well rounded and well experienced in various departments and areas of the church. She holds a total of four degrees two degrees in Journalism, a masters in Theology and an honorary degree.

Bishop Blake would appoint her as the Supervisor of the Southern California Jurisdiction for the first time on May 5, 1988. She would receive her official appointment from General Supervisor Dr. Mattie McGlothen, on November 11, 1988, at the 81st Annual Holy Convocation in Memphis, Tennessee.

Upon the transition of Presiding Bishop G. E. Patterson, Bishop Blake the first Assistant Presiding Bishop would be elevated to the office of Presiding Bishop. He would be the emeritus Jurisdictional Prelate of the Southern California Jurisdiction.

Bishop Joe L. Ealy would be appointed as the next Jurisdictional Prelate of the Southern California Jurisdiction. As the

Prelate, Bishop Ealy would re-appoint Mother Lewis as Supervisor of the Southern California Jurisdiction Department of Women.

As the Supervisor of the First Southern California Jurisdiction Department of Women, Dr. Lewis has been a hard worker in completing projects, moving the department forward and receiving many awards.

Her list of accomplishments and awards include a $ 4.7 million dollar 41 unit senior citizen living facility (the *Hale Morris Lewis Complex*). She is also a published author.

On the state level she holds several offices. She not only serves as the Jurisdictional Supervisor of the First Jurisdiction of Southern California Church Of God In Christ, she is also a member of the Board of Directors.

As part of the Southern California Church Of God In Christ Economic Development Corporation, she serves as President and Chairman of the Board of Directors.

She is a member of Urban League, a member of the RCMA (*Religious Conference Managers Association*) and the NAACP (the *National Association for the Advancement of Colored People*).

On the national level recently in the Church Of God In Christ, Inc., she served under Mother Willie Mae Rivers in the International Department of Women.

Her service under Mother Rivers included Chairperson Special Convention Assistance Committee, a member of the Executive Board, the General Supervisor's Representative for the Western Region of the United States, International Marshal and Chairperson of the Program Committee.

She serves on the C.H Mason Theological Seminary as a member of the Board of Trustees.

Her two son are ordained Elders in the Church Of God In Christ and in January of 2006, Elder Jeffrey Martin Lewis, Sr., would be elevated to role of Pastor of the New Antioch Church Of God In Christ.

When Senior Administrative Assistant Dr. James A. Lewis Sr., would turn over the reins of pastorate to their youngest son Pastor J.M. Lewis, Sr., this would end their 36 years as founding pastoral leadership.

Mother Lewis holds fast to Philippians 4:13 *"I Can Do All Things Through Christ Which Strengthens Me."*

Mother Lewis is appointed

As the newly re-elected Fifth Presid and Seventh Chief Apostle in Succession, in his fourth term, Bishop Blake would in a letter dated February 8, 2017; make known his Quadrennial appointments (*2017 to 2020*)

Bishop Blake would appoint Mother Barbara McCoo Lewis Supervisor of the Southern California First Jurisdiction as the General Supervisor and Sixth President of the International Women's Convention.

Women's International Conventions presided over by Mother McCoo Lewis

See Next Page

Mother Rivers And Mother LMcCoo Lewis 2013

Women's International Conventions presided over by Mother Barabara McCoo Lewis (1)

No.	Year	Location of Convention	Theme of Convention
67th	2017	Orlando, Florida	

Mother Lewis Installed as General Supervisor
by Bishop C.E. Blake, Sr., Presiding Prelate

**Mother Lewis receiving
her Certificate of appointment**
Read by Bishop Lyles, General Sect.

Mother Lewis receiving Congratulations
from the General Board

Mother Lewis embraced by
Bishop Blake

established 1911

Profiles of Other Pioneering Women

Profiles of other outstanding personalities of the Department of Women of the Church of God in Christ.

"Profiles of Pioneering Women" church of God in Christ 1897-1997 (100) Centennial Historical Perspective
Department of Women Mother Willie Mae Rivers General Supervisor

THE TEXAS CONNECTION *Pioneering Women*

National Hospitality Group
Pictured are Dr. Mattie McGlothen National President of Hospitality, Int'l Asst. Supervisor of California with a portion of her group of co-workers as they served the Women of the Int'l Women's Convention

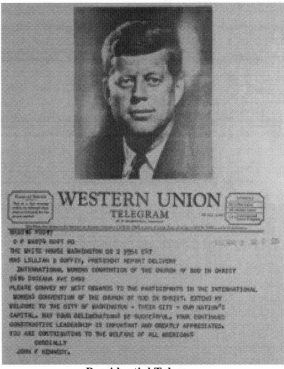

Presidential Telegram
President John F. Kennedy sends Mother Coffey and the women of the Church Of God In Christ a telegram acknowledging the International Women's Convention

Bishop and Mother C.H. Mason

Bishop and Mother O.T. Jones, Sr.

Elsie Washington Mason

Mother Elsie Washington Mason
Wife of Bishop C.H. Mason
1908-2006

Elise Louise Washington was born during the presidency of the 26th President of the United States. President Teddy Roosevelt who would become president after the assassination of President William McKinley on September 14, 1901, six months into his second term.

President McKinley was the third seated American President Assassinated during that time by gun shot.

The first was President Abraham Lincoln the 16th president who was shot on April 14, 1865. He would succumb nine hours after his severe head wound on April 15, 1865. After he would preserve the union after the American Civil War and freeing the American Negro from slavery, during only one term of 4 years and one month in office.

The second was President James A. Garfield who was shot on July 2, 1891, but didn't pass away until September 19, 1891, less than four months in to his term as the 20th President.

The third was President William McKinley September 14, 1901 in Buffalo, NY. Who was the 25th President, six months into his second term.

Elsie's birth would occur during the time when the American Negro, didn't have the right to vote. America was just 43 years from the official end of American Slavery with the signing and ratification of the 13th Amendment to the Constitution on December 6, 1865. Although President Lincoln had issued his Emancipation Proclamation on January 1, 1863.

One year before she was born the (*Pentecostal*) Church Of God In Christ was organized in 1907, after Bishop CH Mason would experience the outpouring of the Holy Ghost at the Azusa Street revival in Los Angeles, California.

Elsie would grow up in the Church Of God In Christ. During this time the women would wear skirts that would drag the floor. She was well trained and was an educator in the Memphis City School Systems.

In 1928, she went to Lexington and taught three years at Saints Industrial School. She was saved and filled with the Holy Ghost under Dr. Arenia C. Mallory at this school.

Miss Elise Washington would become the bride of Bishop Charles Harrison Mason in 1944.

She was a loyal, devoted and dedicated wife who stood by Bishop Mason until his transition. She served the church as Executive Secretary for the Missions Department and National Tithing Fund.

She also served as editor of the church's official organ "The Whole Truth" paper. She has graced the Church Of God In Christ with dignity and is much admired for her humble spirit and devotion to Bishop Mason.

Elsie was a young widow in 1968, when the black sanitations workers met at Mason Temple to rally for the strike, march for fair wages. She is also noted as the first one to donate $90 out of her own pocket to feed those striking. Dr. King would deliver his famous last *"Mountain Top"* sermon from Mason Temple.

She was a living record of the Church Of God In Christ's active role in the civil rights movement. She and Bishop Mason were slowly changing the racial injustice landscape of America by preaching and leading the welcoming message of salvation of the cross to both blacks and whites.

This was before there was an organized civil rights movement. And being one of a few legally organized Pentecostal church organizations at the time. Bishop Mason and the Church Of God In Christ, would license and ordain both black and white ministers as equals.

She would testify of these times during an interview in the 1996, Charisma Magazine article. At the age of 88 she would vividly recall one of the revivals that were held in the south. Bishop *"Mason would attract huge crowds"* and she would say of the revival *"Crutches were lined up against the walls because the people didn't need them anymore"* she would further say about another time during one of the Church of God in Christ's Annual Holy Convocation in Memphis, Tn. *"A lady took sick during our convocation and at that time Doctors were not as prevalent as they are today, and there were hardly any hospitals for Negros. "So they called for Bishop Masson and he prayed until the Lord raised her."*

Mother Mason would later travel to Haiti as a missionary and would found an orphanage.

She would remain faithful until her health wouldn't allow. She would transition from labor to reward at the age of 98 which would occur on January 31, 2006, at Methodist University Hospital in Memphis, Tn.

Two of the wives that undergirded two of the powerful militant preachers of the civil rights movement would be laid to rest just one day apart. Mother Mason would be laid to rest first and Coretta Scott King's funeral would follow on that next day.

All though these two wives would play great roles in supporting their husbands on a course to change institutional racism in religion and in the world. Both women would see their roles change to greater responsibilities after their husbands' transition from labor to reward only a few years apart. Both were young widows.

Both celebrations of life would capture national attention due to each of their respective roles in the life of their husbands, the civil rights movement and spiritual service.

Although Mother Mason's life and work deserved it, her home going celebration (*unlike Mrs. Kings*) was not aired on major cable networks, none of the living Presidents would stop by, her body didn't lay in wake in a rotunda. But it was a celebration worthy of heavens attention.

Mother Elsie W. Mason
Her family
Mother Mason and Bishop C. H. Mason, were married in 1944
no children were born to this union.

Bishop and Mother Mason   *Mother Mason with Bishop F.O. White*

Neanza Zelma Jones

Mother Neanza Zelma Jones
Wife of Bishop O.T. Jones, Sr.

Neanza Zelma was born in St. Louis, Missouri, seventh of eight children born to Mother Joanna Williams Scott. Her father passed away when she was only seven months old.

The family devout members of the Kennerly Avenue Church Of God In Christ in St Louis. At age 12 she gave her life to Christ, thereafter was baptized in the Holy Ghost.

As a graduation present, she attended the Church Of God In Christ's 13th National Holy Convocation in Memphis, Tennessee.

It was during this meeting that she and the then National YPWW President, ("*Brother Ozro*") as he was then called, would meet.

The faithfulness of Elder Jones was recognized by Bishop Mason.

In 1914, Bishop Mason appointed Jones as the President of Young Peoples Willing Department of the Church Of God In Christ, Inc.

In 1916, he authored and edited the Young People Willing Worker (*YPWW*) Quarterly Topics. This Quarterly Topics would grow under his leadership, to one of the largest Pentecostal publications addressing itself to Christian Education.

They were married in 1921 and resided in Fort Smith, Arkansas for the next four years.

During this time, the couple became the parents of their first two children (sons): O.T. Jr., and Walter B.

In 1925, Senior Bishop C.H. Mason requested the young Elder Jones to go to Philadelphia to become pastor of a small band of saints.

This small group would eventually become Holy Temple Church Of God In Christ.

The family established a home, and four more children were born (one son and three daughters): William V., Jean (Anderson), Elma Harriet (Freeman), and Marion Elizabeth Ellison A total of six children were born to this union.

In 1929, Bishop Jones would be the founder of the International Youth Congress of the Church Of God In Christ, which grew under his leadership.

It would become one of the largest annual gatherings of Christian youth and youth workers in the nation.

In 1941, he organized the Youth Department of the Church Of God In Christ, and became its appointed President.

With more than forty years of continued leadership as the President, Bishop Jones would make his most distinguishing contribution as a Christian minister and youth leader.

This distinguished leadership in *Cogicdom* would see nearly thirty new church sponsored youth programs organized for youth work come into being for the benefit of local and jurisdictional departments in *Cogicdom* wide.

He gave leadership and spiritual inspiration and Christian training to virtually all of the future leaders of the Church Of God In Christ (*Cogicdom*) through the training programs which he inspired or sponsored from 1951 until his transition on September 23, 1972.

In the work of her husband, Mother N.Z. Jones was a virtual and virtually indispensable assistant, quietly and always working behind the scenes.

She served as his personal and business secretary, manager of his publications, confidante and as his loving supportive wife.

She severed as Church Mother, organizing strong and helpful groups.

She supported many groups and activities over the years. These would include Home and Foreign Mission, Hospitality, Scholarship Ministerial Assistance and others.

The Jones Children,
Bishop O.T. Jones, Sr., and Mother N. Jones

Mother Neanza Zelma Jones
Her family

Mother Jones and Bishop O.T. Jones, Sr., had six children O.T., Jr. Walter B., William V., Jean, Elma Harriet and Marion

Mrs. N. Z. Jones
Mother

Bishop O.T. Jones, Sr.
Husband

Bishop O.T. Jones, Jr.
Prays for Bishop W.A. Patterson, Sr.
Standing: Bishops R.H.L. Winbush, J.N Haynes, L.H. Ford, O.T. Jones, Jr.

The Jones Children
At the Piano (L to R): Marian, Gene, Elma Harriet
Standing (L to R): O.T. Jones, Jr., William V., Walter B.

Deborah Indiana Mason Patterson

Mother Deborah I. M. Patterson
Wife of Bishop J.O. Patterson, Sr.
08-22-1914 to -06-02-1985

Deborah Indiana Mason was the fifth child among eight born to Bishop Charles Harrison Mason and his second wife Lelia Washington Mason.

She was born September 22, 1914, in Lexington, Mississippi. She attended the Memphis public schools, the Saints Literary and Industrial College in Lexington, Mississippi and Henderson Business College in Memphis.

Her studies and attention to detail caused her to excel and earn her the respect of her peers.

On July 4, 1934, she married a young minister James Oglethrope Patterson and of this union two children were born J.O. Patterson, Jr. and the late Janet Laverne Patterson.

She labored by his side and was a perfect helpmeet. Her entire life was her family and the Church.

She lived to care for the people of God and to love, comfort, and be an asset to her husband Bishop J.O. Patterson, Sr., and her two children.

Mother Patterson served the Church Of God In Christ, as International Marshal of the Women's Convention, Secretary-Treasurer of the Department of Missions and President of the Bishops Wives Circle. She was director of the International Choir. She was also active in all phases of Jurisdictional and local church work. Mother Patterson fell asleep in the loving arms of her savior on June 2, 1985.

Mother Debra I. (Mason) Patterson
a graduate of CH Bible College on November 13, 1979

Mother Debra I. (Mason) Patterson

Mother Debra I. (Mason) Patterson
Parents

Mrs. Lelia Mason
Her Mother

Bishop C.H. Mason
Her Father

Mother Debra I. (Mason) Patterson
Her family

Mother and Bishop J.O. Patterson, Sr., had two children born to this union one son J.O. Patterson, Jr., and a daughter the late Janet Laverne Patterson

Mrs. D. I. Patterson
Mother

Bishop J. Patterson, Sr.
Husband

Bishop J. Patterson, Jr.
Son

Bishop C.H.M. Patterson
Grandson

Early Picture of The Mason Family
Bishop CH Mason, Lelia Mason (wife), her mother and their children.

The extended Mason Family
Bishop CH Mason his children, their spouses and grandchildren.

The resting place of
Bishop J.O. Patterson, Sr. and Mother Debra I. (*Mason*) Patterson

Bishop J. O. Patterson, Sr.
1912 to 1989

Mother Debra I. (*Mason*) Patterson
1914 to 1985

Margaret Ford

**Mother Margaret Ford
Wife of Bishop L.H. Ford**

Margaret *"Babe"* Little was born in Piedmont, South Carolina. After the loss of her father, her family migrated to Evanston, Illinois. Margaret would graduate from the Evanston Township High School. She was persuaded by the spirit to leave the Ebenezer AME Church and to accept holiness in the Church Of God In Christ.

Elder Louise Henry Ford would come from Mississippi to run a revival at the Hovland Court Church Of God In Christ in Evanston, Illinois. During this time Elder Ford and Miss. Margaret Little would meet and would later marry on December 12, 1934.

Elder Louis Henry Ford and Mrs. Margaret (*Little*) Ford would later move to Chicago, Illinois. There they would set up their ministry and their home. To this union were born two children Charles Mason Ford and Janet (*Ford*) Hill.

Elder Ford's ministry would start from his street corner ministry to becoming the founding pastor of the St. Paul Church Of God In Christ in 1936.

He would purchase Chicago's oldest home and land for the new St. Paul Church Of God In Christ. The church and Elder Ford would lease the home that was purchased to Mrs. Ford for her small business.

As a small business owner she operated a restaurant for 10 years in that home that was later sold to the city of Chicago. It is now the Clarke Museum, the oldest home in Chicago which is listed as a national historic landmark.

Her restaurant would serve many, some famous, some not so famous. Some of her well known patrons included among others the Legendary Actress/Singer Lena Horne and the World's Heavy Weight Boxing champion Joe Louis to name a few.

As a first lady with her own style, she was known for her church hat. She would often say *"No well dressed woman should be seen in public without her hat and gloves."*

Mother Ford would be recognized as the *"Model Pastor's Wife"* and described as *"always smiling"* and *"cheering others on."* She was a loyal, faithful and supportive helpmeet to her husband.

Her support for Bishop Ford's ministry would start from his street corner ministry, to him becoming the founding pastor of the St. Paul Church Of God In Christ.

Her support would continue in the late 1940's, when he was appointed the Superintendent of the South Shore District and his appointment as the State Chairman of Illinois.

In the 1950's her support continued to his appointment as State Overseer (*Bishop*) of Iowa.

In 1954, she supported his consecration to the National Bishopric Staff and also his selection as a member of the Board of Education – Saints College.

Also his appointment as the Jurisdictional Prelate (*Bishop*) for Central Illinois, and as the foremost minister in the *"Emmit Till Case"* in 1955.

In 1968 as a supportive helpmeet she would witness history as he was one of the 12 members elected to the first General Board of the Church Of God In Christ, Inc.

Her support would further extent in 1976, when Bishop Ford would be elevated as the Second Assistant International Presiding Bishop.

During this time, she would serve as the President of the State Ministers Wives Alliance for 40 plus years.

Locally she would also serve as a Sunday School teacher at the St. Paul COGIC. Her class was said to be a favorite of the young people of the church.

It was said that her student would *"run to get to her Sunday school class, to hear her teach"*. It was also said *"She had a special gift of working with the young people."*

As his greatest supporter she would see her husband rise to the office of International Presiding Bishop of 8.5 million member Church Of God In Christ. He was the Second elected Presiding Bishop and Fourth Leader in Succession of the Church Of God In Christ.

She would remain a faithful and loyal supporter as the *"Model wife"* until Bishop Louis Henry Ford would transition from labor to reward on March 31, 1995.

Mother Ford was the mother of two children, the grandmother of 10 grandchildren and the great grandmother of 12 great grandchildren.

She would remain active and in attendance for all church services at St. Paul Church Of God In Christ (*founded by her and the late Bishop L. H. Ford and then pastored by her son Bishop Charles Mason Ford*), and for all jurisdictional functions.

Mother Ford would remain faithful to supportive ministries in the church. She was a Sunday school teacher and would lend counsel to other pastor wives.

She shall always be remembered for her faithfulness, for her loyalty to the church and her husband, for hosting of both the famous and the non-famous, for her smile and for always cheering on others.

She would remain faithful until her health wouldn't allow. She would transition from labor to reward on January 2, 2003, at the age of 92 at the Crestwood Care Centre.

Mother Margaret Ford
Her family

Mother Ford and Bishop L.H. Ford, had two children born to this union one son Charles Mason Ford and one daughter Janet (Ford) Hill

Mrs. M. Ford
Mother

Bishop L. H. Ford
Husband

Bishop C. M. Ford
Son

Bishop L.H. Ford
2nd Presiding Bishop
and
Bishop F.O. White
General Board Member

Bishop L. H. Ford *Seating* and
Bishop J. O. Patterson, Sr. *Standing*

Shirley Owens

**Mother Shirley Jennette Owens
Wife of Bishop C.D. Owens**

Shirley Jennette Hardy was born and raised in Detroit, Michigan. She would complete her education in Detroit school system. During this time, which was shortly after high school, the young Elder Chandler David Owens would move to Detroit, Michigan to find work at the Henry Ford Auto Plant and to find the hand of the love of his life.

Shirley Hardy and Elder C.D. Owens would meet and marry at an early age and shortly thereafter his service to the church would be recognized when he would be appointed to a church in New Jersey.

Elder Owens was appointed to his first pastorate at the Wells Cathedral Church Of God In Christ, this appointment was made by Bishop J.S. Bailey.

Elder Owens and Shirley Owens would move twice first to Orange, New Jersey and then to Newark, New Jersey.

This union of Pastor C.D. Owens, Sr., and Shirley Jeannett Owens would see three children born to this young couple two daughters and one son: (*Chandra Stephanie, Chandler David, Jr., and a deceased daughter Shirlitha Shirae*).

Mother Owens was employed by Bell Atlantic in Newark, New Jersey, where she would have a tenure there of over forty years.

Although Mother Owens remained in the background throughout her husbands' career, she has played an integral part in his ministry. Many personal sacrifices have been made by her and she remains steadfast and unmovable for the cause of Christ.

She would see his unusual oratorical gift make him one of the most sought after speakers in the Church Of God In Christ for over thirty plus years. Elder Owens served in almost every area of responsibility including serving as the Chairman of the Commission for the Constitution of the Church.

He has held lead responsibilities in the Department of Evangelism and Youth. Thousands would fill Pentecostal Temple during the Holy Convocation, to hear him preside over the National Musicals. He would travel much as an evangelist, he would cover much ground in the United States and foreign fields such as Caribbean Islands, India and Europe.

Elder Owens was consecrated Bishop of New Jersey Third Ecclesiatical Jurisdiction of the Church Of God In Christ, Inc., while he was pastoring the Wells Cathedral Church Of God In Christ.

In 1976, Bishop Owens made history in the Church Of God In Christ by being the youngest Bishop ever elected to the General Board of the church. He was known as the *Man with the Golden Voice*.

Bishop Owens served as First Assistant Presiding Bishop under Bishop L.H. Ford and when Bishop Ford Transitioned on

March 31, 1995, one of the COGIC's most popular and gifted leaders, had already been groomed to continue this great legacy of Leadership.

And at the transition of Bishop Ford, Bishop Chandler David Owens, Sr., was elevated as Interim Presiding Bishop. Bishop Owens was later elected as the Third Presiding Bishop and the Fifth Chief Apostle to lead the Church Of God In Christ.

It was no surprise that the Church Of God In Christ received him with such a warming confidence. Bishop Owens program for the Church was titled *"Vision 2000 and Beyond"*

He especially targeted concerns such as Evangelism, Church growth, financial solvency, National Auxiliaries, Women in Ministry, Christian education and the C.H. Mason Bible College, as his priority during his tenure.

Bishop Owens was a *"warrior for his principles"* as noted by Dr. David Hall. It was under his administration in April 1997, that Mother Rivers was appointed as Supervisor of the Women's Department of the Church Of God In Christ.

It was also under Bishop Owen administration that AIM (*Auxiliary In Ministry*) was established. This is the summer convention of the Church Of God In Christ that replaced UNAC-5.

Bishop Owens was challenged by Bishop G.E. Patterson for the election as Presiding Prelate of the Church Of God In Christ. Bishop Owens would defeat Bishop Patterson by one (1) vote in November 1996.

By November 2000, Bishop C.D. Owens was defeated in the election by Bishop Gilbert Earl Patterson. Bishop Owens will be remembered as one of the most popular Presiding Officers the Church Of God In Christ has had. He remained a member of the General Board.

Mother Owens would be faithfully by the side of Bishop CD Owens when he went from labor to reward early Sunday morning on March 6, 2011, after a short hospital stay. She remains a faithful member.

Mother Shirley Owens
Her family

Mother Owens and Bishop C.D. Owens, Sr., had three children born to this union one son C.D. Owens, Jr., and two daughters Chandra Stephanie (Owens) Thames and the late Shirlitha Shirae Owens

Mrs. S. J. Owens
Mother

Bishop C. D. Owens, Sr.
Father

Bishop C.D. Owens, Sr,
Preaching the dedication of Temple of Deliverance

Bishop J.O. Patterson, Sr.
Bishop C.D. Owens, Sr.

Office of the Presiding Bishop

Bishop C.D. Owens, Sr.
Bishop F.O. White

Bishop C.D. Owens, Sr.
Mother Shirley Owens

Mother Shirley Owens

Louise D. Patterson

Mother Louise D. Patterson
Wife of Bishop G.E. Patterson

Louise D. Patterson was born January 27, 1940. She is a product of the Memphis School system, Booker T. Washington High School. She was raised in the Methodist Church.

In 1967, Elder G.E. Patterson was the co-pastor of Holy Temple Church of God in Christ in Memphis, Tennessee, which was pastored by his father the Bishop W.A. Patterson, Sr.

It was during this time that two things would occur in her life. She would first meet Elder Patterson. Secondly his preaching would be the cause of her deliverance and salvation. As she would state. *"I experienced the Lord for myself."*

They would began a short courtship that would lead to marriage in 1968, and would last for 39 years until the transition of Bishop G. E. Patterson.

Along with her marriage, she would have to accept and become accustom to the ways and traditions of the Church Of God In Christ. As evident in her humorous statement "I *had to get used to the long prayers."*

As the wife of Elder Patterson, Sister Louise D. Patterson would hit the ground running as a wholehearted believer in his ministry. She would become a Sunday school teacher and a member of the choir among other roles in his ministry.

She has been described as a *"well dressed attractive first lady"* with the brains to match. She is know for her good taste and fashion sense, which emulates the distinction and class of being a woman of holiness; and to say she is compassionate would be saying the least.

Due to the popularity and worldwide outreach of Bishop Patterson's ministry, a new department was organized by Mother Patterson. This department would start with only 80 volunteers and in 5 years would boast 800 volunteers.

Mother Patterson would organize other ministries that would benefit members as well as non-members. These would include ministries that would minister to the very basic needs of man, to the uplift of mankind.

From feeding the seniors, to clothing those in need and encouraging those in tough situations to come out. Her contributions along with Bishop Patterson to education would number scholarships in the amount of over $70,000.00.

She has mentored many across the country from young ladies to Pastor's wives local and nationwide.

Bishop Patterson would acknowledge the importance of his wife's ministry to the women of the church in reaching their destiny in Christ by appointing her the President of the Christian Women's Auxiliary.

She would also assist Bishop Patterson with helping him to pray over, read and answer the many letters he would receive. She would note about this work *"I love doing it because it keeps me in touch with the real world."*

Mother Patterson would remain by the side of Bishop G.E. Patterson until his final days when he would fall asleep in the arms of Christ on March 20, 2007 at age 67.

As the biggest fan of Bishop Patterson Mother Patterson keeps busy these days keeping the legacy of Bishop G.E. Patterson's ministry alive and moving forward for generations to come.

Her efforts would result in purchasing a flame that burns 24 hours a day at the entrance of the Temple of Deliverance. It is in honor of Bishop G.E. Patterson's tireless commitment to his life's work of the Ministry.

She is now serving as the president of the board of directors of Bountiful Blessings, Inc., as the general manager of WBBP radio station, and the president of Podium records.

She can be seen weekly on the Word Network hosting the Bountiful Blessings Broadcast, which features the sermons of Bishop G.E. Patterson. The recordings of Bishop Patterson preaching is still in great demand.

She is also very active in the national church in several departments and ministries. She is among other things, a licensed evangelist missionary of the Church Of God In Christ.

She has served as part of the Bishop's Wives Circle, along Bishop Paterson's side. They would host a yearly pastors and wives dinner during the annual Holy Convocation. She was also honored by the International Sunday School Department. Its yearly pageant was named The Louise Patterson Pageant.

To say the very least she wore well, being the first lady of COGIC. Mother Patterson has described her marriage to the late Presiding Bishop, Bishop Gilbert Earl Patterson as *"It's never a dull moment"*. *"Every day is challenging,"* and *"It's very exciting being married to the bishop."*

Mother Louise Patterson
Her family
Mother Patterson and Bishop G.E. Patterson. No children were born to this union

Mrs. L. Patterson
Wife

Bishop G.E. Patterson
Husband

Bishop G. E. Patterson and Evangelist Louise Patterson

Evangelist Louise Patterson and Bishop G. E. Patterson

Bishop J.O. Patterson, Sr. and Pastor G. E. Patterson

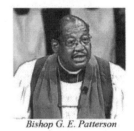
Bishop G. E. Patterson

Mae L. Blake

Mother Mae Lawrence Blake
Wife of Bishop C.E. Blake, I

Mae Lawrence was born to the proud parents of Bishop Elton A. Lawrence and Mother Myrtle Lawrence.

On July 11, 1964 Charles Edward Blake and Mae Lawrence were united in holy matrimony. Bishop Junious Augustus Blake officiated the ceremonies.

Three children were born of this union: Kimberly (*Blake*) Ludlow, Charles E. Blake, II and Lawrence Blake.

First Lady Mae L. Blake is dynamic, warm and gracious. She is acknowledged as an unequaled interior decorator. Her artistic and creative brilliance is evidenced as you enter the beautiful West Angeles Cathedral.

Mother Blake is the founder and president of WAO the Women Affairs Organization which is one of the foremost auxiliaries within the life of West Angeles Church.

Through various fund-raising activities WAO has contributed more than $600,000.00 to the building for the West Angeles Cathedral and hundreds of thousands of dollars on beautification and improvement projects.

Each year the ladies of west Angeles are treated to an awesome inspiring event in which the First Lady gives an encouraging message for all. These events are called "*A Day With Mae.*" Mother Blake uses timely examples and pearls of wisdom in simple, often humorous, language to share the word of God.

Mother Blake commented in her interview with Lady Serita A. Jakes for an article in the Special Spring 2011 Mother's Day Edition of eMotions Magazine: "*When I first became a pastor's wife, West Angeles Church had only 50 members…*"

"*I never dreamed that one day West Angeles would have 25,000 members, and that Bishop Blake would be Presiding Bishop over the entire denomination worldwide.*" She goes on to say "*We give God all the praise and glory.*"

As his help meet over the years she has seen Bishop Blake's go from Pastoring in 1964, to the "*Dark Days*" of the Church.

She was there when his served as the vice chair and the president of the Publishing Board, and as the chair of the Christian Education Board and the Youth Department during the years of 1965 to 1970. During the same time he was editor of the YPWW (*Young Peoples Willing Worker*) topic, from 1996 to 1971.

In 1969, the Blake's life would change when Elder Charles Edward Blake, Sr., would be appointed the Pastor of the West Angeles Church Of God In Christ.

Her support would see his elevation in 1971 to 1993, as a trustee of the Interdenominational Theological Center and a trustee for the Charles Harrison Mason Theological Seminary in Atlanta, Georgia.

THE TEXAS CONNECTION
Pioneering Women (Blake)

She would see her husband be elevated in 1973, when he was consecrated by Bishop J.O. Patterson, Sr., as the Jurisdictional Prelate of the Southern California Jurisdiction of the Church Of God In Christ, Inc.

She would see her husband serve with distinction and honor from 1988 to 2007, as a General Board member of the Church Of God In Christ, Inc.

During the years of 2000 to 2007 she would support his service as he served with distinction and loyalty as the First Assistant Presiding Bishop to the late Presiding Bishop Gilbert Earl Patterson.

This support would see the First Jurisdiction of Southern California grow to more than 250 churches under his leadership.

On the local level she would see West Angeles Church Of God In Christ, grow from 50 to well over 25,000. With more than 80 programs for the psychological, social and economic entrancement of the community.

Bishop C.E. Blake, I, serves as the Seventh Chief Apostle and the 5th Elected Presiding Prelate of the Church Of God In Christ, Inc. He has been elected to serve as Presiding Prelate since 2008 to present.

Mother Blake takes great joy in the fact that she plays a supporting role in the ministry and the support of Bishop Blake, the West Angles church and COGIC worldwide.

Blake Wedding July 11, 1964
(left to right) Bishop Elton A. Lawrence & Mrs. Myrtle Lawrence & Lady Mae (Lawrence) Blake & Elder Charles E. Blake Bishop & Mrs. J.A. Blake

Mother Mae L. Blake
Her family

Mother and Bishop C.E. Blake, Sr., had three children born to this union one daughter Kimberly (*Blake*) Ludlow, and two sons Charles E. Blake, Jr., Lawrence Blake

Mrs. Mae L. Blake — *Mother*   Bishop C. E. Blake, Sr. — *Father*

Elder C. E. Blake, II — *Son*   Sis. K. Ludlow — *Daughter*   Elder L. Blake, Sr. — *Son*

Lady Mae L. Blake

Lady Mae L. Blake   *Bishop C.E. Blake, Sr. Praying during the Holy Convocation*

The Office of General Secretary of the Church Of God In Christ, Inc.

The office of the General Secretary serves as the organ that orchestrates the melodious sound that is the resulting effort of many departments, circles, units and all facets of the Church Of God In Christ. It is the deliberate aim of the General Secretary, to serve, interact, inform and be the herald of the Church's progress.

Over 100 years of history in the Church Of God In Christ can not completely record the devotion and dedicated of its leaders and workers, only their acts and deeds. The Office of General Secretary more than any other save that of the Presiding Bishop relegates itself to the task of serving the church's entire great constituency. Constantly increasing numbers, complex programming and diversified governmental standards elicit from our competent staff the very highest and most skillful performance of duties.

While programs and approaches must change to meet people where they are, the goals and motives of the Office of General Secretary remain constant and unchanging. The Office of General Secretary seeks to demonstrate through diligent and systematic service, the Glory of God to the Saints everywhere.

"The General Secretary" Church Of God In Christ 89th Holy Convocation (100) Centennial Historical Perspective

* Tenure as General Secretary

Elder W.E. Holt
First General Secretary
*1910 to 1920

Bishop J.E. Williams
Second General Secretary
*1920 to 1934

Bishop U.E. Miller
Third General Secretary
*1934 to 1963

Bishop J.O. Patterson, Sr.
Fourth General Secretary
*1963 to 1968

Bishop D.A. Burton
Fifth General Secretary
*1968 to 1976

Bishop German R. Ross
Sixth General Secretary
*1976 to 1991

Bishop W.W. Hamilton
Seventh General Secretary
*1991 to 2001

Bishop A.Z. Hall, Jr.
Eighth General Secretary
*2001 to 2007

Bishop Joel H. Lyles, Jr.
Ninth General Secretary
* 2007 to Present

THE TEXAS CONNECTION　　　　　　　　　　*The Office of General Secretary*

Bishop Mason preaching during the Annual National Convocation
(L to R) Elders Wilson, R.E. Ranger, Overseer V.M. Barker, Eld J. Feltus, Bishop O.T. Jones, Sr., Bishop R.F. Williams, Overseer Samuel S.M. Crouch, Mother Lillian Coffey, Bishop E.R. Driver Overseer J.E. Bryant (insert) Bro. Cooper-radio announcer (at the table) on the Platform in the foreground Elder Utah Smith and Elder C.T. James

Annual National Convocation
The General Assembly to the Annual Convocation
Delegates and Officers at the National Tabernacle

The General Assembly of the Church Of God In Christ, Inc.

Much like Holiness was to the Baptist way, so was Pentecostalism to the Holiness way. After Bishop Mason's return from California a vote on the matter of adding Pentecostalism to the doctrine of Holiness was held by the then general assembly of the Church Of God In Christ (*Holiness*) and the assembly decided to terminate Bishop Mason's membership and all those that believed as he did.

This was done by the general assembly with the simple act of withdrawing "*the right hand of fellowship*" from Bishop Mason and those that held Mason's belief on Pentecostalism.

This decision by the general assembly caused C.H. Mason to leave and take with him some of the congregations of the Church Of God In Christ (*Holiness*). C.H. Mason called a special meeting in Memphis, Tennessee. The ministers that attended this meeting were E.R. Driver, J. Bowe, R.R. Booker, R.E. Hart, W. Welsh, A.A. Blackwell, E.M. Page, R.H.I. Clark, D.J. Young, James Brewer, Daniel Spearman and J.H. Boone.

This group of godly men made-up and organized the first Pentecostal General Assembly of the Church Of God In Christ. This new group of the Church Of God In Christ (*Pentecostal)* decided to keep the name. This new assembly of the (*Pentecostal*) Church Of God In Christ chose as their new leader Overseer C.H. Mason.

"*The General Assembly*" Church Of God In Christ 89th Holy Convocation (100) Centennial Historical Perspective

* Tenure as Chairman of the General Assembly

Bishop C. H. Mason
Chairman of General Assembly

Bishop L. E. Willis
Chairman of General Assembly

Bishop F. J. Ellis
Chairman of General Assembly

Bishop J.O. Patterson, Sr.
Chairman of General Assembly
*2000 to 2011

Bishop James W. Hunt, Sr.
Chairman of General Assembly
*2011 to 2016

Bishop Lemuel F. Thuston
Chairman of General Assembly
*2016 to Present

THE TEXAS CONNECTION *The Office of General Assembly Chairman*

Church Of God In Christ
Annual Holy Convocation December 1932

National Holy Convocation 1970
Bishop J.O. Patterson, Sr., preaching

National Holy Convocation

THE TEXAS CONNECTION — *Auxiliaries In Ministry (AIM)*

The Auxiliaries Convention(s) of the

Church of God In Christ

United **N**ational **A**uxiliaries **C**onventions
1976 to 1994

Auxiliaries **I**n **M**inistry
2000 to Present

The Auxiliaries of the

Church of God In Christ

Intl Sunday School Dept

Intl Dept of Missions

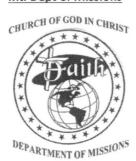

Intl Dept of Evangelism

Intl Music Dept

Intl Youth Dept

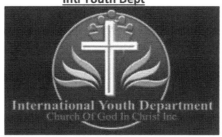

History of the Auxiliaries In Ministry

Established in 1996
Formed 2000

The **AIM** department is **A**uxiliaries **I**n **M**inistry, which is the summer convention of COGIC. This Department is comprised of the five main auxiliaries; with 3 sub conventions; The Department of Sunday School, the Music and Youth Departments (*MY convention*) the Missions and Evangelism Departments (*ME convention*).

The former name for this collective group was UNAC-5 which was the national/international arm and USAC the state or jurisdictional arm.

Predecessor of AIM (*UNAC-5*)
Established 1976

In 1976, during the second term of Bishop J.O. Patterson, Sr., the first elected Presiding Bishop of the Church Of God In Christ, a summer conventions of the 5 major auxiliaries of the church was formed.

This summer international convention of the Church Of God In Christ was given the name of the United National Auxiliaries Convention – 5 the acronym as it was better known was UNAC-5 (pronounced *YOU-NACK*). The number 5 represented the number of participating auxiliaries in the convention.

This summer convention was mirrored by each jurisdiction with its state level convention which was given the name United State Auxiliaries Convention with the acronym USAC (*pronounced YOU-SACK*).

The first UNAC-5 convention was hosted by the COGIC saints in Dallas, Texas. The theme of the first summer convention was **Maranatha** (*Our Lord Come*).

UNAC had two convention chairmen in its history which has from 1976 to 1996. The first chairman was Bishop Roy L. H. Winbush and second was Bishop F.E. Perry.

Bishop R. L. H. Winbush
First Chairman of UNAC-5
*1976 to 1993

Bishop F.E. Perry, Jr.
Second Chairman of UNAC-5
*1993 to 1994

It was under Bishop Owen's administration that AIM (*Auxiliary In Ministry*) was established.

After the dissolution of UNAC-5 under the administration of Bishop Gilbert Earl Patterson the new national auxiliary convention was organized as the **Auxiliaries In Ministry** with the acronym **AIM**. It served the same purpose as UNAC-5, with also a jurisdictional level convention also called **AIM**.

The first AIM chairman was Supt. Jerry Wayne Macklin, who served this department well from 1996, until he was elevated to the office of Bishop. During Supt. Macklin's tenure as the AIM chairman many wonderful things were brought to the summer conventions of the Church Of God In Christ, Inc.

Supt. J.W. Macklin
First Chairman of AIM
*1996 to 2001

Supt. J. Drew Sheard would serve as the second chairman of the AIM summer Convention of the Church Of God In Christ.

Supt J. Drew Sheard
Second Chairman of AIM
*2001 to 2013

Supt. Sheard would serve from 2001 to 2013. His administration would lead in many organizational changes to the department. He would surround himself with departmental leaders that would be future leaders of both the department and the church at large.

Under his tenure many successful summer conventions were held across the country, where many of the delegates would be blessed and many were saved. He would serve this position well until his elevation to the office of Bishop.

Supt Linwood Dillard, Jr.
Third Chairman of AIM
*2013 to Present

Presiding Bishop Charles E. Blake named Superintendent Linwood Dillard of Memphis, TN as the new Chairman of AIM.

Supt Dillard was the former president of the International Youth Department and is the pastor of the Citadel of Deliverance Church Of God In Christ, in Germantown, Tenn.

Having served in many capacities at every level of the church, the chairman brings a wealth of administrative and organizational skills to the position.

Supt. Dillard holds a Bachelor of Science degree in engineering from the University of Tennessee at Chattanooga.

He is also a graduate of the W.L. Porter Bible Institute (*which is accredited by the Evangelical Training Association*). In February 2006, Supt. Dillard was featured in EBONY Magazine as one of 30 young leaders under the age of 30.

He was highlighted for his work with various social and professional organizations such as the National Association for the Advancement of Colored People, the National Society of Black Engineers, and the American Institute of Chemical Engineers.

A recipient of numerous awards, recognitions, and commendations for his academic, ministerial, and social involvement and accomplishments.

Chairman Dillard assumes leadership of the denomination's largest summer convention. that comprises of five of the major departments of the church.

It is not known to many outside of the church, that there are three sub-conventions going on during the annual AIM convention.

These sub-conventions are as follows: *The Sunday School convention*, the *MY convention* (*Music and Youth*) and the *ME convention* (*Missions and Evangelism*). The departments share in three conventions all in one setting.

His first convention as AIM chairman was held in Baltimore, MD, July 1 – 5, 2013, which drew tens of thousands of delegates.

The goal of AIM is effectiveness in ministry. Its primary goal is training for a more effective domestic and global outreach, and its mission is to advance Kingdom work through training, worship, evangelism, discipleship, fellowship and service.

Chairman Dillard is happily married to the lovely Stephanie Marie Dillard. They are the proud parents of two children, Faith Marie and Linwood, III.

The 3 Sub Conventions of AIM

The Sunday School Convention

The MY Convention (*Music and Youth*)

The ME Convention (*Missions and Evangelism*)

Bishop Marvin Winans preaching in AIM 2016
(*L to R*) *Supt Dillard, Bishop Winans and Bishop Blake*

The 3 Sub Conventions of AIM

The Sunday School Convention

The MY Convention (*Music and Youth*)

 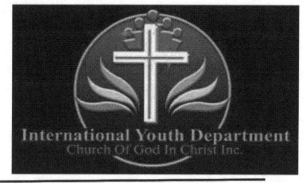

The ME Convention (*Missions and Evangelism*)

History of the Sunday School Department

Established in 1914

The first Sunday School was started in Lexington, Mississippi, by Professor L.W. Lee in 1908, Professor Lee was the Principal of the College at Natchez, Mississippi. He was saved under Elder C.P. Jones in 1895. He was the first Sunday School Superintendent of the Church.

In 1916, in St. Louis, Missouri Elder F.C. Christmas (*Father Christmas*) led Sunday School classes with nine women and three men. After two months he introduced quarterlies.

Some of the Saints battled against these books. Bishop Mason was called to St. Louis. After seeing the results of the Sunday School and the benefits of the teachings from these quarterlies, he saw that it was good for the Church.

In 1917, Overseer C. Bostic of Missouri had Elder Christmas come to the National Convocation to present the Sunday School Professor Courts of Lexington, Mississippi was in charge of the National Sunday School.

After hearing Father Frank C. Christmas, Professor Courts acknowledged that he was the man for the job. Mother Lizzie Robinson also believed that Father Christmas was the man for the job.

Elder F.C. Christmas
First Supt. of Sunday School
***1924 to 1944**

In 1924, Elder F.C. Christmas was appointed National Superintendent of Sunday School by Bishop Mason. After building the Sunday School Department in every state, an Assistant was needed. Elder L.C. Patrick was added to the National Sunday School. In 1944, Bishop Patrick became the National Superintendent.

Elder L.C. Patrick
Second Supt. of Sunday School
***1944 to 1967**

In 1945, Bishop S.M. Crouch of Northern California appointed Elder H.C. Johnson as State Sunday School Superintendent.

He in turn appointed Missionary Lucille Cornelius to be his Chairlady, the First woman to work with the women in the Sunday School Department.

A National Sunday School Congress along with a YPWW Congress began to meet in 1946. In 1951, the First National Sunday School Convention was held.

Bishop C.W. Williams
Third Supt. of Sunday School
*1967 to 1993

Mother Jones of Arkansas became the first National Field Representative under Bishop Patrick. In 1967, Bishop C.W. Williams became the National Sunday School Superintendent.

In 1968, under the direction of Bishop Roy Winbush of Louisiana, the Publishing House in Memphis, Tennessee was started.

Supt. Jerry W. Macklin
Fourth Supt. of Sunday School
*1993 to 2000

In 1993, Supt. Jerry Macklin of California was appointed National Superintendent. Along with him was Sister Gloria Smith of Washington as his National Field Representative.

In Memphis 1999, the International Sunday School was truly International, the Sunday School was live on the web during the World's Greatest Sunday School.

Under the administration of Presiding Bishop C.D. Owens, Sr., in 1996 AIM was established and Supt. Macklin was elevated to organize this new summer convention of the Church Of God In Christ. (*AIM would replace UNAC-5*) In 2000 Supt Macklin would be appointed as the first chairman of AIM. Also during this time he would be elevated to the office of Bishop.

Bishop Alton Gatlin
Fifth Supt. of Sunday School
*2000 to Present

Bishop Alton Gatlin of Louisiana was appointed to take the Sunday School Department to new and greater levels along with Missionary Georgia Macklin-Lowe of Tennessee as the National Field Representative of Sunday School.

Presiding Bishop Charles Blake, Sr., has reappointed Bishop Gatlin and National Field Representative Mother Macklin-Lowe to continue their leadership of the World's Greatest Sunday School.

Mother Lowe would step down to care for her husband Bishop Lowe. Evangelist Cleolia Wells-Penix would be appointed by Presiding Bishop Charles E. Blake, Sr., as the next International Field Representative of the Sunday School Department.

Bishop A. Gatlin **Mother Cleolia Wells-Penix**
Intl S.S. Supt *Intl Field Rep*

History of the Youth Department

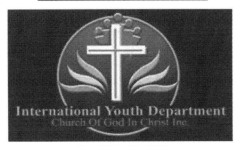

Established in 1912

The history of the Young People's Willing Workers Department is rich and inspiring. It is an incredible journey of a department formed in an era of political and social unrest, both internal and external. While the African-American community struggled with the injustices of the political void of the spiritual, the African-American church struggled with the spiritual over saturated with the political.

In 1915, the racist hate groups that had plagued Reconstruction, reorganized and in 1916 brought the *"Back to Africa"* movement of Marcus Garvey. In 1919, racial tensions came to a head.

African-American population in northern cities grew and discharged black war veterans entered the job pool. In the decade from 1910-1920, Detroit's African-American population grew by more than 600 percent, Cleveland's by over 300 percent, and Chicago's by 150 percent.

The mass migration from the Deep South to the industrial north created a brush fire of racial violence across the country. In July 1919, the worst rioting up to that time erupted when a black teenager was purposely drowned after drifting over to a *"white"* section of Lake Michigan.

It is into this setting that as Joshua ushered Israel's new and young generation into the land of promise, amidst turmoil and adversity, the great forefathers of our church lead the youth department into the promising future of spiritual education, enrichment and evangelism.

The Young People Willing Workers department is the International Youth Department of the Church Of God In Christ.

Elder M.C. Green
First YPWW President
*1912 to 1917

In 1912, Elder M.C. Green of Arkansas was appointed National YPWW Leader. At this time the national activities of the young people were confined, more or less, to sessions in the National Convocation.

Bishop O.T. Jones, Sr.
Second YPWW President
*1917 to 1962

In 1917, Bishop O.T. Jones, Sr. of Fort Smith, Arkansas was appointed as the National President.

Under his administration, YPWW grew to a large training organization. With the increasing number of philosophies and doctrinal dogmas circulating and targeting America's youth, it became vitally imperative for the youth of the church to be educated in biblically based doctrines of the Church Of God In Christ.

In 1929, the first National YPWW Congress was held in Kansas City, Missouri. Since that time, the Congress has grown to such proportions that its attendants fill some of the largest convention centers in the country.

It was under the tenure of Bishop O.T. Jones, Sr. that the Young People Willing Workers Topics were created. They began humbly with only a subject and a scripture.

Bishop O.T. Jones, Jr.
Third YPWW President
*1962 to 1968

The son of Bishop Jones would become the next Department head. Under the leadership of Bishop O.T. Jones, Jr., the department continued to evolve, motivated by a spirit of excellence. Bishop O.T. Jones, Jr., propelled the commitment to Christian education by moving the YPWW Topic from a subject and a scripture, to a complete manuscript curriculum.

Bishop C.D. Owens was the next International President of the YPWW Department. His charismatic personality and *"silver tongue orator"* delivery gave the department unequivocal exposure.

He is credited with moving the responsibility of the YPWW Topic to the COGIC Publishing House.

Bishop C.D. Owens
Fourth YPWW President
*1969

Bishop H.J. Bell then became the first author after the change and gave the YPWW Topic the name COGIC Training Union.

Bishop William James
Fifth YPWW President
*1973

The Youth Department continued to excel under the leadership of the next two Presidents, Bishop William James and Bishop Charles Brewer.

Bishop Charles Brewer
Sixth YPWW President
*1985 to 1997

The department's emphasis shifted from the pedagogical to include the evangelical.

Manny young people experienced the ecstasy of divine power and the magnanimity of divine grace as the "latter rain" fell mightily in the Youth Congress services.

Supt. J. Drew Sheard
Seventh YPWW President
*1997 to 2000

President J. Drew Sheard was appointed International President after Bishop Charles Brewer. He served as the catalyst in expanding the scope of youth ministry with creative and innovative youth programs.

Regional youth rallies provided the impetus for reparation and reclamation of enthusiasm and department synergy.

The contribution of women in the youth Department has been undeniably intrinsic. Women like Mother J.V. Hearne, Mother Clara Clemmons and Evangelist Deborah Thomas paved the way for women working in youth ministry serving as International Chairladies.

Evangelist Joyce Rodgers' passion for youth ministry led her to being appointed International Chairlady in 1999.

She has enhanced the programs of the International Youth Department by developing exciting new programs including *"Sister to Sister,"* Created to Praise *(Praise Dancers)* and Young Women in Ministry (*YWM*).

In the year 2000, Pastor Brandon Porter was appointed International President by Presiding Bishop, Bishop G.E. Patterson.

Bishop Brandon Porter
Eighth YPWW President
*2000 to 2004

Pastor Porter accepted the challenge for global ministry. With visionary goals, he introduced various ministries. He was responsible for the publishing of the first Youth Department magazine-Youth LINC.

Pastor Michael Hill
Ninth YPWW President
*2005 to 2008

Pastor Michael Hill was appointed in January 2005 as the ninth President of the International Youth Department. Pastor Hill's passion for ministry and commitment for excellence has taken the department to a greater level. He built upon the foundation of his predecessors, and has 'lengthened the chords' and extended the arms of youth ministry to reach a changing generation. Pastor Hill has approached this opportunity in a fresh and innovative manner revamping exiting auxiliaries, establishing new programs, and has unveiled a new departmental logo.

He established the first International Youth Council which consists of the young people of the Church Of God In Christ.

Pastor Linwood Dillard
Tenth YPWW President
*2009 to 2013

In the year 2009, Pastor Linwood Dillard was appointed the tenth President of the International Youth Department and Evangelist Joyce Rodgers was re-appointed as Chairlady of the department.

Under the leadership and extensive plan of Pastor Dillard, the department took a quantum leap into the 21st Century, with utilizing technology, a contemporary organizational structure and a *"team"* strategy to meet the challenges of today's youth. Pastor Dillard has proposed and implemented the development of a strategic plan for the department as well as developed commissions to meet the ever changing environment that our youth deal with daily.

Those commissions include Education, Juvenile Crime Prevention and Reduction, recreation and Organized Sports Commission, information Technology, Spiritual Empowerment, College and Career Preparatory, College Campus Ministries.

As in 1914, the political and social climate of the world is full of tensions, even as we have embarked upon a new millennium. Young people are inundated with threats of biological and nuclear warfare. Terrorism and hideous acts of violence plague our nation's schools and communities.

However, with anointed, gifted, executive, administrative teams and a host of committed willing workers, the International Youth Department is well equipped to meet the challenges of global youth ministry.

Pastor Benjamin Stephens, III
Eleventh YPWW President
*2013 to Present

In 2013, Pastor Benjamin Stephens, III was appointed President of the International Youth Department and Evangelist Joyce Rodgers was re-appointed as Chairlady of the department.

Under the creative leadership and visionary plan of Pastor Stephens, the department looks to build on the solid foundation that has been laid in our prosperous history.

Pastor Stephens has a plan to embrace the youth, youth leadership, and parents with innovative ideas that will lead countless souls to Jesus Christ with a belief that these steps will nurture their growth in faith.

On these proposed fundamental and refined techniques given by Pastor Stephens, the International Youth Department is poised to march forward into the future.

History of the Department of Evangelism

Established in 1927

In February of 1927, Bishop C.H. Mason appointed Elder L.C. Page as leader of the "Group of Evangelists" within the Church Of God In Christ. By his own admission, Elder Page did not know the first thing to do, so he just preached the gospel. Bishop Mason later gave Elder Page a second charge in the fall of 1933.

Bishop L.C. Page
First President of Evangelism
*1927 to 1980

He instructed him to organize and supervise the National Evangelist Board. Not long after these instructions, Elder Page began having Evangelist Board meetings in different parts of the country.

The first meeting was held in Memphis, Tennessee around 1937. The early conventions of the Evangelist Board were basically crusades led by Evangelist Page and a few other Evangelist from across the country. Those in attendance were few and the delegates stayed in private homes.

The first year the convention had headquarters in a hotel in 1969, in Dallas, Texas. This was the first convention following Elder D.L. Austin's appointment as the first Convention Chairman in the Boards history. Bishop Page was officially installed as President of Evangelism in 1977. Bishop L.C. Page was a noted soul-winner and these conventions reaped large numbers of converts who received the Baptism of the Holy Ghost.

In 1981, Bishop J.O. Patterson, Sr., appointed Dr. Edward Lee Battles President of the Department of Evangelism. During his administration, Dr. Battles organized Regions to oversee evangelistic ministry in various regional areas across the country.

Dr. Edward Lee Battles
Second President of Evangelism
*1981 to 1996

He also instituted the Annual Prayer Breakfast, conducted Evangelistic Crusades across the country and developed the Church Of God In Christ National Evangelist Crusades across the country and developed the Church Of God In Christ National Evangelist Registry. Dr. Battles served as president until his transition in December of 1996.

In 1997, Bishop Chandler D. Owens appointed Evangelist Richard *"Mr. Clean"* White as President of the Department of Evangelism. Evangelist White continued to seek the Lord in prayer for direction in leading the department to a *"Higher Level of Excellence"*.

Bishop Richard "Mr. Clean" White
Third President of Evangelism
*1997 to 2004

He continued to build on the department through expansion of the Regional Administration into 10 geographical locations across the country.

He appointed Regional Presidents to serve as Liaisons to the Jurisdictional Presidents. Through his leadership and vision he emphasized the importance of *"Deliverance, Development and Demonstration,"* which resulted in a new department theme…*"It's All About Souls!"* Evangelist White stood on the premise that after a soul has received deliverance through salvation, he or she must be taught and trained for spiritual development to become a strong and mature believer.

In 1951, Dr. Reatha Herndon was appointed as Elect Lady of the Evangelist Department. She served faithfully for many years with Bishop Page, Dr. Battles, and Evangelist White. In January 2001, she was emeritized and Evangelist Maria Gardner was appointed International Elect lady by Presiding Bishop Gilbert E. Patterson.

Bishop Patterson also re-appointed Evangelist Richard White as International President. Evangelist White served until his elevation to the Office of Jurisdictional Bishop in 2004. Elder Dennis L. Martin, Sr. was appointed as International President of the Evangelist Department in 2005.

Elder Dennis L. Martin
Fourth President of Evangelism
*2005 to 2009

In 2009, our visionary leader, Presiding Bishop Charles E. Blake, Sr. appointed Pastor Willie James Campbell to the office of President of the International Department of Evangelism and Evangelist Rita Womack as International Elect Lady.

Supt. Willie James Campbell
Fifth President of Evangelism
*2009 to 2013

Through Bishop Campbell's world renowned preaching notoriety, as with former president (*Bishop Richard White*) he would secure the visibility of the department. Supt. Campbell would serve until his elevation to the office of Bishop in 2013.

Supt. Elijah H. Hankerson, III
Sixth President of Evangelism
*2013 to Present

THE TEXAS CONNECTION — AIM Department (Evangelism)

In 2013, Dr. Elijah H. Hankerson, III, was appointed by Presiding Bishop Charles E. Blake, I, as the International President of the Department of Evangelism. Dr. Rita Womack was reappointed as International Elect Lady and Dr. Dorinda Clark Cole was reappointed as Assistant International Elect Lady.

Following the sterling leadership of Presiding Bishop Charles E. Blake the Department's direction is to evangelize the world!

The emphasis is not only on the itinerant *"evangelist"*, but also encouraging every believer to practice *"evangelism."* This has led to a collaborative team approach between Evangelism, different departments and organizations within our Church.
New resources have been created and a new focus to evangelize areas that have not received our distinctive *"COGIC"* approach to the Gospel has come to fruition.

Through the fine tuning of financial procedures the Department has also ventured out into foreign soil to win the lost! **THE FLAME OF EVANGELISM MUST NEVER GO OUT!**

As the newly re-elected Fifth Presiding Bishop and Seventh Chief Apostle in Succession, Bishop Charles E. Blake, I in his fourth term would in a letter dated February 8, 2017, would make known his Quadrennial appointments (2017 to 2020).

He would after much prayer and counsel choose to not reappoint Evangelist Rita Womack as the International Elect Lady. The Assistant Elect Lady, Evangelist Dr. Dorinda Clark-Cole would be elevated to the office of Elect Lady.

Members of the General Board officially installing Bishop L C Page as President of the Department of Evangelism (1977)

(L to R) Bishop J.O. Patterson, Sr., Bishop L.H. Ford, Bishop J.A. Blake, Bishop F.D. Washington and Bishop L. C. Page

Supt. Hankerson was elevated to the office of Jurisdictional Prelate (Bishop) in November of 2015, at the 108th Holy Convocation. This was due to the growth of this district. The name of this new ratified jurisdiction is Missouri Midwest Ecclesiastical Jurisdiction (MMEJ).

Bishop Elijah H. Hankerson, III
Sixth President of Evangelism

Evan. Dr. Dorinda Clark-Cole
Int'l Elect Lady

THE TEXAS CONNECTION   *AIM Department (Evangelism)*

Established in 1927

History of the Department of Missions

Established in 1925

The Home and Foreign Missions Department had its beginning in 1925. The House of Prayer International Home and Foreign Mission Board (*of Portland, Oregon*) was under the leadership of Elder Searcy, who later became affiliated with the Church Of God In Christ. This group remained with the church until June, 1926.

Elder Searcy
Missions Worker
*1925 to 1926

Elder J.R. Anderson
First President of Missions
*1926 to 1937

When the House of Prayer withdrew the small balance that remained in its treasury was given to Bishop C.H. Mason. He was to take disposition of it in the cause of Foreign Missions.

In 1926, upon the recommendation of Mother Lizzie Robinson, Elder C.G. Brown of Kansas City Missouri, was appointed the first Executive Secretary-Treasurer of the Home and Foreign Missions Department by Bishop C.H. Mason.

On December 2, 1926 at our headquarters in Memphis, Tennessee, the Elders' Council met and organized the first Missions board of the Church Of God In Christ. This board consisted of five members, namely:

Elder J.R. Anderson, President, Milwaukee, WI

Elder V.M. Baker, Vice-President, Kansas City, MO

Elder C.G. Brown, Exc. Sec. & Trea., Kansas, MO

Elder C. Pleas, Recording Sec., Kansas City MO

Elder C. Range, Corresponding Sec., Chester, Pa.

Mother L.M. Cox, Representative Trenton, N.J.

The Missions Board met annually at the National Holy Convocation in Memphis or at the request of the Executive Officer; Elder Brown.

In 1927, the call was made for workers to go to serve the Lord in foreign lands. Mrs. Mattie McCaulley of Tulsa, Oklahoma was the first to respond to the call. She was sent to Trinidad, one of the islands of the West Indies. After spending some time there she was then sent to Cristobal, Canal Zone.

She also spent some time in Costa Rica and then returned home. It was during this time while attending the National Convocation that a native of Turks Island, British West Indies volunteered to return to his homeland to minister to his people. He served faithfully for ten years. He transitioned at sea while on a voyage traveling to reach his people.

After the loss of Elder Hall, the work was carried on by Elder R.E. Handfield who had been assistant to Elder Hall. He served in the Turks Island faithfully until his transition in 1949.

In 1929, Miss. Elizabeth White, who had already done three years of service with the Assemblies of God at Cape Palmas, Liberia, became a member of the Church Of God In Christ and volunteered to continue her work in Africa under the banner of the Church. She was sent back to Africa by the Mission Board in 1930.

There she worked alone among the natives at the Bonika Mission Station. As a result of her work, a small congregation was started. The work increased until it was necessary to send another Missionary. Mother Robinson recommended Mrs. W.C. Ragland of Columbus, Ga., to the Mission Board to be the assistant to Miss. White. At the close of the Holy Convocation in 1931, Mrs. Ragland was appointed. In the first part of the year of 1932, she sailed to Liberia, West Africa. Here those two women supervised the erection of a stucco church building; our first in Africa.

After spending four years in the severe heat, Missionary White returned home for a much-needed rest. Missionary Ragland remained in Africa carrying on the work until Missionary White returned in 1935.

In 1937, Miss. Beatrice Lott of Dallas joined the missionaries and a work was began at Tubake and at Wissikeh. When World War II began, and the forces of combat surged around the continent of Africa, the missionaries were called home by the US government to wait until the conflict ended.

While the returned missionaries were busily engaged in ministering in different areas, it was through their inspiring messages that Miss. Dorothy Webster, a teacher in the public schools of Cleveland, Ohio, and Miss. Martha Barber of Chicago, Illinois, felt the call of the Lord to go to the mission field. Miss. Weber was led to choose the Republic of Haiti for her field of ministry, while Miss. Barber went with Miss. Lott back to Liberia.

Also in 1937, the Board reorganized and became known as the Department of Home and Foreign Mission of the Church Of God In Christ. Bishop Samuel Crouch of Los Angeles, California, was appointed president of the Department. Bishop Crouch visited the foreign work and appointed Bishops over various fields.

Bishop Samuel Crouch
Third President of H&F Mission Dept
*1937 to 1968

He set conferences and held them in several states. Bishop Crouch was later joined by Bishop Richard L. Fidler of Racine, Wis., who brought together the work of Cuba and much of the Spanish-speaking people of the Americas. Under Bishop Fidler, *"Mission Outlook"* became the official paper of the Department. He served well with Bishop S.M. Crouch. In 1968, Bishop Crouch was elevated as the Second Assistant Presiding Bishop of the Church Of God In Christ. Bishop S.R. Martin of Seaside, California, was appointed President of the Department of Home and Foreign Missions. Bishop Martin led the Department until 1973, when he was elevated to Jurisdictional Bishop of California N.W.

Bishop S.R. Martin
Fourth President of H&F Mission Dept
*1968 to 1973

In 1939, Overseer A.B. McEwen was appointed Bishop of the Foreign Fields. He later succeeded in having Elder Joseph St. Juste, a native minister, appointed overseer of Haiti, with some 96 churches affiliated with the Church of God in Christ.

After the transition of Overseer St. Juste, Bishop Courtney was consecrated the Prelate of Haiti. He was succeeded by Elder Lopez Dautruche, a native of Haiti. Elder Dautruche was consecrated Bishop of Haiti in 1947. Under his leadership the church grew and has continued to grow. There is now some 42 schools, one orphanage, an apartment complex and over 159 churches.

In 1945, Bishop C. Pleas was appointed Bishop of Liberia. He arrived in Monrovia in September, 1948. He formed an acquaintance with some of the government officials, among whom was his Excellency President Tubman, the President of the Republic of Liberia. He was treated with every courtesy due a prominent executive of the Church.

There was no church edifice or other group in Monrovia. Bishop Pleas set about with Elder Valentine Brown, a native minister of the church and they procured a sight on top of a hill located along Broadway Street to erect a house of worship. In four weeks the walls were completed and the building was ready for roofing.

Bishop Pleas held the first Holy Convocation of the Church Of God In Christ in Africa. In the summer of 1949, Elder O.T. Jones Jr., of Philadelphia was sent to Monorovia to encourage the work. In the same year, Mrs. Francina Wiggins was sent to Liberia to assist Mother White at the Wissikeh Station. Mother Wiggins later went to the Monalu Station and was instrumental in building a church, a school and a mission complex.

Elder Charles Kennedy and his wife Mary Beth went to Liberia in 1959, to serve at Wissikeh where they served the Lord by being in charge of the Mission Station, conducting a school with both elementary and high school levels, a clinic and other needed ministries until they returned home about five years later.

Interim H&F Missions Committee

F.D. Washington **J.A. Blake** **C.L. Anderson**
Chairman **Member** **Member**

In 1973, the Department was then placed under the supervision of an interim committee:

Bishop F.D. Washington, Chairman
Bishop J.A. Blake
Bishop C.L. Anderson

Under this committee, Bishop R.L. Fidler became the Executive Secretary. In November 1975, at the National Holy Convocation in Memphis, TN., with the consent of the General Board, Elder Carlis Moody, Sr., of Evanston, Illinois, was appointed by Bishop J.O. Patterson to be president of the Department of Home and Foreign Missions.

Bishop Carlis Moody, Sr.
Fifth President of H&F Mission Dept
*1975 to 2015

Elder Moody immediately began to reorganize the Mission Department, giving new guidelines. A new mission board was selected. The officers were:

Elder Carlis Lee Moody, Sr. - *President*
Elder J.W. Denny - *Executive Sec.*
Mrs. D.M. Patterson - *Treasurer*
Mr. Oknewa Onwuckewa - *Finance Sec.*
Elder Benjamin Crouch - *Chairman of Finance Committee*
Elder W.W. Covington - *Vice-Chairman of Finance Committee*

Through this board a new organizational structure was established, written, and approved on April 6, 1976; then on November 1, 1977, it was amended.

One of Elder Moody's first task was to visit Haiti and reregister all of the Church Of God In Christ properties. President Moody has been busy checking on the progress of the work on the mission field, and encouraging the support of the national church for missions. He has visited the work in Haiti, Canada, Jamaica, Mexico, Belize, Nassau, Germany, Dominican Republic, Puerto Rico, Virgin Islands, Liberia, Ghana, Nigeria, Panama, England, India, Sri Lanka, Kenya, Columbia, Trinidad, Malawi, Brazil, South Africa and Barbados. President Moody also added these ministries to the mission Department:

1) Youth On A Mission (YOAM) – a ministry of young people visiting the mission field to serve each summer.

2) Student Aid – a ministry of support to foreign students.

3) Touch a Life- Child Support Ministry

4) Nurses Aid Ministry – Nurses taking their skills to the mission field.

5) Sister Church Support Ministry – A church in the USA giving support to a church on the mission field.

6) The Voice of Missions - a bimonthly magazine

In 1983, Bishop Moody, with Mother Irene Oakley, with the help and support of Mother Mattie McGlothen and the Women's Department, began the reconstruction work on a building in Haiti. It was completed in the summer of 1984. This housing unit has ten finished apartments.

The late Bishop J.W. Denny, who was then Elder J.W. Denny the Executive Secretary, worked close by the president's side. A vote of thanks goes to all of the Mission Board Members. They have been a constant source of encouragement to the president.

THE TEXAS CONNECTION — AIM Department (Missions)

After 40 years of faithful and admirable service as the president of the International Missions Department, Bishop Carlis Moody, Sr., would step down. With the approval of the General Board, Bishop Charles E. Blake, Sr., the Presiding Bishop would on February 25, 2015, appoint Bishop Vincent Matthews, Jr., as the new president of International Missions Department.

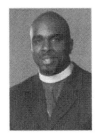

Bishop Vincent Matthews, Jr.
Sixth President of H&F Mission Dept.
*2015 to Present

Bishop Matthews is the Jurisdictional Prelate of South African First Jurisdiction and Pastor of the Tabernacle Church Of God In Christ of Ivory Park, Johannesburg. He brings with him to this new post a heart for missions.

His ambitions to reach men and women around the world for the cause of Christ, will keep the department on task of its mission of *"empowering people to transform their communities."*

His educational accomplishments includes a BA from Wayne State University, an MA from University of Illinois and a Doctorate of Theology from the North Carolina College of Theology.

Bishop Matthews is also the author of six books. Along with his wife Sharon of more than 21 years, they have been fulltime Church Of God In Christ missionaries for more than ten years. This decision to become a fulltime missionary would cost him what was said to be a lucrative career in education.

Bishop C. Moody, Sr. and Bishop Vincent Matthews, Jr. at AIM 2016

The handbook for the Department of Missions

THE TEXAS CONNECTION *AIM Department (Missions)*

Established in 1925

History of the Music Department

Established in 1940

Music in the Church Of God In Christ, has a long and rich history in the church and can be traced back to its very roots.

Like the Church Of God In Christ, music in the church is lead by the Holy One. Elder C. P. Jones and Elder C.H. Mason both authored songs that are still used to this day.

The National Music Department of the Church Of God In Christ, formally began in 1940, in Jacksonville, Florida. Having been impressed by God to pave the way for an organized Music Department, Elder Lawrence C. Patrick, The National Sunday School Superintendent, was given permission by Bishop Mason for this Ministry in song.

Elder L.C. Patrick

Prior to this time, great emphasis was placed upon congregational singing. In fact, it is often stated that "Dad Mason" as Bishop Charles Harrison Mason was affectionately called, did not want formal choirs, because he believed that the congregation would just sit back and allow the choir to do all their singing and eventually all of their praising.

Pioneering officers include Elder L.C. Patrick President, along with Mrs. D.D. Douglass as Vice President. Other Vice-Presidents included Overseer W.D.C. Williams and Elder I.A. Lawrence. Mrs. L.R. Ewing was Recording Secretary and Mrs. E.B. Washington, along with Mrs. W. Turner served as Correspondent Secretaries with Mrs. M. Christian.

The first Choir Director was Elder C.T. James, whose directing style was legendary. Other directors included Mrs. Alice Thomas, Mrs. D. Douglas and Mrs. Deborah Mason Patterson. Instrumentalists were Overseer Williams, Mrs. C.T. James, Mrs. J.O. Patterson (*Deborah*) and Mrs. Shaw. Later Elder James Whitehead, Sr., Mrs. Anna Crockett Ford and others were added to the musical staff. Overseer A.T. Moore was the Director of Recordings.

At this time, choirs were being organized across the nation and especially in the urban areas. In addition, the fame of Rosetta Tharpe and Arizona Juanita Dranes as Gospel Artists, as well as various quartet groups, had reached across the land. The original intent of the organized choir was to glorify God and enhance Worship through inclusion and full participation. Praise and Worship needed to be the personal responsibility of the congregant – and not solely the professional Artist – according to Psalms 34 and 103.

Anna Broy Crockett Ford
President of the National Choir

In 1936, Faides McCardell (*Wagoner*) was asked to begin formation of the Choir. She had worked diligently with Elder C.T. James in California. In 1937, she attended Saints

Industrial School in Lexington, Mississippi with Anna Broy (*Crockett Ford*) – whose mother was a teacher on campus and Dr. Adrenia C. Mallory. Faidest played and trained the school choir on the order of Fisk Jubilee Singers. After Mother Anna Broy Crockett Ford moved to Chicago, Illinois, she was selected to lead the National Choir, along with Bishop Mason's daughter, Mrs. Deborah (*Mason*) Patterson

Her specialty was hymns and anthems. Music Advisors, Emily Bram (*Bibby*), Ernestine Washington, and Jessie Mae Renfro Sapp, were named to assist in the organizing and participation of those outside of Tennessee.

Mother Anna Crockett Ford, along with the late Deborah Mason Patterson, served faithfully in the capacity of President and Director of Music for twenty-five years.

Mrs. Patterson would often say……*"Singing is a ministry; not entertainment. We are the preached word put to music."*

Mother Ford's administrative tenacity laid the foundation (*nationally and internationally*) for her musical successors including Dr. Mattie Moss Clark, Lu Vonia Whittley, Professor Iris Stevenson, and currently, Dr. Judith Christie McAllister. As a composer, she has over two hundred (*200*) gospel songs to her credit.

Simultaneously, Mother Ford served as the Minister of Music in Chicago – at St. Paul Church Of God In Christ, pastored by Bishop Louis Henry Ford.

The division of duties was as follows: Anna Broy directed the choir during the week and Deborah Mason Patterson directed Bishop Mason's Official Day. On Official Day, the Tennessee State Choir was asked to render all the music.

Professor Samuel Flagg played the organ and then eventually turned the reins over to Brother Samuel Spann – who in turn, trained the Tennessee State Choir and played organ/piano, while Deborah Mason Patterson directed.

Madame Ernestine Beatrice Thomas Washington, wife of Bishop Frederick Douglas Washington of Brooklyn, NY was considered the National soloist.

Greatly influenced by Arizona Juanita Dranes, she would sing before the Sermon on Official Day. Often she was accompanied by Alfred Miller (*Organist of Washington Temple Church Of God In Christ, in Brooklyn, NY*). It was not referred to as the "*sermonic solo*" until the administration of Bishop J.O. Patterson, Sr., so named by Jesse Delano Ellis.

As an ardent worker in the Church Of God In Christ Women's Department. Mother Ford served in several capacities under the leadership of the first National Supervisor Mother Lizzie Woods Robinson, who was later succeeded by Mother Lillian Brooks Coffey.

During the tenure of Mother Coffey, she was appointed the Director of Music for the Women's International Convention Choir, as well as the head of the Transportation and Hospitality Committee.

Mother Ford was greatly assisted by her Assistant Directors: Mrs. Vernon Oliver Price, Ms. LaBarbara Whitehead, Ms. Natalie Green Neal, Ms. T. Lynn Smith and others.

Mother worked untiringly through the administrations of Mother Annie L. Bailey, Mother Mattie McGlothen, Mother Emma Crouch and Mother Willie Mae Rivers.

Dr. Mattie Moss Clark
President of Int. Music Dept
1968 to 1994

Dr. Mattie Juliet Moss Clark remains one of the most influential and important figures in the history and progression of gospel music as well as in the history of the Church Of God In Christ. Her legacy has created and helped to shape some of the most successful gospel artists including Vanessa Bell Armstrong, Donald Vails, Commissioned, Esther Smith, Keith Pringle, Rev. Rance Allen, the Rev. James Moore and her own daughters, The Clark Sisters. She taught that one should never try to sing, preach, teach, or reach without prayer and that Christ must always be the center of attraction and the center of one's life.

Born the seventh of nine children to Fred J. Moss and Mattie J. Walker in Selma, AL, she began playing the piano at age six. By 12, she became the musician for mother's services at the Church of Christ and Prayer. After high school, she attended Selma University and received training in classical music and choral singing. In addition, she continued to travel with her mother and play at her mission services.

She moved to Detroit in 1947, to be with her sister Sybil Burke and became a member of Greater Love Tabernacle Church Of God In Christ. There, under the leadership of Bishop W. Rimson, she was baptized in the Holy Ghost and subsequently became the Minister of Music. She served an historic tenure as Minister of Music for both Southwest Michigan Jurisdiction and Bailey Temple Church Of God in Christ, under Bishop John Seth Bailey. Soon she was in demand to train choirs at churches throughout the brotherhood of COGIC. She married her first husband, Mr. Cullum and that union produced two children Leo and Jacqueline. Her next marriage was to Elder Elbert Clark and unto their union four daughters were born, Denise, Twinkie, Dorinda, and Karen.

In 1958, she recorded *"Going to Heaven to Meet the King,"* with the Southwest Michigan State Choir, becoming the first person to commit the sounds of a choir to record. She was also the first person to separate vocal parts into soprano, alto and tenor. She received three gold albums with the Southwest Michigan State Choir, and went on to write and arrange hundreds of songs and record over 50 albums.

She directed Cadillac Motor Company's Christmas choir for eleven years and also conducted community wide mass choirs for the prestigious NAACP Freedom Fund Dinners. In 1979, she founded the Clark Conservatory of Music in Detroit, which established itself as one of the most prestigious schools of its kind in the country.

In 1981, Trinity College in Pennsylvania conferred upon her one of their highest honors, the degree of Doctor of Humanity. After the transition of Bishop Bailey in 1985, she continued as State Minister of Music for Southwest Michigan Jurisdiction No. 1, attending Greater Mitchell Church Of God In Christ, under Bishop J.H. Sheard.

She was also one of the editors and contributors to the hymnal published by the Church Of God In Christ entitled *"Yes, Lord."*

When the late Bishop J. O. Patterson, Sr., appointed her the International President of The Music Department in 1968, she worked to instill within musicians and choirs a responsibility to Christ as well as capability for Christ.

Throughout her efforts, young people especially received her and many were saved, and uplifted by her music and message.

She completely revolutionized the music department. She gave definition to the role of State Minister of Music, traveled year round to every state in the country conducting workshops, rehearsals and musicals to prepare choirs for service on the National Church level and organized the structure of the National Music Convention of the Church Of God In Christ.

Dr. Clark introduced the workshop and seminar concept to the convention, and along with her staff, structured classes for the convention and created *"A Song Is Born,"* the program where new talent was introduced before thousands.

As her health declined, Dr. Clark never lost the fire and passion for her mission, and she learned to give all she had with whatever God gave her and believed He would do the rest.

An accomplished musician, singer, arranger, composer, leader, director, teacher and exemplary woman of God, Dr. Clark transitioned on September 22, 1994.

The legacy of Dr. Mattie Moss Clark is one that will stand as a testament to the anointing of God and his gifts. What she accomplished is matched by only a handful of anointed vessels, cementing her standing as the true "*First Lady*" of gospel music.

Evangelist LuVonia Whittley
President of Int. Music Dept
*1994 to 2000

In 1994, Presiding Bishop Louis Henry Ford appointed Evangelist LuVonia Whittley of Chicago, Illinois to be the National Music President. Evangelist Whittley continued the legacy of her predecessors and brought a level of exceptional administrative organization to the Department.

During the administration of Dr. Mattie Moss Clark, Evangelist Whittley served with Sara Jordan Powell in the Church Of God In Christ National Fine Arts Department for over twenty-five years – as a scholarship judge and as Fine Arts Music Activities Coordinator. She is also credited with organizing the Church's National Orchestra, under the leadership of the late Presiding Bishop J.O. Patterson, Sr.

In addition, she served the National Music Department as Coordinator of the Jurisdictional Presidents & Ministers of Music, and Department Vice-President – along with Madame Bibby.

During her tenure, Dr. Whittley wrote an informative, insightful Music Department resource entitled "*The Choir Member and the Music Ministry*". After her productive term of Presidency, Dr. Whittley continued serving faithfully as AIM Secretary under former AIM Chairman Bishop Jerry Macklin and with Supt. J. Drew Sheard, while serving with Mother Willie Mae Rivers and the International Women's Department as a Jurisdictional Supervisor.

Professor I. Stevenson
President of Int. Music Dept
*2000 to 2008

In the year 2000, Presiding Bishop Gilbert Earl Patterson appointed Professor Iris Stevenson of Los Angeles, California as President of the International Music Department. Professor Stevenson is a scholar, Artist, Music Educator by profession, Activist and a world traveler spreading the gospel message in song. She continued as President until 2008, her notable tenure ending under the leadership of Presiding Bishop Charles Edward Blake, Sr.

During her years of preparation, Professor Stevenson served in many capacities. Dr. Mattie Moss Clark gave her the opportunity of recording her original music, directing and training the choir, writing the Church Of God In Christ hymnal, playing keyboards, playing classical piano for the National Fine Arts Department and the J.O. Patterson, Sr., Grand Orchestra, serving as Music Liaison for the

National Fine Arts Department while working with Sister Sara Jordan Powell.

Professor Stevenson also served as Assistant Director of the Mass Choir, Workshop Clinician throughout the country (*while representing the President*) National Coordinator of the Teen Choir (later the International Youth Choir), Dean of Instruction and Vice President. Dr. LuVonia Whittley fine-tuned her administrative, organizational and re-structuring skills.

Dr. Stevenson believed in a Leadership Team approach; and her Vice-Presidents were Evangelist Barbara E. Jackson, Evangelist Dorinda Clark Cole, Psalmist Bettye Ransom Nelson and Pastor Frank Anthon White.

During the 2004, tenure Psalmist Bettye Nelson was appointed as the Coordinator of the Women's International Convention Choir, thus providing an opportunity for Dr. Judith Christie McAllister to serve as Vice-President with the Leadership Team. Dr. Curtis Lewis was the Dean of Instruction. Dr. Vernard Johnson was the Executive Director of the Instrumental Division and Conductor of the Grand Orchestra.

The Executive Board, at the time, consisted of nearly 225 Jurisdictional Ministers of Music and Presidents, an Executive Staff, an Advisory Board, thirty Regional Coordinators (*including vocal & instrumental*), four Administrative Assistants, Pastor Timothy Wright, Superintendent David Blakely, Sr., Elder Edgar Madison (*who served as Chairman of Finance*) and Brother Mance Aytchan. Dr. Valda Slack served as Executive Director of the Committee on Departmental Excellence; and Dr. Rickey Payton served as the Executive Director of the Office of the President.

Because of the Church's emphasis on Global Ministry, President Stevenson developed cultural exchange programs, sharing through "*Common Ground*" experiences, and spreading the Gospel in the native languages of COGIC constituents from around the world. Church Of God In Christ, Artists have traveled abroad since our beginnings and the mantle of Global Ministry had been placed upon Professor Iris Stevenson since the late '70's Under her leadership, the following programs were implemented:

"Sista 2 Sista", "Go All Out Praise Festivals", "The Soulful Soiree", "It's Yo Time", "Choir Mania", "It's Family Affair", "RE'CHOIR'ED", "A Song is Born"

Unprecedented support for the Local church, District and Jurisdiction was emphasized through the Power-shops, including Class Outlines, designed to empower the Anointed Music Ministry.

The Committee for Departmental Excellence was being established as an outgrowth of the Music Department's Visionary Leadership Forum with the huge responsibility of equipping its Leaders with systems thinking and strategic planning for incredible personal growth and effective leadership.

Professor Stevenson made it possible for Worship Resources to be obtained by access to the web site, www.cogicmusic.com. She focused on Outreach for more souls; In-reach for Church Of God In Christ artists with secular musical careers; and Preservation of the rich musical history through documentation, research and International musical encounters.

**Dr. Judith Christine McAllister
President of Int. Music Dept
*2009 to Present**

During the Leadership Conference held in Phoenix, Arizona in January of 2009, Presiding Bishop Charles E. Blake, I, appointed Dr. Judith Christine McAllister, President of the International Music Department. Dr. Judith

McAllister is probably best known for her impact as one of the forerunners of the Praise and Worship movement in the African American Church.

The Inaugural Celebration for the newly appointed President was celebrated by the international body on Friday September 4, 2009, with *'A Night of Praise and Worship'* at West Angeles COGIC- North Campus at 7:00pm.

On Saturday, September 5, 2009, the celebration continued at the Sheraton Gateway hotel. The events began with various workshops and an Inaugural Celebration Luncheon at 12:30pm.

On Sunday, September 6, 2009, the celebration convened at West Angeles Cathedral for a Morning Worship Celebration where the Presiding Bishop Charles Blake served as the keynote speaker.

Often referred to as *"The First Lady of Praise & Worship,"* she served for 17 ½ years as Worship Leader at the West Angeles Church Of God In Christ *(under Bishop Blake's visionary, exemplary leadership)* and had a 13-year tenure as the church's Executive Director of the Music & Worship Arts Department.

During this term of service, she developed a style and approach to Praise & Worship that has earned her accolades from Coast to Coast.

But more than this, Dr. McAllister is a Wife, Mother, Author, prolific Bible Teacher, Prophetic Psalmist and CEO of 3 ministries.

The first, **Judah Music Incorporated**, serves as the springboard for her recordings – *"Send Judah First"*, *"Raise the Praise"*, *"In His Presence"* and *"Sound The Trumpet.* In 2005, she founded Inheritance of **Judah Ministries International**, thorough which she imparts to the next generation the foundational principles required for the pursuit of excellence in worship ministry.

The newly formed **Never Ending Worship (N.E.W.) Enterprises LLC** serves as the foundation for all of her workshops, seminars and ministry products.

Dr. McAllister stands as a trailblazer, providing a new paradigm for kingdom excellence in ministry; and in addition to mentoring worship leaders all around the globe, her insightful teaching continues to impact the body of Christ by elevating the understanding of *radical, reverent and revelational worship.*

The life of this servant of God is aptly summarized by her personal mission statement:

"To fulfill the purpose of God for my existence to its fullest capacity, to die empty: having maximized every gift, passed on every ounce of wisdom having been blessed to obtain, completed every assignment and accomplished all that God has ordained for my life."

With this mission in mind, Dr. McAllister realizing the urgency of time; has selected a strategic leadership team who has worked faithfully during this administration to fulfill the vision of the Presiding Bishop within the context of the International Music Department.

Included in this team of leaders are – Evangelist Jackson-Sago, (*Memphis, TN*), Elder Edgar (*Petey*) Madison Jr. (*St. Louis, MO*), Dr. Rickey Payton, Sr. (*Washington, DC*) Evangelist Kim Burrell (*Houston, TX*), and the incomparable Pastor Timothy Wright as Vice President Emeritus.

These individuals, along with eight appointed Administrative Assistants *(Elder Zaccheus Hayslett, Elder Michael Virgil, Ms. Cassandra Scott, Pastor Keith Newton, Evangelist Sybil Finney, Dr. Phillip Hall, Elder Kevan Beamon, Evangelist Rosalind Jones)* has lead the International Music Department into a greater level of excellence – in anointing and in approach to music ministry.

The Office of the President was founded under the administration of Professor Iris Stevenson;

and it remains in the current administration to be a source of presidential output to the constituents within the International Music Department.

This sector, led by Executive Director, Evangelist Cynthia Benning (*Buffalo, NY*) with assistants, Minister CJ Faulk (*Atlanta, GA*), Pastor Joseph Lindsey *(Baton Rogue, LA)*, also includes; Executive Director of Administrative Support, Mrs. Nikki Thorpe (*Pittsburg, PA*), Executive Assistant, Evangelist Markita Knight (*Los Angeles, CA*) Assistants Ms. Siantra Richardson (*Nashville, TN*) and Alonzo Graves (*Memphis, TN*) Dean of Education Evangelist Vandalyn Kennedy (*Brooklyn, NY*) and Executive Director of the J.O. Patterson fine Arts Orchestra, Elder Ezra Howard (Starksville, MS).

One of the first appointments under Dr. McAllister's administration was that of Dr. Curtis Lewis to the **COGIC Heritage Singers / IMD Historians**. Dr. McAllister sought out the expertise of this great historian to direct and oversee all aspects of these newly formed musical and educational aggregations. The burning desire within Dr. McAllister's heart, was to create a medium by which the youth of our church would be able *"to partake of their musical heritage"* (*We will not forget from whence we have come*), and bring awareness of and appreciation for those whose shoulders we now stand upon.

Dr. McAllister has also commissioned Dr. Curtis Lewis and his team to compile a written history of the International Music Department, which due to its massive nature, is targeted to be complete by Holy Convocation 2013.

These two aggregations (***COGIC Heritage Singers / IMD Historians***), will serve as a means by which all IMD constituents will learn of and embrace the heritage of the past, while reaching for the promise of our future.

The IMD logo, the development of job descriptions for all executive assignments within the department, the creation of the IMD Leadership Consecration Liturgy and the following Vision/Mission Statement (*predicated on the vision of Presiding Bishop Charles E. Blake*) were all created within the first year of Dr. McAllister's administration; and they are the first of many legacies that she will leave for the music leaders of future generations.

The Vision/Mission Of the International Music Department – COGIC

1. We will promote the authenticity of worship by embracing and fulfilling our roles as Levitical priests.
(***Ezekiel 44:9-11, 15; Ephesians 5:19, Colossians 3:16, I Chronicles 15-16***)

2. We will maintain the fire and exuberance of the former rain, while embracing the promise of the latter rain. (***Proverbs 22:28, I Samuel 7:12, Joel 2:23***)

3. We will centralize our focus on Jesus and His kingdom; and this focus will be the goal of all departmental activities. We will endeavor to remove attention away from man and/or tradition, realizing that the commandment of God take precedence over the traditions of man. (***Mark 7:6-9***)

4. We will embrace the vision set forth by the Presiding Bishop; and each of its Components will be made applicable to all constituents of the International Music Department.
(***Habakkuk 2:2, Hebrews 13:17***)

The current visionary focus includes the following:

a. Spiritual Emphasis
b. Financial Accountability & Integrity
c. Missions
d. Global Interaction Through the Digital Divide (*Internet*)
e. Urban Initiatives
f. Increase in Educational Opportunities

THE TEXAS CONNECTION — AIM Department (Music)

5. Through teaching and mentoring, we will equip each constituent of the International Music Department with the tools necessary to minister with excellence and anointing within their Music & Worship Arts Components (*local churches, districts, regions and jurisdictions*).
(*I Chronicles 15:22, Psalm 33:3*)

6. We will encourage, utilize and bring to the forefront the hidden talents and gifting's of those who serve in our department.
(*II Timothy 1:6*)

7. We will support and encourage opportunities which allow each gift to be utilized to its maximum potential.
(*Proverbs 18:16, Ephesians 3:20*)

8. We will continually endeavor to make the International Music Department the greatest within the brotherhood of believers.
(*I Corinthians 10:31*)

Armed with this targeted vision, her knowledge, experience and a passion for God's presence, Dr. Judith C. McAllister has been equipped to lead the International Music Department, as it embraces the opportunities and challenges that accompany this season of global ministry.

Pastor Timothy Wright

The Clark Sisters

Album Cover from U.N.A.C.-5 C.O.G.I.C.
Title: *A Song is Born*

Pastor Kim Burrell

Dr. Mattie Moss Clark

1990 Album Cover from U.N.A.C.-5 C.O.G.I.C.
Title: *"Go Tell It"*
Live From San Francisco

Richard *"Mr. Clean"* White

Rev. James Moore

The Winans Brothers

These are just some of the products of the
Music Dept.
of the
Church of God in Christ

> *"Singing is a ministry; not entertainment. We are the preached word put to music."*
> **Director Deborah Mason Patterson**

Chapter 2

The Texas Jurisdiction

Chapter 2
THE CHURCH OF GOD IN CHRIST in TEXAS

Where does the Church Of God In Christ get its start in the Great State of Texas? This was the question for me that started the research that caused this book to be compiled.

My novelist style of research lead me to a people with a hunger for a deeper religious experience in this great lone star state called Texas. This experience for a true call to Holiness was made and a group of saints began to gather in Houston, Texas, sometime around the late 1800's.

Some of this group may have also included a remnant of the original Pentecostal movement that was started in the face of the segregated south by Pastor J.W. Seymour and Charles Fox Parham.

Pastor Seymour would find his way to Houston, Texas sometime in 1903, in search of siblings of his parents; whom were sold during slavery times. This search would serve as a catalyst for the Azusa Pentecostal revival awakening.

While in Houston Seymour would find work as a janitor and a place to worship as he believed. The place of worship would be a small holiness church pastored by Lucy Farrow, a freed slave. Farrow was the niece of Frederick Douglas.

In 1899, Charles Fox Parham would hold a New Year's Eve revival at the Bethel Bible School in Topeka, Kansas; in which one of his students requested that she be filled with the Holy Ghost by the laying on of hands.

On one of his visits to Houston, Texas, Charles Fox Parham would ask Pastor Farrow to come to his home in Topeka, Kansas to be the Governess in his home.

Farrow's acceptance of this request to fill this position of Governess created a need for leadership for the church she pastored. This need was met by Minister Seymour. This would be his first pastoral assignment.

After spending a short period of time as the governess for Parham in Kansas, Farrow would return to Houston and visit the church she pastored. She brought back with her the gift of speaking in tongues.

During this same time Parham would come to Orchard, Texas and Houston, Texas. This would be the first time that Seymour would hear the teachings of Parham on this new Pentecostal experience.

At the local request of some of Parham friends, he would move the bible school to Houston, Texas to train workers in the ministry.

On July 13, 1905, Parham and the Bible Training School (*formerly the Bethel Bible School of Topeka, Kansas*) would move to Houston, Texas at 503 Rusk St. in downtown Houston (*the present site of the Federal Courthouse*).

One year and a month after this move, the local paper, the Houston Chronicle would run an article entitled *"Houstonians Witness the Performance of Miracles."* This service was held at the then Bryan Hall.

This article would run in the Houston Chronicle on August 13, 1905.

Houston Chronicle Article
August 13, 1905 edition

Parham is given credit as the founder of the Apostolic Faith Movement and the modern Pentecostal/Charismatic revival. Parham taught the initial evidence of the baptism in the Holy Ghost was speaking in tongues.

Seymour wanted to learn more about this new move of God upon his people. He was ready to spread the word. There was only one problem. Texas and much of the south had laws that separated the races. These segregation laws didn't allow what was called, the *"mixing of the races."*

These widely observed segregation laws would seem to be the barrier that would not allow Seymour to learn this new doctrine. Even though it seemed this would not be, Pastor Seymour would enroll in the Bible Training School in October of 1905.

This enrollment of Pastor Seymour presented a problem for Parham. Due to the laws of Texas, he could not allow Pastor Seymour to sit in the same class with the other (*white*) students. So Parham came up with an inventive way for Pastor Seymour to still get the benefit of his class room teachings on the experience of Pentecost.

The solution was simple, when the class was conducted, Parham would simply leave the door open and Pastor Seymour would sit on the floor outside the classroom to hear the teaching.

It is recognized that Pastor Seymour was a quick study. After hearing and receiving this new doctrine for only a few weeks on the baptism of the Holy Ghost, with the initial evidence of speaking in tongues, he began to teach this new doctrine on his own, *even though at that time he was not a recipient of this experience.*

The segregation laws of Texas again proved to be a problem which caused Seymour's teaching of this new doctrine to be limited to only blacks, but again this would be solved by the joint meetings of Parham and Seymour. In these meetings Parham would address the white audience and Seymour would address the black audience.

This arrangement would seemly work to Parham's advantage, because Parham saw this as an opportunity to reach the African American community in Texas, through Seymour. This would help to spread the Apostolic Faith message among them.

Seymour would carry this message through revivals in Texas, Mississippi and other states.

Charles Fox Parham
"The Leader of the Bible Training School"

William J. Seymour
"The Leader of the Azusa Street Revival"

Little did Parham know that God would use Pastor Seymour to spread more than just the Apostolic Faith message. God would carry Seymour from Houston to California, and this move came about because of a faithful visit of Sister Neely Terry.

Terry was a resident of Los Angeles and a member of the Second Baptist Church in Los Angeles, California. This would lead to the Azusa Street Revivals.

The Anointed Handmaid

Farrow would also go to Azusa to assist Seymour. She was known as the *"anointed handmaid"* because of the ministry of the laying on of hands. The use of this ministry caused many to receive being filled with the Holy Ghost with the evidence of the gift of tongues. She would then go to Portsmouth, Virginia, where 150 would be *"baptized with the Holy Ghost"* at meetings conducted by her.

Lucy Farrow
"The Anointed Handmaid"

Farrow would by December 1906, answer the call to do mission work abroad. This call would be answered when she would first travel to New York and meet up with others on similar journey locations in Africa.

This journey would start for her in Monrovia, Liberia and would settle in Johnsonville, Liberia, a short distance from Monrovia. She would stay in Johnsonville until August of 1907.

(*The saints at the Azusa Mission were said to be the main sponsor of this trip*). As in times before, many heard the message, believed, and were added to the church. Some were healed, sanctified and 20 said to receive the *"baptism of the Holy Ghost."*

By November of 1907, she was headed back to the Azusa Mission. This journey back to the Mission would take her back through Virginia and then the mid-south.

While traveling through the south she would stop over in Littleton, NC and conduct services at one of the Apostolic Mission Church.

Farrow would make it back to the Azusa Mission just before the end of 1907. Upon her return she would continue her ministry work. This work of the ministry was said to have taken place in a small *"faith cottage in the back of the Mission."*

The Mother group of COGIC Saints

The original group of saints were considered as the mother group of the Church Of God In Christ, in Texas. This group was disenfranchised with the religious landscape of the 1900's. This was only a short time after slavery and saints were just one generation removed from slavery, the issuing of the Emancipation Proclamation in 1863, and the passage of the Thirteenth Amendment to the Constitution of the United States.

(*It was June 19th, 1865, and the location is in Galveston, Texas. General Gordon Granger and Union Soldiers have landed in Texas with news that the Civil war was over and slavery had ended. Hence the Annual Juneteenth celebration among African American communities in Texas.*)

The 13th Amendment made slavery illegal for the first time in American History. This newly freed people took with them some of their religious traditions of slavery with them.

This next generation of the newly freed American Negro saints (*as Seymour was*) would meet in Houston with no national structure of leadership. At best, maybe some local leadership and no suitable meeting place.

This reality caused the meeting places of the saints to be of various types, such as a front porch when available, which would serve as the pulpit for an outdoor gathering.

Another such gathering place would be the Brush Harbor. The Brush Harbor was a clearing that slaves would clear to meet in secret to practice their religion *(it was illegal for slaves to practice their religious traditions)*. These traditions of theirs or their parents were still fresh. For they were just a generation or so from the reach of slavery.

Brush Harbor
Artistic drawing

And yet another such meeting place was called the So-so mission, because it was an old saloon called the "*So-So.*" This location was a popular meeting place for the saints in the formative years of the church in Texas.

These disenfranchised saints were former members of organized denominations such as the Baptist, Methodist and other such groups. Many, if not all, of these organized groups were not accepting of these new doctrines of Holiness, Sanctification and Pentecostalism. Many of the saints were dis-fellowshipped from local and state conventions for their beliefs.

Elder D.J. Young
Assigned to the work in Texas
by Bishop Mason

Amongst this new group of saints we find Elder D.J. Young who was born sometime in 1861, in Chester, South Carolina on a small farm owned by his father. He was called into the ministry from early childhood as a member of the African Zion Methodist Church.

He was sent to a country school with his eleven brothers and two sisters. He would be so successful with his studies, that his parents would send him to Brainard College of South Carolina, which a few years later he would graduate from.

After graduation, although quite young, Elder Young would travel to nearby towns ministering where he become known as a quick study and liked by everyone he came in contact with. He was adored by both the young and the old.

As his ministry improved he began to travel through adjoining states to his birth state of South Carolina. Such as North Carolina, Georgia, Alabama, Florida and Mississippi. While traveling for the ministry to Water Valley, Mississippi he would meet and marry Miss. Pricella Louise Jones.

It was shortly after his appointment in Chicago, that God, in His omnipotent power, began to speak to him telling him of a higher life.

Being somewhat exalted in his way and perhaps over his high position, Elder Young hesitated and ignored the voice of God calling him to a higher life. Still, as the Voice continued to trouble him, Elder Young became unsatisfied and greatly troubled and decided to obey the voice of the Lord.

God working in a mysterious way, lead Elder Young to a band of sanctified people, better known as the *"Burning Bush"* people. He remained with them about two years.

It was while he was with this religious sect that Elder Young became sanctified. After receiving a new light, he began to evangelize, telling of the wonderful new light which he found.

He traveled far and near preaching conversion and sanctification to people everywhere. In his evangelistic travels he came to Memphis, Tenn; where he met Elder C.H. Mason and Elder C.P. Jones, who were also sanctified preachers.

After his acquaintance with Elder C.H. Mason, Elder Young made his temporary home in Memphis, but continued his ministerial work in Tennessee and Arkansas.

While in Arkansas doing evangelistic work, he came to Pine Bluff, Arkansas where he moved his family a little later.

In the meanwhile, Elder Young heard of a great revival in Los Angeles, California. As the news of it was spreading far and wide, he decided to go to Los Angeles to see what it was about.

In company with Elder C.H. Mason and others, Elder Young went from Pine Bluff, Arkansas to Los Angeles, California to attend this great revival.

One day as he sat in the revival, the Holy Ghost came as a mighty rushing wind and baptized many with the Holy Ghost and with fire.

Being overjoyed of the greatest light which he had found, Elder Young returned to Pine Bluff, Arkansas preaching the gospel in its fullness and purity, in which many believed.

He was made the first pastor of the new church which sprang from the sanctified Church. In this office he worked and discharged this duty to the best of his knowledge.

As the truth began to spread, God burdened Elder Young's mind with the thought of spreading it far and wide by means of a religious paper called the *"Whole Truth."*

This paper was sent all over the world to foreign countries as well as over the United States.

After pastoring in Pine Bluff, Arkansas for seven years, God sent him to Beaumont, Texas. Here he was pastor of a small band of fifty members.

Elder Young was favored through God with an increase in membership to about two hundred and fifty members.

Having proved faithful in discharging his duty, Elder Mason appointed him to oversee the work in Texas. He would remain overseer for a while but finally gave it up in favor of the Elder E.M. Page.

Soon after his resignation Elder Young began to do evangelistic work in various parts of the north.

In 1916, Elder Young came to Kansas City and started a church in Kansas City, Kansas. He was very successful. Later he was appointed overseer of Kansas, where he served until he was forced to resign on account of ill health.

In the spring of 1916, Elder Young was appointed by Elder Mason as publisher and manager of the Sunday School literature of the Church Of God In Christ.

The Saints in Houston
The Mother Group

The saints in Houston would eventually organize themselves in to a legally recognized congregation and call the name of the church First Church Of God In Christ.

This Church was often called Center Street Church Of God In Christ and many thought that this was the name of the church.

First Church Choir 1943 Bishop JH Galloway, Pastor (seated) located 3014 Center St Houston, TX

In 1916, the official building was erected at 3014 Center Street. Since the church was located on Center Street it was often times call Center Street Church.

The First Pastor of this Church was Elder Willie Harris and he served as Pastor from 1911 until 1918 and it is from this point we start the history with the personal history of the first appointed Bishop of Texas.

Bishop Emmett Moore Page
First Bishop of Texas 1914 – 1944
Diocese #1

Emmett Moore Page was born on May 19, 1871, on a farm in Yazoo County Mississippi to Mr. Richard Page and Mrs. Polly Ann Page. He was converted in 1884, when he was only 13-years-old. He was a member of the Union Paradise African Methodist Episcopal Church in Yazoo County Mississippi (*although at this time neither of his parents was converted*).

Even though Richard and Polly were neither converted, nor active members of a church, they still instilled in their children to pray each night and in the morning; to go to Sabbath School; and to church for worship.

At the age of 23-years old Emmett, was ready to experience more of life than what the simple farm life of his birth place could offer. So sometime in 1894, he would leave the farm at Yazoo County Mississippi and head for the city life of Jackson, Mississippi.

No account is given of his early or late childhood schooling, but during his residence in Jackson, Mississippi he was able to enroll and attend College at Lane College. Sometime later Emmett was employed by ICR (*Illinois Central Railroad*). ICR would remain his employer for many years thereafter.

In October of 1902, Emmett would receive the experience of sanctification. A Brother Milan preached that one must live a clean life and receive divine healing, but as Emmett would later testify *"……..but he did not preach the whole gospel. But it was so much richer than any I had ever heard, so I accepted it."*

By the following year Emmett would met another preacher preaching a message of Holiness. It is now 1903, Emmett would travel to Memphis, Tennessee where he would meet as he described him, *"precious Elder C.H. Mason."* He would later testify Elder Mason was teaching a message that was blanketing the south at that time, the message of Holiness.

The following is Emmett's testimony of the message he heard preached by Elder Mason: *"I shall not forget the first sermon I heard Brother Mason preach on Virginia Ave. Memphis, Tennessee. His text was, He has translated us into the kingdom of His dear Son."*

This God arranged meeting of these two men of God had a great impact on the life of Page. The impression of Mason on the life of Page was so great until he moved to join the Holiness movement of Mason, that of the Church Of God In Christ (*Holiness*) and support the work faithfully in all aspects.

Mother Molly Page
Wife of Bishop E.M. Page

Page would soon realize his call into the gospel ministry, but he didn't openly confess it. By 1907, two great growth changes came in his spiritual life. In his own words, *"In 1907, the Lord baptized me with the Holy Ghost and fire. Amen" …..and when He baptized me my heart was made willing, and I said, yes to God."*

Also during this time there was a new movement that would have a lasting and life changing effect on those that were members of the Holiness movement named the Church Of God In Christ (*Holiness*).

This change would happen when Page's new mentor and spiritual leader, in the person of Charles Harrison Mason, would be lead to attend the Azusa Street Revival held in Los Angeles, California.

The Bible Training School (then)
503 Rusk St Houston TX

Bob Casey Federal Building (now)
515 Rusk St. Houston, TX

There at the Azusa Street Revival, Elder Mason would receive the baptism of the Holy Ghost with the evidence of speaking in tongues. This new Pentecostal experience for Mason would forever change his life and those who were his contemporaries.

Upon his return to Memphis, Mason would come home preaching this new doctrine of Pentecostalism and he also saw a need to incorporate this into the holiness message. This decision and message was not met with agreement by all.

A group within the Church Of God In Christ (*Holiness*) led by its General Overseer Elder

C.P. Jones, felt that this was a delusion, and Jones and others decided to withdraw the right-hand of fellowship from Mason and all those that believed as Mason did.

This move by Jones and others would cause Mason to make a call of all those that believed as he did to come to Memphis, Tennessee for a meeting.

This was a call that organized the *(Pentecostal)* Church Of God In Christ. Among those that answered the call and were present at this meeting that were departing from what was then the standard of Holiness belief, to include with its practice and belief, the addition of a Pentecostal experience was Emmett Moore Page.

Page and others stood as part of the original sixty charter members of the *(Pentecostal)* Church Of God In Christ.

(Although Jones was the General Overseer of the (Holiness) Church Of God In Christ, Elder Mason was the register agent and the incorporator of the organization.)

At this meeting Elder Mason was elected as the General Overseer and Chief Apostle of the *(Pentecostal)* Church Of God In Christ. He was given complete authority by the general Assembly to establish new auxiliaries of the church and was given the authority to establish doctrines for the church and appoint State Overseers (*Bishops*).

These first appointments were Dr. Hart for Tennessee; Elder J Bowe for Arkansas and sometime later he appointed another, the Elder J.A. Lewis for the state of Mississippi. Elder Page was one of what was called a blazer of the Church Of God In Christ, he was one of the men who blazed the way.

While he was working on a secular job he was also working for the church on the weekends. During the weekends Elder Page would work out churches and preach. Because of diligent efforts of men like Elder Page, the Church Of God In Christ began to grow.

It is now 1911 and by this time the work had grown enough so that Page was able to quit his regular fulltime job and go into the ministry full-time in the Memphis area.

By 1914, the Church Of God In Christ had grown so much and so in other areas and regions of the country that this growth caused the following appoints to be made to the office of State Overseer's: Elder E.M. Page for Texas; Elder R.R. Booker for Missouri; Elder E.R. Driver for California and a few years prior Elder W.B. Holt as National Field Secretary.

The appointment of Bishop Page to Texas by Bishop Mason would occur in later 1913. Bishop Page would later state about this appointment to Texas. *"It hurt me so bad to think of going to Texas." "But after humbling myself before the Lord for five hours in prayer, the Lord spoke to my soul and I said: Yes, Lord! Not one moment did I resist anymore."*

In January of 1914, Bishop Page would leave Memphis, Tennessee headed for Texas. Page would make it to the Dallas, Texas area by the evening of January the 27th, 1914. He would meet with the saints who were happy to welcome him and in his words, *"to take charge of the work at Dallas, which was in a backslidden state, being without proper attention."* (*Bishop Page was sent to oversee the work in Texas, that was formerly headed by Elder D.J. Young*)

Upon his arrival in Texas the work consisted of some churches, a number of missions and a few buildings. Bishop Page had a God given mandate to ensure the growth and success of the Church Of God In Christ in Texas.

Bishop Page would further note: *"For five months I labored, without leaving my Church to go anywhere. More than 100 persons were saved and reclaimed."*

In May of 1914, Bishop Page took with him a small band of workers to Waco, Texas. He would state of this trip that *"the Lord broke through and saved one hundred and twenty-five souls in six weeks."*

In July of 1914 Bishop Page would host his first State Convocation as the State Overseer in Houston, Texas. He would state concerning this meeting, *"Again In this meeting the Lord saw fit to appoint me as overseer of Texas through our Chief Apostle."* He would further state about his appointment *"To me that was the worst mistake I thought Elder Mason made. I had several hearty cries about it but, went doing the best I could."*

In the face of the segregation laws that spilled over into discrimination of every facet of the newly freed American Negro, Bishop Page would set out to accomplish his mandate by using two mediums. First, starting a school to educate and secondly, a monthly state wide distributed tabloid.

The school would be aptly named the Page Normal Industrial School and Bible Institute (*it was later called the Page Industrial and Literary School*). The Page School would find its home just outside of Hearne, Texas on Henry Prairie Rd.

The school's focus of education for those that attended would be the need for one to be both scripturally equipped and to achieve success in the secular world by using the vehicle of education. Bishop Mason would show his support for the school by sending his son Bob Mason to attend the Page Industrial School.

Bishop Mason and Bishop Page

Bishop Mason and Bob Mason
At the Page Industrial School

In 1932, the school would experience a loss to its facilities due to a fire.

Page School
Class of 1931

Page School
Class of 1933

This fire would not detour the will and drive of Bishop Page and the people. They would work hard to raise funds to restore this great work.

As aforementioned also during this time Bishop Page would start the communication medium for the new Texas Jurisdiction (*Diocese One*) the first jurisdiction of Texas. This medium would be called The Texas Bulletin.

A monthly magazine to keep the Texas saints informed of what was going on in the jurisdiction. This monthly publication was the first of its kind. It was an affordable way for the leadership of this new jurisdiction to keep its members informed on the church and the school.

The bulletin would prove affordable at the then low rate of only $1.00 for a full year's subscription. Assistant State Overseer Galloway would give recaps of the instruction given at the school. Overseer Galloway would also offer practical preaching tips and techniques that still hold firm even today.

Bishop Page would found and pastor the Page Temple Church Of God In Christ at 3204 Thomas Ave. Dallas Texas.

As he would later state, *"This meeting was quite a coming together of the Lord's people."* By 1919, Bishop Page would report that *"These five years I have endeavored to prove my works. ......The Spirit, through our chief apostle, appointed me as State Overseer. Thank God, I can say I have not caused him to regret the appointment. ... In five years we had about eighty churches and missions and about thirty-five or more creditable churches. The church property at Dallas and Houston is worth $20,000. All the glory to our blessed Christ. Pray for brother Page that I may keep in the center of His will."*

This growth was continued and by 1925, the Church Of God In Christ in Texas numbered some 135 congregations. Bishop Page would report 150 ministers (*50 local Elders and licensed preachers*) and at least four evangelistic women helpers. These areas of growth would include: *Abilene, Amarillo, Bastrop, Beaumont, Blooming Grove, Bonham, Brenham, Bryan, Cleburne, Como, Conroe, Crockett, Dallas (Oak Cliff), Denison, Electra, Ennis, Fairbanks, Farmerville, Ferris, Fort Worth, Franklin, Galveston, Garland, Grayburg, Silsbee, Hillsboro, Houston, Jasper(Honey Island), LaFrange, Lincoln, Magnolia, Magnolia Springs, Marshall. Maypearl, Nacogdoches, Nolan Orange, Palestine(West Side), Paris, Plum Port Arthur, Prairie, Rosebud, Sulphur Springs, Tehuacana, Trinity, Wichita Falls and Waxuhachie.*

The Lord, through my earnest labor with my brethren, has brought the work from twelve churches to more than one hundred churches in these eleven years. Many thousand souls have been saved, church houses built, 268 acres of school land bought and paid for, and school being erected.

I am glad to say Texas produced good preachers and well trained men, which shows for itself. I have had eleven State Convocations and raised $18,308.58

We have held eleven ministers' and workers meetings and raised $10,265.91 and we raised $10,150.00 for the State in 1925. Making a grand total of $38,825.19 Thank the Lord for all he has done for us. I have not looked for myself I have looked for the people.

The Lord moved me to go to Oklahoma in 1917, the church at Muskogee was established, Tulsa was revived and also Sand Springs and Shawnee, where they burned two houses to get the holiness out of town.

Went to Oklahoma City and there founded another good church which stands as one of the leading churches in the state today.

With the cooperation of my elders and workers in Oklahoma, the state is going to the top. We purchased one whole block of land in Oklahoma City for our state headquarters, built a large tabernacle where thousands are gathered all the summer, also large kitchen and dining room, well furnished with enamel plates and cups to match, with knives and forks. Watch Oklahoma. We are workers and not shirkers.

The national Church Of God In Christ recognized Bishop Page's accomplishments

THE TEXAS CONNECTION — COGIC in Texas

and his selection by Bishop Mason as one of the original five Bishops of the Church Of God In Christ. This was not known by many but the original name of his jurisdictional territory was called *"Diocese One"* which covered Texas, Oklahoma, Kansas, Western Missouri, Eastern Illinois, Iowa and the State of Wisconsin.

He served the church well during his tenure as Jurisdictional Prelate of Texas and these other regions. His service as Bishop was with distinction and integrity. Bishop Page's services as the first Prelate of Texas had seen the growth in Texas of the Church Of God In Christ grow from one Jurisdiction in Texas in 1914 to the present day count of 19 Jurisdictions.

Bishop E.M. Page's health began to fail him in 1939. He went from labor to reward on Tuesday, January 4, 1944, at St Paul Hospital. His Home-going Celebration was held on Wednesday, January 12, 1944, at Page Temple Church Of God In Christ on Thomas and Ellis in Dallas, Texas. Bishop C. H. Mason was the eulogist.

The State of Texas

The Flag of Texas

Bishop Page Church in Oklahoma

Church Of God In Christ
212 North Byars Street
OK City, OK
Bishop E.M. Page, Pastor

The State of Oklahoma

The Flag of Oklahoma

Bishop Mason at the pulpit
Bishop Mason Eulogizing Bishop Page
At Page Temple January 12, 1944

Bishop Page's funeral notice

Bishop Page Funeral Set for Wednesday

Churchmen are gathering in Dallas from several states to join Texans in the last rites for Bishop E. M. Page whose funeral will be held Wednesday noon at the Church of God in Christ, Thomas and Ellis. Senior Bishop C. H. Mason, Memphis, Tenn., will deliver the eulogy. Bishop Page died Tuesday at St. Paul Hospital.

He was Overseer of Diocese No. 1 which included Texas, Oklahoma, Kansas, Western Missouri, Eastern Illinois and Iowa. He was 72 and had been in failing health since 1939. He lived in Dallas twenty-nine years and was head of the church where the funeral will be held.

Bishop Page is survived by five daughters: Morley, Ruby, Pearl, Louise and Charliaemason Page; two sons, Lieut. M. R. Page of the United States Army Air Forces and R. S. Page, who has followed in his father's footsteps twenty-two years. His passing is also mourned by twenty-three other close relatives now serving in the United States armed services.

Henderson-Wren funeral directors for Negroes will be in charge.

The resting place of Bishop and Mother Page

Bishop and Mother Page's headstone

Bishop Emmit Moore Page 1871 to 1944

Mother Mollie Page 1874 to 1956

The next leader of Texas

The next Leader of the work in Texas was the assistant Bishop to Bishop E.M. Page in the person of Bishop J. H. Galloway.

Joseph Houston Galloway was born in 1891, to the proud parents of Wesley Galloway and Josephine Clegg Galloway in Pine Bluff, Grant County, Arkansas.

Bishop J.H. Galloway
Second Bishop of Texas 1944 – 1951
Texas Jurisdiction

Not much is known about his education or work history. The little we do know about his education is that he received his education from the rural school system there in Grant County.

He was saved at an early age and was a member of his local African Methodist Episcopal Assembly.

He later joined a local Church Of God In Christ under the pastorate of Elder D.M. Welch which was located in Malvern, Arkansas. He was setting a pattern in his walk that earned him honor and respect as a local member of the Church Of God In Christ for 29 years.

This honorable walk was furthered when in 1912 Brother Joe Galloway acknowledged his calling to a greater work of service, that of the preaching the gospel.

Bishop J.H. Galloway

Three years after acknowledging this life changing call Rev. Joseph Houston Galloway met and fell in love with Miss. Elma Mildred Wade.

Mrs. E. M. Galloway
wife of Bishop J.H. Galloway

On August 3, 1915, in Dallas, Texas Rev. Joseph Houston Galloway married Miss. Elma Wade. Bishop E. M. Page officiated and also served as the witness to the marriage. This union was blessed with the birth of nine children (*6 boys and 3 girls*).

The 25th wedding Anniversary march of Bishop and Mrs. Galloway at First Church Of God In Christ Houston, Texas.

Mrs. Elma Mildred (*Wade*) Galloway was born in 1896, to Lewis Wade and Emma J. (*Koontz*) Wade in Texas. Mother Galloway has been described as *"the good wife"* and *"faithful mother"* who is credited with educating the first five of their children, the latter four were enrolled in school.

She would start her Christian experience in 1911, when she was converted under the ministry of Rev. F.F. Bosworth. She was a faithful member of the St. Paul A.M.E. Church. She would later convert to the Church Of God In Christ under Rev. Eddie Scott. Her church work has been described as a *"serviceable Christian"* and a *"faithful worker and lover of her church."*

She has been further described as possessing a loving disposition, a pleasant personality, plus many friends. She stood very high in her community and church circles, locally and nationally. Mother Galloway would serve faithfully by Bishop Galloway side in the Ministry. Bishop Galloway would describe her as a *"true and faithful wife for 25 years and an inspiration and wonderful helper in the church work."*

His call was further acknowledged in 1917, when Rev. Galloway was ordained into the gospel ministry by Bishop Charles Harrison Mason, the Senior Bishop of the Church Of God In Christ.

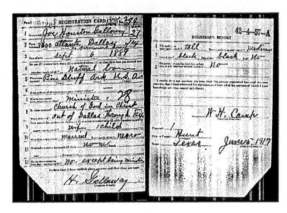

Registration Card from Hunt, Texas filled out and signed on June 5, 1917 by Bishop Galloway. He lists his occupation as a minister of the Church Of God In Christ.

The spirit filled, God given sermons of Elder Galloway was said to have *"edified the most highly educated and feeds the most humble."* His leadership ability was described as the *"essentials for good leadership"* and he was loved and respected by many; said to be *"a humble man"*.

Bishop Galloway (center) with four of his nine children (6 boys, 3 girls)

He was further described as *"a wonderful personality,"* which *"can be counted on as a true friend,"* *"conscious of his work"* and *"honest and upright in all his dealings."*

Before being elevated to office of State Bishop, Elder Galloway held many important positions in the church, both locally and nationally.

One of these positions in the national church was the editor of the Church Of God In Christ's largest and national self-published newspaper, *"THE WHOLE TRUTH,"* for a number of years.

Other national positions held by Elder Galloway was that of secretary of the National Publishing Board, recording secretary of the Home and Foreign Mission Board. He was also the president of the National Benevolent Burial Association.

Certificate of Membership
For the National Benevolent Burial Association of the Church Of God In Christ

Bishop Galloway *was the founding President of the Association in 1918*

He was also one of the instructors at the Page School in Herne, Texas and a contributor and editor of the *"Texas Bulletin,"* the jurisdictional newspaper.

As the editor, Galloway would instruct ministers in the Texas region via *"The Texas Bulletin."*

Bishop Galloway who lived in Houston would suggest that a sermon should only last for 30 to 35 minutes at the most. He would also suggest that the Pentecostal art of a closing should include (1) knowing when to close the sermon. (2) Never close a sermon lower than you started, and (3) close the sermon when it is at its peak.

He would also prescribe *"learn to build your sermon"* and *"don't start off too rapidly, but build up to your climax, then close."* Bishop Galloway would then instruct: *"Let's quit boring our people,"* *"if we don't, we will not have anybody to bore."*

Sometime in 1931, Elder Galloway would become the third Pastor of the First Church

Of God In Christ (*also known as the Center Street Church*).

On the state and local level Elder Galloway was appointed as the pastor of the oldest Mother COGIC church in Texas that of First Church Of God In Christ, located at 3014 Center Street, Houston, Texas 77071. *(Often referred to as the Center Street Church, because of its location).*

Elder Galloway was also selected by Bishop E. M. Page as the assistant Bishop of Texas. He also served as the chairman of the General Council of Texas.

In 1931, Galloway Tabernacle COGIC was established in San Antonio, Texas, after Bishop J.H. Galloway conducted a 90-day tent revival in the city (*renamed Blue Bonnet COGIC in 1936 and later renamed Childress Memorial COGIC*).

Upon the transition of Bishop E. M. Page on Tuesday January 4, 1944, Bishop C.H. Mason appointed Bishop J. H. Galloway of Houston, Texas, as the new State Bishop of Texas.

Bishop Galloway served faithfully in this position as State Bishop from 1944 until his transition in 1951.

The Start of the Women's Work in Texas
Hannah Chandler was a convert of the Methodist Episcopal Church at an early age. The Methodist Church was the first organized African American religious group of people that taught and practiced sanctification. These doctrines were taught to Chandler by her pastor.

Mother Hannah Chandler
First Supervisor of Dept. of Women
Appointed by Mother Lizzie Robinson
*1914 to 1944

Chandler accepted these teachings and was ready for the next step in her religious walk with God. The next step was the *"Baptism of the Holy Ghost."* The year is now 1910, and Emma James of Memphis, Tennessee is visiting Dallas on an evangelistic missionary journey.

While on this mission, James would introduce the doctrines of being baptized and filled with the Holy Ghost. Chandler would later recall *"I never heard this teaching before."* It was *"expounded in such a simple way...."*

James would explain that after being sanctified, the next step was the *"baptism of the Holy Ghost."* After teaching, James would then start *"begging God"* to baptize Chandler with the Holy Ghost.

Chandler would return to her church with her new spiritual work that the Lord had done in her life.

Chandler's excitement about her new experience was met with opposition that many of her day felt. She was rejected by the leaders of her church due to her acceptance of this new doctrine and being baptized with the Holy Ghost.

She was excommunicated from the Methodist Episcopal Church. After that she would then join James on a similar evangelistic mission trip to Tyler, Texas.

There was a great out pour on Chandler's first mission trip with James. It was said of this trip that the *"Lord gave...a great field of labor"..."many souls were saved and added to the church."*

In Little Rock, Arkansas Chandler would attend the Church Of God In Christ State Convocation also in that same year of 1911.

She would attend her first of many trips to Memphis, Tennessee for the 5th Annual National Church Of God In Christ Convocation.

Chandler would serve faithfully in various areas of the church. Her service would include, among other things, all areas of need. This would include both spiritual and physical labor. She would truly adhere to the saying of *"whatever your hands find to do."*

She would do her part, from first naturally, as the church janitor, and then spiritually, as an evangelist. Her hard work and faithfulness didn't go unnoticed. She would receive a letter that would forever change her life and responsibilities.

These new responsibilities would add a new job title to her resume. Chandler was honored with the new awesome appointment as State Mother of the Women's Work in Texas.

This new jurisdiction would be called Diocese No. 1. *(Which would include Texas, Oklahoma, Kansas, Western Missouri, Eastern Illinois and Iowa).*

She would say about reading the letter of appointment, that she would become *"almost unnerved"* by the announcement which came as a total surprise. It would make her immediately start *"praying to the Lord, to give wisdom,"* to do this new and challenging position.

Mother Chandler would record, *" I went into with all my heart."* (She would join the newly appointed Jurisdictional Overseer, Bishop E.M. Page in proselytizing the message of the Church Of God In Christ in Diocese No. 1.)

Below is a part of the testimony of Mother Chandler recorded in year book of 1926:
"I have worked these eleven years with Elder Page and we have not had any trouble at all. We are glad to say that women's work is well organized in Texas."

Mother Chandler would serve as the State Mother for Texas and Oklahoma. Mother Chandler would serve faithfully until her transition in 1944.

Upon the transition of Mother Chandler, Bishop Galloway would appoint one of her assistants, Mother Bertha M. Polk to be the next Supervisor of Texas.

Mother Polk would serve in this position with Bishop Galloway until his transition in 1951, and she would continue as State Supervisor when Bishop Mason, the Senior Bishop of the Church Of God In Christ would serve as the interim Bishop of Texas from 1951 until 1956.

Texas is divided
Four new Jurisdictions are formed

THE TEXAS CONNECTION   COGIC in Texas

After the transition of Bishop Galloway in 1951, the then State Secretary of Texas Pastor R.E. Ranger described the work in Texas in a letter to Bishop C.H. Mason as a *"Tent without a top on it."*

The work in Texas had grown so vast in number of churches, comprising of four to five hundred, that the need of more presiding officers (*Bishops*) became a necessity.

The decision by Bishop Mason to split this one jurisdiction into four jurisdictions was ratified by the General Assembly of the Church Of God In Christ and enacted by the Executive Commission of the church.

The then Commission members were Bishops A.B. McEwen, J.S. Bailey, S.M. Crouch, O.M. Kelly and O.T. Jones, Sr.

The Four new Bishops of Texas

Bishop F.L. Haynes
Texas Northeast

Bishop R.E. Ranger
Texas Southeast

Bishop T.D. Iglehart
Texas Southwest

Bishop J.E. Alexander
Texas Northwest

Bishops pictured at Mason Temple includes two Texas Bishops. (Left to right) Bishop John White, Bishop E.E. Hamilton, Bishop Barker, Bishop L.H. Ford, Bishop F.L. Haynes-Texas NE, Bishop R.E. Ranger-Texas SE and row behind Ranger Bishop Bradford.

The New Supervisors of Texas

Mother Bertha Polk
Texas Northeast

Mother Fern Smith
Texas Southeast

Mother Bertha Polk
Texas Southwest

Mother Emma Crouch
Texas Northwest

The new Jurisdictional Prelates of Texas would hold a combined State Convocation as one jurisdiction on April 23-29, 1956 at the Buck Street COGIC. The four new bishops of Texas would be consecrated on December 10, 1956, to their new jurisdictions.

Texas is divided
Four new Jurisdictions are formed
1956

The home of Bishop F.L. Haynes at 713 Bailey St Denton, TX

COGIC in Texas is divided into 4 Jurisdictions
December 10, 1956

Bishop J. E. Alexander
Texas Northwest

Bishop F. L. Haynes
Texas Northeast

Bishop F.L. Haynes and Elders at Page Temple

Bishop T. D. Iglehart
Texas Southwest

Bishop R. E. Ranger
Texas Southeast

Flyer for the first
Inter Jurisdictional Convocation
Of the Texas Jurisdictions

Mother Polk's funeral at Page Temple

While researching the history of Church Of God In Christ in Texas the Lord allowed me to meet one of Bishop J.H. Galloway's granddaughters.

After I explained this project to her and the historical story I wanted to record, she provided some of her family pictures of Bishop and Mother Galloway's home which was located in the Third Ward Area of Houston.

At the time I lived only a few blocks from the location of the Galloway family home. I was so excited when she emailed me the pictures that I walked the few blocks over to find their family home.

It was located a few blocks from Texas Southern University. Upon my arrival to the location many things had changed.

The original home in the pictures no longer existed, but I could make out some of the features of the property I saw in the pictures.

The following seven pages feature this magnificent Galloway family home. Thanks to the Galloway family for allowing us to share this rich pictorial history with the world.

Following the pictures of the Galloway family home are other pictures of Bishop and Mother Page; Bishop and Mother Galloway and other early Texas histories.

Pictures connected to that history include the church Bishop Galloway pastored on Center Street. The church was renamed by its current Pastor Supt E.E. Hamilton, Sr., to Greater First COGIC.

Elder Hamilton was appointed to this church in 1982 by Bishop R.E. Woodard, Sr. The Center Street property was sold due to the unrepairable condition of the building and a new building was built in 1986, on Deams Street just north of Fifth Ward.

The Home of

Bishop Joseph Houston Galloway and Family

2602 Barbee Street Houston, Texas 77004

(*3 blocks from Texas Southern University*)

The residence of Bishop Joseph Houston Galloway and family

Dining room of the Galloway Family

Living Room of the Galloway Family

Morning Porch of the Galloway home

Kitchen of the Galloway Home

The side bedroom of the Galloway home

Bishop Galloway's bedroom during his illness

Master bedroom in the Galloway home

The Attic in the Galloway home

The side lawn of the Galloway home

The First and Second Bishop of Texas

The Page's

Bishop E.M. Page
1st Prelate of Texas

Mother M. Page
wife

The Galloway's

Bishop J.H. Galloway
2nd Prelate of Texas

Mother E.M. Galloway
wife

34th Holy Convocation Official Program

Some of the first Bishops of COGIC with the Mayor of Memphis.
(L to R) Bishop E.M. Page – Dallas, TX
Bishop R.F. Williams – Cleveland, OH
Senior Bishop C.H. Mason – Memphis, TN
Bishop Walter Chandler – Memphis, TN
Bishop WM Roberts- Chicago, IL
Bishop O.T. Jones, Sr. – Philadelphia, PA

Other notable Women from Texas

When Bishop Mason appointed 4 new Bishops to the work in Texas, Mother Bertha Polk, who was the second State Supervisor of Texas would serve as the first State Supervisor of two of the new four jurisdictions. These two jurisdictions were Texas Northeast and Texas Northwest.

Also appointed was Mother Fern Smith as the first State Supervisor for Texas Southeast and Mother Emma F, Crouch as the first State Supervisor for Texas Southwest.

Counted as some of the other notable women in the Church Of God In Christ, with a Texas Connection, was the fourth General Supervisor Mother Mattie (Clark) McGlothen of Tehuacana and Mexia, Texas.

Mother Nancy Gamble, another notable woman, was born in 1873 in Arkansas eight years after the end of slavery. She was saved and sanctified in Tyler, Texas. She would go on to be the first mother of Illinois.

Mother Emma Frances (Searcy) Crouch was born in Texas to Mr. and Mrs. Searcy and she would be the fifth General Supervisor.

First Church Of God In Christ Choir – 1943
Bishop J.H. Galloway
3014 Center Street • Houston, Texas 77007

First Row Left to Right: *Sis Thelma Baker, Sis Gussie Robinson, Sis Loretta Logan, Mother Elma Galloway, Pastor - Bishop J.H. Galloway, Corrine Price, Lillie Marilyn Williams, Ceola Williams*

Second Row: *Rev. Butler of Chicago, Choir Director - Erma Galloway Ighner, Sister Lonella Williams, Ben Hillard, Eunice James, Orelya Lane, Rosa Lee Galloway, Sister Franks, Ollie Masterson, Sister Lucille Lewis, Willie Lee Johnson, Mother Graves*

Third Row: *Esther Williams, Dorothy Hilliard, Junior Baker, James Harold Galloway, Eva Crawford, Esther Galloway Jenkins, Willie Williams, Audrey Galloway Fejey, Vivian Ighner, Charles Graves, Ronald Galloway*

First COGIC
(L to R) Elder E.E. Hamilton, Sr. Pastor
and Elder Carroll
Original Location
3014 Center St
Houston, TX 77007

Pastor E.E. Hamilton and Elder A. Carroll in front of the sign and church at the original location.

Greater First COGIC
Supt. E.E. Hamilton, Sr.
Pastor

Current location
2619 Deams St
Houston, Tx 77093

Pastor Hamilton relocated the church to its present location a more suitable one. He also added Greater to the name to signify its acclaim.

The Women's work of the Church Of God In Christ in Texas has produced many notable women for the work of the department of women for Cogicdom worldwide.

We will cover other notable men and women in and from Texas that have made sizable contributions to the Church Of God In Christ, Inc. The Church Of God In Christ worldwide has grown from 10 congregations in 1907, to 15,500.

Texas, as of the printing of this volume is comprised of 19 Jurisdictions. The histories of each is covered in the following chapters 3 through 21, chapter 22 covers the Texas Inner-Jurisdiction, and chapter 23 covers other churches and fellowships that share doctrine beliefs similar to the Church Of God In Christ. Chapter 24 covers news worthy COGIC events in Texas.

From the 1926 Year book
The above is the likeness of Elder J. Houston Galloway, Austin Texas. The Assistant Overseer of Texas and President of the National Benevolent Burial Association, who has been instrumental in legislating for the success of the Benevolent Burial Association since 1918, and through our legislation we have been able to obtain membership in several states. Saints everywhere, take note of this, and avail yourself of this protection by taking out membership at once.

The Report of Bishop E.M. Page to the Church Of God In Christ in the 1926 Year Book

Dear Readers:

It is a pleasure to me as well privilege to tell how the Lord has blessed and how He will bless those who will surrender to Him, thank God. In the latter part of 1913, the Lord, through Elder C. H. Mason, our Chief Apostle, called me to go to Texas. It hurt me so bad to think of going to Texas, but after humbling myself before the Lord for five hours in prayer, He spoke to my soul and I said: "Yes, Lord." Not one moment did I resist any more. In January, 1914, I left Memphis for Texas. Arrived in Dallas on the 27th, met the Church that night and they received me gladly.

For five months I labored, without leaving my Church to go anywhere. More than one hundred persons were saved and reclaimed. In May, 1914, I took a little band of workers and went to Waco, Texas, where the Lord broke through and saved one hundred and twenty-five souls in six weeks.

And in July, 1914, I went to Houston, and met the first convocation after coming to the state. In this meeting the Lord again saw fit to appoint me State Overseer of Texas through our Chief Apostle. To me that was the worst mistake I thought Elder Mason ever made. I had several hearty cries about it but went, doing the best I could.

The Lord, through my earnest labor with my brethren, has brought the work from twelve churches to more than one hundred churches in these eleven years. Many thousand souls have been saved, church houses built, 268 acres of school land bought and paid for, and school being erected. I am glad to say Texas produced good preachers and well trained men, which shows for itself. I have held eleven State Convocations and raised $18,308.58. Eighteen thousand three hundred and eight dollars and fifty-eight cents. We have held nine ministers' and workers' meetings, and raised $10,365.91. Ten thousand three hundred sixty-five dollars and ninety-one cents. And in 1925 we raised for the State $10,150.70. Ten thousand one hundred and fifty dollars and seventy cents, making a grand total of $38,825.19. Thirty-eight thousand, eight hundred and twenty-five dollars and nineteen cents. Thank the Lord for all He has done for us. I have not looked for myself, I have looked for the people.

The Lord moved me to go to Oklahoma in 1917, the church at Muskogee was established, Tulsa was revived and also Sand Springs and Shawnee, where they burned two houses to get holiness out of town. Went to Oklahoma City and there founded another good church which stands as one of the leading churches in the state today. With the co-operation of my elders and workers in Oklahoma the state is going to the top. We purchased one whole block of land in Oklahoma City for our state headquarters, built a large tabernacle where thousands are gathered all the summer, also large kitchen and dining room, well furnished with enamel plates and cups to match knives and forks. Watch Oklahoma. We are workers and not shirkers.

Yours for the Master,
E. M. PAGE.

Holy Convocation Quick Reference Table
1907 to 1988

1.) 1907	2.) 1908	3.) 1909	4.) 1910
5.) 1911	6.) 1912	7.) 1913	8.) 1914
9.) 1915	10.) 1916	11.) 1917	12.) 1918
13.) 1919	14.) 1920	15.) 1921	16.) 1922
17.) 1923	18.) 1924	19.) 1925	20.) 1926
21.) 1927	22.) 1928	23.) 1929	24.) 1930
25.) 1931	26.) 1932	27.) 1933	28.) 1934
29.) 1935	30.) 1936	31.) 1937	32.) 1938
33.) 1939	34.) 1940	35.) 1941	36.) 1942
37.) 1943	38.) 1944	39.) 1945	40.) 1946
41.) 1947	42.) 1948	43.) 1949	44.) 1950
45.) 1951	46.) 1952	47.) 1953	48.) 1954
49.) 1955	50.) 1956	51.) 1957	52.) 1958
53.) 1959	54.) 1960	55.) 1961	56.) 1962
57.) 1963	58.) 1964	59.) 1965	60.) 1966
61.) 1967	62.) 1968 (1st*) 1st	63.) 1969	64.) 1970
65.) 1971	66.) 1972 (2nd*) 2nd	67.) 1973	68.) 1974
69.) 1975	70.) 1976 (3rd*) 3rd	71.) 1977	72.) 1978
73.) 1979	74.) 1980 (4th*) 4th	75.) 1981	76.) 1982
77.) 1983	78.) 1984 (5th*) 5th	79.) 1985	80.) 1986
81.) 1987	82.) 1988 (6th*) 6th	83.) 1989 1st Int Bd trans(7th)	84.) 1990 (7th)
85.) 1991 JO Patt (7th)	86.) 1992 (7th*) 8th	87.) 1993	88.) 1994

Table Legend
62.) 1968(1st*) 1st
(Line Item used 62. example above)

62.) - Convocation number (*62nd Convocation*)
1968 - Convocation and Scheduled Election Year (*Quadrennial*)
(1st) – Quadrennial Board Number (*if on election schedule*)
1st – Actual Board Number
(Highlighted Items w/notes are unscheduled changes to the board)

Legend of the table
Convocation Number; 4 digit Yr.; (*elected board#) Actual board #

GENERAL BOARDS OF COGIC
13 Quadrennial elections so far
3 Interim Boards
1 Replacement Board
1 Vacancy Board
(18 Total Boards to-date)

Holy Convocation Quick Reference Table
1989 to 1958

89.) 1995 2nd (9th)	90.) 1996 (8th*) 10th	91.) 1997	92.) 1998
93.) 1999	94.) 2000 (9th*) 11th	95.) 2001	96.) 2002
97.) 2003	98.) 2004 (10*) 12th	99.) 2005	100.) 2006
100.) 07/08 3rd GE (13th)	101.) 2008 (11th*) 14th	102.) 2009 15th trans Owens	103.) 2010
104.) 2011	105.) 2012 (12th*) 16th	106.) 2013	107.) 2014
108.) 2015	109.) 2016 (13th*) 17th	110.) 2017	111.) 2018
112.) 2019	113.) 2020 (14th*) 18th	114.) 2021	115.) 2022
116.) 2023	117.) 2024 (15th*) 19th	118.) 2025	119.) 2026
120.) 2027	121.) 2028 (16th*) 20th	122.) 2029	123.) 2030
124.) 2031	125.) 2032 (17th*) 21st	126.) 2033	127.) 2034
128.) 2035	129.) 2036 (18th*) 22nd	130.) 2037	131.) 2038
132.) 2039	133.) 2040 (19th*) 23rd	134.) 2041	135.) 2042
136.) 2043	137.) 2044 (20th*) 24th	138.) 2045	139.) 2046
140.) 2047	141.) 2048 (21st*) 25th	142.) 2049	143.) 2050
144.) 2051	145.) 2052 (22nd*) 26th	146.) 2053	147.) 2054
148.) 2055	149.) 2056 (23rd*) 27th	150.) 2057	151.) 2058

Table Legend
62.) 1968 (1st*) 1st
(Line Item used example above)

62.) - Convocation number (*62nd Convocation*)
1968 - Convocation and Scheduled Election Year (*Quadrennial*)
(1st) – Quadrennial Board Number (*if on election schedule*)
1st – Actual Board Number
(Highlighted Items w/notes are unscheduled changes to the board)

Legend of the table
Convocation Number; 4 digit Yr.; (*elected board#) Actual board #

GENERAL BOARDS OF COGIC
13 Quadrennial elections so far
3 Interim Boards
1 Replacement Board
1 Vacancy Board
(18 Total Boards to-date)

THE TEXAS CONNECTION — Index

Indexes The six indexes included in the Texas Connection will help you locate histories of the International Church Of God In Christ and Church Of God In Christ in Texas. These are the stories of the local churches, districts, jurisdictional histories in Texas and a limited International Church of God In Christ history.

International Officers This index list the 2 Senior Bishops of the Church Of God In Christ, the 5 Presiding Bishops. It lists the 6 General Supervisors of Women and other national officers both past and present.

Jurisdictional Officers This index lists the past and present Presiding Prelate of each of the 16 Jurisdiction in the great State of Texas. It lists the past and present State Supervisors of the Women's Department for each of the 16 Jurisdictions in Texas. It also lists other jurisdictional officers past and present.

District Officers This index lists the past and present District Superintendents and District Missionaries in the 16 Jurisdictions of Texas. It also lists other district officers of each district.

District's This Index lists the Districts of each Jurisdiction

Local Churches This Index lists the local Churches of each Jurisdiction.

Others This Index lists Fellowships and other Churches that may have once been a part of the Church of God in Christ or that shares similar doctrines.

THE TEXAS CONNECTION   Index

International Officers
This index list the 2 Senior Bishops of the Church Of God In Christ, the 5 Presiding Bishops. It lists the 6 General Supervisors of Women and other national officers both past and present.

Senior Bishops (2)
Mason, Charles Harrison..........................
Jones, Sr., Ozro Thurston............................

Presiding Bishops (5)
Patterson, Sr., James Oglethorpe........................
Ford, Louis Henry................................
Owens, Chandler David..........................
Patterson, Gilbert Earl..............................
Blake, Sr., Charles Edward............................

General Supervisors of Women (7)
Robinson (Woods), Lizzie............................
Coffey (Brooks), Lillian.............................
Bailey, Annie L.................................
McGlothen, Mattie..............................
Crouch, Emma Frances...........................
Rivers (Smalls), Willie Mae........................
Lewis, (McCoo) Barbara.........................

National Officers
Patterson, Sr. J.O..........
Patterson, Jr. J.O..........
Jones, Sr. O.T..............
Jones, Jr. O.T..............
Patterson, Jr. J............
Jones, C.P..................

National Officers

SAMPLE ENTRY

Jurisdictional Officers This index lists the past and present Presiding Prelate of each of the 16 Jurisdiction in the great State of Texas. It lists the past and present State Supervisors of the Women's Department for each of the 16 Jurisdictions in Texas. It also lists other jurisdictional officers past and present.

District Officers This index lists the past and present District Superintendents and District Missionaries in the 16 Jurisdictions of Texas. It also lists other district officers of each district.

District's This Index lists the Districts of each Jurisdiction.

Local Churches This Index lists the local Churches of each Jurisdiction.

Others This Index lists Fellowships and other Churches that may have once been a part of the Church of God in Christ or that shares similar doctrines.

Made in the USA
Columbia, SC
06 February 2019